GEORG SIEGMUND

Buddhism and Christianity
A Preface to Dialogue

Translated by
Sister Mary Frances McCarthy

THE UNIVERSITY OF ALABAMA PRESS
University, Alabama

Library of Congress Cataloging in Publication Data

Siegmund, Georg, 1903-
   Buddhism and Christianity.

   Translation of Buddhismus und Christentum.
   Includes index.
   1. Christianity and other religions—Buddhism.
2. Buddhism—Relations—Christianity. I. Title.
BR128.B8S513   261.2   77-23809
ISBN 0-8173-6703-9

Translated into English from *Buddhismus und Christentum*
Copyright © 1968 by Verlag Josef Knecht
English translation copyright © 1980
by The University of Alabama Press
All rights reserved

Manufactured in the United States of America

CONTENTS

Preface	vii
1. A Preface to Dialogue	1
2. The Basic Experience of Buddhism	11
3. Man Between All and Nothing	30
4. Buddhist versus Christian Doctrine of Suffering	47
5. "Freedom from Suffering" by Means of Self-Redemption?	60
6. On the Meaning of Suffering	67
7. Buddhist and Christian Concepts of the "Soul"	92
8. The Perfect Man	102
9. God or Atman	113
10. In Search of the Absolute	126
11. Buddha and Christ	152
12. From Emperor Worship to Belief in God	170
Notes	185
Index	193

PREFACE

For many years, I have wanted to make an intensive study of Buddhism. But it was not until a trip to Eastern Asia in 1966, on which I was able to visit Japan, Korea, Hong Kong, Formosa, and the Philippines, that I had the opportunity of encountering Buddhism directly and, in particular, of enriching my knowledge of religious conditions in Japan. As a result, I decided to attempt the comparison between Buddhism and Christianity that is presented here. Since the religious face of Japan is shaped not only by Buddhism but also by Shintoism, it seemed justifiable to exceed the theme of the book by devoting the last chapter to a consideration of this latter religious movement.

Fulda-Neuenburg   GEORG SIEGMUND
April 20, 1968

Buddhism and Christianity

1

A PREFACE TO DIALOGUE

Some years ago, when the foreign correspondent for financial affairs of a German newspaper visited a Zen Buddhist monastery in Japan, he asked one of the monks: "Do you believe in God?" He did so in the belief that he was posing a relatively simple and unequivocal question. But he discovered to his surprise that his Japanese companion—a student of German—had difficulty translating the question into Japanese. The translator had to decide whether he should translate the question as literally as possible, knowing that if he did the monk would answer with a simple negative and that the journalist would feel justified in reporting at home that, in Japanese monasteries, even the monks no longer believe in God. Or should he, the translator, adapt the journalist's question to the Japanese mentality and reword it accordingly? If he did that, the question would touch off a discussion that the journalist had not intended.[1]

This small incident shows what an abyss separates the intellectual world of the East from that of the West, and how easily misunderstandings can arise that militate antecedently against a genuine confrontation. In the intellectual world of the West, which has been formed by ancient classical and Christian traditions, *God* means first, and in a proper sense, the one Creator-God who transcends the world, who is and remains the raison d'être of the world, and to whom it returns. In the West, every other concept of God is derived from this first and basic one. This concept of God, which has been formed by centuries of intellectual effort, has come to be accepted without question by the intellectual world of the West whether one believes in this God or rejects him. "Belief in God" and "denial of God" have meaning only in a world to which "God" is no stranger. Such a concept of God is lacking, however, in Eastern thought. For that reason, one cannot simply inquire of a Japanese whether he believes in God. He will be confused by the question. This is not to say that the Japanese do not know "gods"; their "kamis" play an important role in their mythology. But these *kamis* are so fundamentally different from the Christian *God* that many Christian missionaries long refrained from using the term *kami* to refer to the Christian God. They preferred to speak of the "Lord of the World." Under the imperceptible influence of Christian thought, however, the concept *kami* gradually lost its polytheistic primitiveness. In everyday speech, as a result, its meaning now approximates the monotheistic concept of God. Only in most recent years have missionaries yielded their reluctance to speak of the Christian God as the "kami."

In the course of just a few centuries, the various churches of the Christian world have grown so far apart that it is difficult for them to rediscover the basic concepts they have been interpreting so one-sidedly throughout their history and just to understand each other again even though unity is still impossible. So long as this condition persists, the difficulties in the way of an understanding between the fundamentally different worlds of East and West are well nigh insurmountable.

The two great religions of Japan are Shintoism and Buddhism. When the Western Christian hears of them, he involuntarily thinks of religious groups so distinct from one another that membership in the one automatically excludes from membership in the other. In our society, one who is a Protestant is, for that very reason, not a Catholic or a Muslim. But for the Japanese, Shintoism and Buddhism are not two mutually exclusive entities. On the Festival of the New Year, he goes to the Shinto shrine; on the Festival of the Dead, he visits the graves of his native place and usually thereafter the nearby Buddhist temple. He is married by a Shinto priest, but he summons the Buddhist monk to recite the sutras over the cremated remains of a departed relative. Japanese cities have taken over from the West the hubbub of the Christmas market. As a logical consequence, there are also Christmas celebrations for children. Even in non-Christian circles the Bible has found wide acceptance. The result of all this is that, for the uncritical masses, the intellectual and religious worlds are inextricably confused. But those who are intellectually more alert are beginning to compare and to test.

In the Far East, moreover, the era of strictly hermetic delimitation has yielded to an era of mutual receptivity. In the religious sphere, this development has brought new goals into view; simple believers as well as theologians find themselves confronted with new tasks—among them, the opening of a door to non-Christians. If the tendency of our age is to form out of many separate, individual nations a single, all-embracing one; if the fates of individual nations can no longer operate in isolation from the fates of neighboring nations; if a threat to one nation is at the same time a threat to all mankind; then there will be everywhere apparent, in our awakening awareness that we are all in the same boat, the determination to set aside the barriers that separate us and to work for the preservation of human nature and of the human race.

In particular, the intellectual meeting of East and West received new impetus from Vatican Council II and from the personality of Pope John XXIII. An English edition of his encyclicals, entitled *Pacem in Terris* (Peace on Earth), became a best-seller even in Japan. By the human warmth of his manner, he was able to achieve what philosophical discussions and church dogmas had been unable to effect. Through the person of

A Preface to Dialogue

this pope, as Heinrich Dumoulin of Tokyo says, the word "fraternity" gained a tone that is new and a content that is rich in hope. His fraternal attitude toward men of all races and religions opened more hearts than could have been opened by proclamations alone. In November 1962, he granted an audience in his private library to thirty Buddhists of various sects. The Buddhists had sought this audience with the intention of delivering to the head of the largest Christian church a plea for the cooperation of all religious organizations for the preservation of world peace.

We do not know the exact words John XXIII spoke at this audience, but we do know what impression the pope's words made on his visitors. The leader of the group, Zen Abbot Iwamoto, reported in Tokyo that

> the address surprised and delighted both himself and his companions. They had expected the Pope to thank them for their visit and then to explain that the Christian religion is the supreme one that must be accepted by all men. Instead, the Pope recognized their religious belief and said, in effect, that belief in God and belief in Buddha rest on a common ground and that all those who believe should do good together for the well-being of mankind. By no word did he indicate superiority. And it was this fact that confirmed them in their own resolution to work together, regardless of the differences of sect that existed among them, for the good of all. The Buddhist Abbot told them, with visible emotion, of the further events of the day.[2]

Since that time, contacts between Japanese Buddhists and the pope have not been lacking. In the autumn of 1966, Pope Paul VI received fifteen Japanese bonzes. To the introductory address of their speaker, the pope answered with a short speech in which he joyfully acknowledged that there had arisen in recent years, because of the numerous visits of Japanese Buddhists to the Vatican, a relationship of friendship between the Catholic church and the Buddhists. In view of the threat to world peace, the pope admonished, it was the duty of all religious persons to contribute effectively to the creation of favorable circumstances in which the peace so longed for by mankind could thrive. In conclusion, the pope expressed his expectation that, in the spirit of tolerance and mutual respect among the religions of the world that had been created by Vatican Council II, the visit of the Japanese Buddhists would influence favorably their knowledge of Christianity and would lead them to treasure even more highly the contribution of religion to the well-being of mankind and to the culture and development of the human family.[3]

What is especially noteworthy in the pope's remarks is their obvious recognition of Buddhism as a religion although—if we are to judge by the discussion about the status of Buddhism—this is by no means a matter to be taken for granted. For there are not only Buddhists who refuse to regard Buddhism as a religion in the Western meaning of the word; there are many

Christian thinkers who look upon Buddhism as a philosophy rather than a religion.

What began in the personal meetings of Buddhists with the head of the Catholic church has been fostered in the proclamations of the second Vatican Council, which, by its courageous "Declaration on the Relationship of the Church to Non-Christian Religions," provided the necessary basic clarification. "In our times," we read there, "when every day men are being drawn closer together and the ties between various peoples are being multiplied, the Church is giving deeper study to her relationship with non-Christian religions. In her task of fostering unity and love among men, and even among nations, she gives primary consideration in this document to what human beings have in common and to what promotes fellowship among them."[4]

The common source and goal of all peoples in God is given as the basis of the rapprochement demanded by the times. From this proceeds also the common existential condition of all mankind. Everywhere those questions are being raised that are the intimate concern of religion.

> Men look to the various religions for answers to those profound mysteries of the human condition which, today even as in olden times, deeply stir the human heart: What is a man? What is the meaning and the purpose of our life? What is goodness and what is sin? What gives rise to our sorrows and to what intent? Where lies the path to true happiness? What is the truth about death, judgment, and retribution beyond the grave? What, finally, is that ultimate and unutterable mystery which engulfs our being, and whence we take our rise, and whither our journey leads us? (p. 661)

From even the most ancient times until the present, there has been observable among the various peoples a certain awareness of a hidden power that is present in the course of the world and in the history of mankind and that has frequently resolved itself into a recognition of a supreme God, even of a Father-God. As civilization advanced and language became more sophisticated, the basic questions were raised again by the great religions and were given answers that reflected the basic beliefs of each. This is especially true of Hinduism, Buddhism, and Islamism. "Thus in Hinduism," the *Declaration* continues,

> men contemplate the divine mystery and express it through an unspent fruitfulness of myths and through searching philosophical inquiry. They seek release from the anguish of our condition through ascetical practices or deep meditation or a loving, trusting flight toward God. Buddhism in its multiple forms acknowledges the radical insufficiency of this shifting world. It teaches a path by which men, in a devout and confident spirit, can either reach a state of absolute freedom or attain supreme enlightenment by their own efforts or by higher assistance. Likewise, other religions to be found everywhere strive

A Preface to Dialogue

variously to answer the restless searchings of the human heart by proposing "ways," which consist of teachings, rules of life, and sacred ceremonies. (pp. 661–62)

Of particular importance in this statement is the reference to the "restless searchings of the human heart" *(inquietudo cordis hominum)*. It is, in fact, the common basis of all religions. In the difficulties that threaten every attempt to initiate a fruitful dialogue, in the sense of the Vatican *Declaration*, we are reminded again and again of this restlessness. Only from that basis is it possible to conduct a meaningful dialogue.

In the brief formula of the council text, the multiplicity of the various forms of Buddhism is indicated. Briefly, but unmistakably, it characterizes the two chief forms—the *Mahayana branch,* which strives for the highest enlightenment, and the *Hinayana branch* (today often designated as the Theravada), which strives for *nirvana* (in Pali: *nibbana*). The word was translated, after much deliberation, as the "state of absolute freedom" *(status perfectae liberationis)*. The translation indicates the negative character of the much-discussed word *nirvana,* but it also—as Dumoulin says in his excursus on the council text—"accords with the usual Buddhist teaching on the subject by leaving no doubt as to the positive content of the designated beatitudinal goal."[5] As a result, a high degree of positive characterization has been successfully incorporated into the brief text.

This document represents only a first step toward a goal that will not be reached for a long time. Initial goodwill has permitted the differences in basic orientation to recede into the background and is even inclined to underestimate them. But they will reemerge as soon as the discussion of these questions in dialogue begins in earnest and will make it manifest that much patience and goodwill are necessary if the road to the goal of intellectual and religious understanding is to be traversed.

At times something special occurs in human relationships that causes persons who, for a long time, have been passing one another without notice to meet one another on a new human basis and to become open to one another. It is only to be expected that, in the first joy of such an encounter, they will overemphasize and overestimate what they have in common while underemphasizing and underestimating what tends to separate them. This may well be the case with those Christians and Buddhists who are becoming open to one another today. The manifestations of reverence; the preparations for and methods of meditation; the cult of the dead; the use of candles, incense, and formulas of prayer; the customs of contemplation and pilgrimage; monastic life and convents—all these may well give the uninitiated a first impression of great inner proximity and relationship.

But when the actual content of Buddhism as it has been formulated by its contemporary scholars comes under scrutiny, it becomes immediately obvious that there are significant differences between the two. For example, a propagandistic pamphlet published in Germany states in all clarity:

> The teaching that Buddha left as his legacy to mankind knows no divine Creator of the world, no Ruler of the world, no Redeemer, no divine revelation, no soul if, by this word, one means an unchanging entity, and no religious dogmas or doctrinal statements that one must believe in order to attain the highest good, eternal peace; on the contrary, Buddha warned against accepting religious dogmas on the authority of another. Can one say, then, that Buddhism is a religion? Certainly not, if the word religion is to be understood in its usual sense.[6]

From this statement, the author concludes that Buddhism and Christianity move on different levels: Buddhism is simply a philosophy, based on one's own pure insight; Christianity, on the contrary, is a religion, based on faith in an authority.

From the time of St. Francis Xavier (d. 1552) to the present, intellectually prominent Christians who have attempted to establish a dialogue with scholarly Buddhists have had the initial experience that the ground on which they had hitherto been standing was slipping away under their feet. From this ground, they had been able to conduct dialogues with Christians of other sects. But a Christian who really "encounters" a representative of an Eastern religion suffers, initially, the painful and shocking experience of swinging for a time in airless space; feels—as Klaus Klostermaier says in his discussion of Hinduism—that "all concepts on which one had hoped to build knowledge and experience are breaking and crumbling away; that one is falling into ever deeper abysses and uncertainties. Gradually, one again finds ground under one's feet—deeper, more precipitous levels of reality. It is still impossible to say how near one is to the reality. New impressions present themselves, new abysses, new depths."[7]

The fundamental difference in mental attitude is made radically clear when a commentator on Nishida Kitaro, who is regarded as Japan's greatest philosopher, says that it is a traditional concept in the East to regard "nothingness" as the basis of all existence. However mysterious the concept may be to Western thought, it is commonplace in Eastern thought. The idea of "absolute nothingness" is the concept that causes the most difficulty for the Western Christian. But it is here that the usual course of Eastern thought begins. In the religion of the West, God is regarded as the highest Being, as the Existence of all existences. It is otherwise in the East. For Mahayana Buddhism, clinging to existence is looked upon as a form of not-knowing. *Absolute nothingness* is expressly raised to a metaphysical principle: the last stage for everything that has being is to be without being. If nothingness has the metaphysical function of being the last hiding place of everything that has being, this seems to be in direct opposition to the Christian concept, which ascribes this function to God.

Buddhism, for its part, repeatedly emphasizes that its concern is with

A Preface to Dialogue

"absolute nothingness." If this were so, there could be no bridge of understanding between the two contrary positions. It is not particularly convincing when representatives of Western thought seek again and again to prove that this so-called absolute nothingness is not really an absolute, but a relative nothingness. In such a controversy, it is very likely that the two parties will succumb to the pitfalls of their own thinking and that the "dialogue" will end in petty warfare.

There are certain indispensable prerequisites for the inauguration of genuine dialogue. There must exist a common intellectual platform from which clarifications may be sought and speculative progress made in a philosophical give-and-take. For this, there must be a certain at least minimal area of common ground, of the will and the ability to recognize and acknowledge the common element as such so it can become the basis of further agreement.

By its nature, dialogue aims at the clarification of facts, at the discovery of "truths." But Eastern religions are not primarily concerned with intellectual clarifications; they proceed from quite different premises. Their difference of attitude is not to be underestimated. Every Westerner who attempts such a dialogue suffers again and again from the realization that "truth" as a concept is not meaningful in the East. The Easterner thinks with his feelings; he has an explicit dislike of logical sequences; he disavows the evident principle of contradiction; he resists analysis and differentiation. He believes that one should think "wholly" in an undifferentiated unity of thinking and feeling, intellect and emotion. Again and again, he confuses abstract thinking and concrete experience. Because the non-Christian religions require no personal decision, whether moral or intellectual, he believes that it is possible to live now with this "truth," now with that; that it is permissible to use Shintoism, Buddhism, Hinduism, and Christianity interchangeably as "necessity" demands in the vicissitudes of his life situation. The postulates of Eastern thought are not intended metaphysically. On the contrary, they are intended "soteriologically." Their first and central concern is with "saving" man from the trouble and misery in which he is involved. Obviously, then, only spiritual matters can be legitimate starting points for the establishment of a cordial dialogue between East and West.

Whereas in Western philosophy and theology, in more than a millenium of intellectual exertion, concepts have been determined and a conceptual language has been created that make possible a common intellectual effort, this has not occurred in the East. The understanding of basic concepts such as God, soul, spirit, conscience, good, evil, person, sin, salvation, redemption, grace, and immortality cannot be expected of the representatives of Eastern religions, for they do not exist in the East. Nor does the attempt to substitute verbal designations of somewhat similar content meet with any success, for they, too, have their source in a totally different intellectual world.

A significant impediment to fruitful dialogue is the fact that this lack of clarity with respect to good and evil easily introduces confusion into the dialogue. The non-Christian has no certain feeling or judgment about sin; he has no clear concept of what is meant by sin. He tends to relativize good and evil. But this is an obstacle to any serious understanding of the Christian message.

For the most part, believers of Eastern religions have lived in a completely closed world that no person or thing has ever placed in question. Their formation is limited to the intellectual mastery of the texts that contain the teachings of the sect to which they belong. Because they have not learned to think for themselves or to appraise critically, they react sharply and negatively to any attempt to discuss matters objectively, for they regard such an attempt as an attack on the substance of their thought, which they steadfastly defend.

Religion—and this must be remembered in every attempt at dialogue—is more than a matter of insight and feeling. Religion is ultimately a matter of personal decision made within the human heart; it is and remains rooted in man's freedom. For this reason, no religious dialogue can really limit itself to purely objective clarifications; it must progress to appeals for a decision. A comparison between Socrates and Jesus Christ will show how true this is of religion. Socrates, the teacher of wisdom, could conduct with his disciples dialogues aimed solely at conceptual clarifications, for they all held basically the same notion and the same concept of morality. Only those who were not numbered among his disciples took exception to his teachings. But it was otherwise with Jesus Christ. He was more than a teacher of wisdom. He forced men to come to a decision; he demanded of them conversion, opening of the heart, penance. Thus he became a sign of contradiction; in him, the thoughts of many hearts were revealed. He came as the Light into a world in which many loved darkness more than the light. In a similar manner, today's effort to understand Eastern intellectuality is not concerned solely with "information," with the removal of mutual prejudices, but with decisions that fall—just as they do in the Western world—on one side of an alternative.

Eastern man's readiness to listen to his Christian partner in dialogue has also been considerably lessened by the fact that it has often been the disappointed or fallen-away Christian who, in his search for something new, has turned to Buddhism or Hinduism, both of which were originally regarded as relatively identical entities. Thus Arthur Schopenhauer, in his comparison of Christianity and Buddhism, gave the preference to the latter because it presented a consistent pessimism, whereas Christianity presented only a fragmented one. In the excess of his joy of discovery, he overestimated the agreement between his own teaching and that of Buddhism. In his day, the literature about Buddhism was noticeably incomplete and overlooked, in particular, the multiformity of Buddhism in its historical development. Today, the attempt of Paul Deussen (d. 1919), the disciple of Schopenhauer, to explain away the differences between Christianity and Buddhism is also regarded as a failure. Schopenhauer's prophecy that Buddhism would basically alter our knowledge and thought has not been fulfilled. If Buddhism, with its remarkable adaptability, has today become fashionable in some psychological and psychotherapeutical schools of the West and if the methods of enlightenment that are proper to Zen Buddhism, for instance, have been compared with Christian asceticism and mysticism, even that is "an alienation and distortion . . . [for it equates] the essence of Buddhism with religion,"[8] an attitude that Buddhism permits with great equanimity.

Since the beginning of the century, organizations like the "Buddhistic Society of Germany" (1903) and the "German Buddhistic Union" (1958) have been making their appearance; the adherents of "theosophy" (Helena Petrovna Blavatsky) and of "anthroposophy" (Rudolf Steiner) have formed societies to study the modes of Eastern thought; individual enthusiasts have even found their way into Buddhist monasteries. On the other hand, the East has also made attempts to win followers for Buddhism in the West, even to propagandize it. The books about Zen Buddhism by Professor D. T. Suzuki (d. 1967) have found a wide circle of readers. After World War II, the Buddhists became aware of their membership in the one worldwide community and of their duty to extend it. As a result, they have begun to oppose their own Buddhist mission to the Christian one. In recent years, Buddhist councils have decided to undertake a Buddhist mission to the West (p. 21).

In the years during which Japan was struggling to free itself from the suggestive influence of the dialectical materialism of the Soviet Union and to reaffirm its own values, a slogan originated there about the "intellectualism of the East and the materialism of the West"; "more and more blind enthusiasts were to be found who were neither aware of the intellectualism that actually exists in the West nor disconcerted by the materialism rampant around them in every aspect of their own lives, even in religion; in fact, the slogan was even echoed in Western lands that had become alienated from their own intellectual heritage."[9] Out of this reaction to materialism grew the enthusiasm for the "Messianism of the East" that has flourished in Europe in recent years. Klaus Mehnert summed up the basic thrust of the movement in the slogan: "The cure for the West lies in the East."[10] Already Westerners in search of "salvation" have traversed the Far East, among them Arthur Koestler, who sought everywhere to discover whether the wisdom of the East might not offer an intellectual cure for Western civilization.[11]

Once Buddhism had followed European models and had established universities of its own, it was compelled to relinquish its previous reserve and self-sufficiency, to distinguish itself from other world views and religions, and thereby to achieve, in its own right, a higher intellectual level. Today, in consequence, Buddhism finds itself more and more in the situation of having to undertake a dialogue with the Western religions, especially with Christianity.

On the other hand, Christian missionary activities today are also motivated by a new impulse. To what extent Christianity can and ought to enter into dialogue with the East is shown paradigmatically in the case of Hugo Lassalle, who has been active for some decades as a missionary in Japan. For more than twenty years, he has been taking part regularly in the exercises of Zen Buddhist monasteries, has discovered from within the meaning and value of Zen meditation for a deepened Christianity, and is in the process of evaluating his experiences. As a Zen master, he has assumed a Japanese name. He has truly penetrated the inner sanctuary of the opposite side.[12]

2

THE BASIC EXPERIENCE OF BUDDHISM

Buddha and Sartre

Just as Christianity derives from Jesus of Nazareth, who is called Christ, so Buddhism derives from Siddharta Gautama, who is called Buddha. The basic difference between Christ and Buddha lies in the way in which each of them became the founder of the religion that owes its origin to himself. Jesus Christ not only proclaimed the way of salvation to which he pointed, but designated himself as both the bringer and the way of salvation, so Christianity cannot be thought of apart from his person. Buddha, on the contrary, simply proclaimed a doctrine, the salvific way of an enlightenment that each person can achieve for himself. Buddha demanded no "faith"; indeed, he refused to be regarded and revered as a religious authority. Shortly before his death, he admonished his disciples to seek their salvation and refuge only in themselves and nowhere else. Each was to strive independently for the enlightenment that was to be his. Thus it was possible for everyone who sought his salvation along the paths pointed out by Buddha to repeat the basic experience in his own way, to develop and re-form it.

The fact that Buddha's teaching and his way of salvation found an amazingly widespread reception in the Far East and that the many nations in East Asia that adopted Buddhism did not hesitate to develop and change it is essentially due to the modes of thought and experience that are deeply ingrained in these nations. No one in the East would regard the separation of the gospel of salvation from its founder or the changing of it as a "defection," as the West does when attempts are made to separate "Christianity" from "Jesus Christ." The common core of Buddhism is not exclusively dependent—as Maurus Heinrichs has pointed out [1]—on the historical Buddha per se; it is rooted much more deeply in the similarly based mode of experience and way of life that are peculiar to Eastern man. If Buddhist sects today do not regard the historical Siddharta Gautama as being in any way essential, but place their emphasis instead on a common Buddha nature (in Chinese: *fo-hsing;* in Japanese: *bus-shô*), no ones sees in this fact a "defection" from the true founder, but rather a further development that is completely in accord with his original intention. The visitor to the famous Zen monastery Ryoanji in Kyoto is given a brochure of which the opening words may be translated as follows: "Zen is a religion without God or Buddhas. Zen is a religion without any object to be venerated. Zen is a religion that venerates the 'self.' Zen is a religion that strives for a deep awareness of 'self.' "

It is important that we keep in mind this quite different attitude of the founder of the Buddhist doctrine of salvation if we are to gain a real understanding of Buddhism as a whole. For we must understand not only the basic experience of Buddhism, but also the later fulfillment of this basic experience, in which, in the last analysis, all Buddhism has its roots.

Today, it is generally assumed, on the basis of our knowledge of philological and archaeological sources, that the man who is credited with the founding of Buddhism actually did exist.[2] But the historical details of his life history were very early overgrown with legendary features that can no longer be clearly distinguished from the historical ones. In an analysis of the basic Buddhist experience, however, historical details are not really significant. Far more significant is the typically common element that spoke to men of the East and that the disciple of Buddha seeks to reexperience in his meditations in order thereby to achieve the same enlightenment that his Master achieved. When we deal with the basic Buddhist experience, it is permissible, for purposes of psychological and existential illumination, to evaluate not only the meager details of the life of Buddha himself, but also the legendary excrescence and the reports of analogous experiences. What we can no longer reconstruct from historical reality, we can thus discover in the genuineness of human experience.

To do this, we must return to the roots of Buddhism in the soil of the country in which it originated. There is no doubt that the Aryan immigration contributed as much as did the geographical location, above all in the valley of the Ganges and in the vicinity of the Himalayas, to the great influence that emanated from Indo-Aryan India, spread far and wide beyond the cultural circle of India, and affected many other peoples and cultures of middle and eastern Asia. The immigration of the Aryans from the northwest into the land of the five rivers probably took place in the beginning of the second millenium before Christ and seems to have been attributable to their military and cultural superiority. The Aryans were familiar with agriculture and brought with them laws and community organization, some knowledge of heavenly portents and the reckoning of time, religious concepts, and sacrificial hymns. In the following centuries, the land of the five rivers was subjugated, Aryan dominion was increased and strengthened, and the caste system was established more and more rigidly. The dark-skinned original inhabitants were partly suppressed, partly enslaved. Finally, partial kingdoms were established, and a more or less sedentary period succeeded the periods of unrest. In time, the warlike nobility had no more pressing tasks to accomplish. As a result, a certain lethargy ensued, and the ruling classes found the life of inactivity more and more burdensome.

Admittedly, the soil, which bore fruit throughout the year, required no constant or long-sighted cultivation, but the people, because of their largely passive attitude, were equally exposed to the favor or the disfavor of nature; natural catastrophes, for which they were not prepared, often had ruinous consequences. We will never be able to analyze properly the factors that cooperated in India to produce a certain sluggishness in the Aryan temperament. "The contact with the original inhabitants, the lethargic effect of the climate, the steadily increasing affluence, an attitude toward life that was oriented much more, among the upper classes, to pleasure than to war or work, as well as a skeptical confusion about former traditions may well have caused a definite change in the temperament of the conquerors, but none of these factors was so important as a later development in turning the Aryans into Hindus."[3]

It was not until much later that the Hindus came into contact with the Hellenic world. When Alexander the Great came to India, Buddha had been dead for more than a century and a half. The people had developed their own modes of living and thinking, and their norms were not suitable for other nations. The Hindus had become a nation of dreamers; their feet were not planted in the soil of their own age and they lacked the incentive to comprehend or shape it. No past lived in their memory to form the present. They had no present that they had determinedly made their own in love or in hate. They did not plan purposefully for the future that lay before them. Instead, the thinkers of India dreamed "pale proud dreams of that which was above all time and of their own kingdom in these eternal realms. Even the teaching of Buddha and the life forms of his disciples reveal the imprint of this Hindu characteristic in all its sharpness and strangeness."[4]

At the time when Buddhism originated, there was no central power in India. Many small states and, among them, many free cities existed side by side. If there were occasional feuds among the princes or between the princes and the cities, such feuds excited neither the great mass of the people nor the learned brahmins. Nor were peasants, citizens, or priests more deeply affected.

In the land and of the tribe of the Sakyas ("the mighty ones"), Siddharta Gautama was born the son of a prince. At the time of the Sakya domination, the land was highly cultivated. The rice fields stretched out between high forests; the cultivation of rice is expressly mentioned in the Buddhistic Scriptures. The water of the rainy season and the floods remained for a long time on the excellent soil of the deep-lying plains, where it fostered the cultivation of rice and made toilsome artificial watering unnecessary. Thus the Hindu lacked even then the incentive that springs from dire need to procure for himself by planned and strenuous manual labor the necessities of life. He had no need of "labor improbus" because every inch of soil was fruitful throughout the year. In consequence, the people did not learn by experience how arduous struggle against the resisting forces of nature forms the human personality, awakens self-consciousness, and stimulates energy and inventiveness. Instead, there existed a certain satiety that lay like a blight upon the common mood and curtailed vigor and versatility.

As an intellectual movement, Buddhism proceeded from no necessity either of daily life or of an intellectual and religious nature; neither did it arise as a reform movement in protest against religious corruption. On the contrary, its roots lay deep in a bourgeois satiety that knew no incentive to the active removal of need and that made no appeal to the heroic aspects of man's nature. What gnawed at the souls of men was the dissatisfaction that results from oversatiety in an assured state of affluence. A similar frame of mind must have existed in France during the youth of the Existentialist Jean Paul Sartre, for he reports: "In that period, the western world was choking to death: that is what was called 'the sweetness of living.' "[5]

Although the real political power of the Sakyas over their neighbors was slight, nevertheless a haughty disposition reigned in their ancient tribe; the "Sakya pride" was proverbial. When brahmins came to the Sakyas, they were in no way honored as befitted their intellectual dignity, but were rather treated with presumptuous hauteur. It is understandable, therefore, that the young Siddharta was infected with an "arrogance" that he later expressly rejected. Along with this arrogance of "life," Buddha speaks also of the arrogance of youth and of riches. Although the celebrated and surely often exaggerated wealth of the Sakyas may not have been exceedingly great, they were nonetheless a tribe that knew how to enjoy life. The sources speak of them as a "tribe blessed with prosperity and great enjoyment" (Oldenberg, p. 101).

It is only in his stubborn wrestling with the unfertile soil, in his struggle against opposition, that man is able to construct for himself out of living experience the self-awareness of personal unity. This vital experience of personal unity is wanting in the child and the immature person. Only one who has become clearly aware of himself in struggle, only one who has dared and won, knows himself as really "one," as a genuine inner unity, not merely as a coincidence of many elements. Because this rousing life experience was generally lacking to the Hindu, he was able to believe that the human entity was composed of elements, of material and intellectual as well as personal and eternal elements. It was assumed that the material elements decomposed at death. "The personal and eternal element is the migratory element and is named, according to circumstances, the self (atman), the vital principle (jiva), or even man (parusa) and so on. This eternal and changeable element, however, was rejected by the various materialistic sects because, in their view, man is composed only of material and perishable elements and decomposes after death. In consequence, they were not troubled by the problem of redemption" (Bareau, p. 9).

The man who lives in a satiated late era has lost the spontaneous feeling of being at home in the world. He is inclined to plaintiveness. He sees the world as a place of division, unpeacefulness, limitation, and pain. He accuses the mighty ones of having inflicted this fate upon him. When

The Basic Experience of Buddhism 15

Buddha appeared, the great framework of a pessimistic world view that placed the blame for the state of the world upon Brahman, the original being, had long been promulgated by Brahminism and had been accepted as one of the basic tenets of mankind.

It seems likely that Buddha's father was no more than a landed proprietor of the Sakya tribe, not a king as later tradition would have it. His mother, Maya, is also supposed to have belonged to the Sakya family. Her confinement is said to have taken her by surprise as she was on her way to visit her parents. Since she died seven days after giving birth, her sister Mahapajapati, who was a second wife of Buddha's father, Suddhodana, seems to have assumed the role of foster mother for the newborn child.

In a civilization in which man has become dull and tired, birth is much more frequently an event that proves fatal to a young woman than it is in a society that is healthily close to nature. It is impossible to say with certainty today whether Siddharta's mother actually did die soon after his birth. But the death of the noble lady, untried by suffering, in the course of an unavoidable natural occurrence is quite compatible with the description of life at the Hindu royal court from which Buddha takes his origin. We know from manifold experience that the attitude of the mother-to-be has a decisive influence on the course of the birth. Many primitive peoples regard parturition as a completely natural event that women approach without anxiety. As soon as the first labor pains are perceived, the pregnant women go into the bush and are able to care for themselves soon after giving birth without danger to the child or to themselves. If birth in our contemporary society has become an event that can hardly take place without the assistance of a doctor, this state of affairs is properly viewed as an alienation from nature that is attributable to civilization. In any event, the death of the mother in the first days after the birth of Gautama fits perfectly into the context of a life alienated from nature by luxury.

We know practically nothing about Buddha's childhood and youth. There is mention of a stepbrother and a stepsister. The education of a prince's son in those days would surely have stressed physical fitness, not the acquisition of the wisdom of the Veda. Nor have the Buddhists ever attributed Vedic learning to their master.

According to tradition, the growing Siddharta Gautama was provided, as befitted his rank, with three palaces furnished so they could be occupied in winter or summer or in the rainy season according to the change of season. In them, the customary court life of the era must have been whiled away with the monotonous repetition of various "pastimes."

As was the custom in the royal courts of the day, the young prince probably married at an early age. It would seem that one of his cousins was not his only wife. Besides the one legitimate wife, he seems—as did his father before him—to have had other wives. At least, the names of several wives have been handed down to us.

If Gautama had inherited the haughty disposition of his ancestors, the confines of an inactive court life must soon have become too "oppressive" for him. In reports of the young prince's flight from home, "oppressiveness" is stressed as the principal motive. "Oppressively confined is life in the house, a place of gloom. Freedom means leaving the house; and while he was thinking this, he left the house" (Oldenberg, p. 106).

We cannot—and do not need to—know in detail what the young boy did to escape the stultifying monotony of inactive repose and the satiating pleasures of court life. To understand the great decision of his life, it is sufficient to know that the world in which the young Gautama grew up was a sated, in fact oversated, world that made no appeal to the actively heroic side of his nature, a world in which there was nothing that could have presented to his spirit the ideal of an active hero. On the contrary, his father, it is expressly emphasized, had attempted to keep far from his son everything that might have reminded him of the suffering that existed in the world. We can understand, therefore, that the prince, restlessly driven by a vague thirst for daring and fighting, endowed with an earnest and strong disposition, and dissatisfied with pleasures that were all too easily attainable, should at last have found the atmosphere of his home unbearable and should have felt himself compelled by some inner impulse to flee from it.

Suffering and sensitivity to suffering stand in a uniquely reciprocal relationship one to the other. Whoever seeks to flee from the sufferings of this life will find his sensitivity to suffering immeasurably increased. Moreover, the sufferings of life will eventually overtake the fugitive and the very shadows of suffering will cast him to the ground. From time immemorial, parents and teachers have striven to keep far from the children entrusted to them the suffering that they themselves have experienced in their lifetime and that has marked their very being. They want life to be better for these children than it was for them. But parents fail to realize that their efforts are thwarted from the outset by that secret law that creates an inner bond between suffering and sensitivity to suffering. Instead of being hardened in the school of life's suffering, such children remain soft and yielding.

Obviously, this was also true of the Hindu prince's son who was to become the founder of Buddhism. His father had been anxious to "spare" him every suffering. Thus Gautama was reared in the untroubled "happiness" of life at a wealthy court and was married at an early age. But, in his case, too, the removal of every opportunity of being tested in the real sufferings of life greatly increased his sensitivity to pain. Even those scenes of age, frailty, sickness, and death that are inseparable from the human condition were sufficient to fill him with such pessimism toward life that he came to realize the nothingness of the world, to leave wife and child, and to withdraw totally from the world—in a word, to do precisely what his father had hoped to prevent his doing.

Undoubtedly there was also operative in this choice of a way of life the protest of a young man who sought greater things, who had grown weary of the Talmi happiness of his home, and who was no longer content that his father should lead him like a child. Whenever Buddha spoke to his disciples about his youth, he always stressed the luxury that had surrounded him at home in his palaces: "With such wealth was I endowed, my disciples, in such magnificence did I live" (Oldenberg, p. 103).

We will perhaps be better able to understand what was taking place within the young Gautama if we turn our attention to the autobiographical description of the childhood of a man who grew up in very similar circumstances. It is to be found in Jean Paul Sartre's analysis of his own youthful development, to which he has given the (at first impression unusual) title *The Words*. He was "the coddled child who is bored on his perch" (p. 181). The condition of the age in which he spent his youth has been described as "the sweetness of life"; yet it was an age that was "choking to death" (p. 149). He and his companions were "coddled and . . . sensitive" (p. 223).

The young Sartre was not allowed to view real dying or death. For that very reason, however, the image of death pursued him and tortured him with fantastic grimaces. "I saw death. When I was five, it lay in wait for me. In the evening, it would prowl on the balcony, press its nose against the window. I saw it, but I dared not say anything. . . . In that period, I had an appointment with it every night in bed. . . . During the day, I recognized it beneath the most varied disguises. . . . When I was seven years old, I met real Death, the Grim Reaper, everywhere, but it was never there" (pp. 94–96).

However credible Sartre's statement that he suffered from a neurosis in his youth, it is impossible to explain that fact in terms either of psychoanalysis or of the psychology of the individual. He did not suffer from an Oedipus complex. His father had died young; his mother was like an older sister to him. Nor was he the victim of an inferiority complex for which he had to compensate by great achievements or by taking refuge in sickness. Even as a child, he was regarded as the genius of the family, upon whom they looked with amazement and from whom they expected great things. What increased the young Sartre's secret fear of death, which he dared not voice for fear of being laughed at, to the point of neurotic terror, was the realization of his metaphysical rootlessness. In his search for the causes of this "genuine neurosis," the thought intruded itself upon him:

> . . . as a spoiled child, a gift of providence, my profound uselessness was all the more manifest to me in that the family rite constantly seemed to me a trumped-up necessity. I felt superfluous; therefore, I had to disappear. I was an insipid blossoming constantly on the point of being nipped in the bud. In other words, I was condemned; the sentence could be applied at any moment. Nevertheless, I rejected it with all my might. Not that my existence was dear

to me; on the contrary, because I wasn't keen on it: the more absurd the life, the less bearable the death. (pp. 96–97)

If we turn now to one of the other Lives of Buddha and, without questioning the historical reliability of the details that are reported there, look only for a description of the milieu in which the young Gautama grew up, we gain a striking confirmation of the foregoing in the portrayal of a "happiness" unmarred by tensions. In a Tibetan Life, it is reported that from the day of his son's birth the "king's" wealth of elephants, horses, friends, and water supply for the harvest was on the increase. Great was the fame of his many cows, which gave much milk and bore excellent calves that "were good and without passions. They were fat and peaceful."[6]

There were no political tensions. The prince's "enemy became neutral; he who had been neutral became his friend; friendship was strengthened to an astonishing degree. As there were only two parties for him, there was no enemy" (p. 14). Even nature lost its terrors. "The voice of the thunder was like a gentle wind; the cloud was adorned with an encircling wreath of lightning" (Ibid.).

This blessed nature relieved men of toilsome labor. "Even when little effort was expended on field work, the grain of seed grew and brought forth fruits according to the season. And these, in turn, became . . . healing herbs, remarkable for their juices and efficacy" (p. 15).

Among the people there was order; subjects were respectful to their lords. "Freed from hunger and fear and sickness, it was as though a happy mankind enjoyed heaven itself. No one transgressed against the rights of another—neither man against woman, nor woman against man." There was no need to fear either thieves or enemies. The prince was subject to no restrictions from one higher than himself. "The king enjoyed happiness and a good harvest" (p. 15).

The prince was eager to secure the dominion to his own clan. He was "like the Lord of Creatures (Prajapati) at the beginning of time when he wanted to beget creatures." For this purpose, "he relinquished the sword. . . . He retained dominion for the sake of his son, the clan for the sake of fame, fame for the sake of heaven, heaven for its own sake; he desired his own continuance because of the law of religion; he prayed suppliantly: 'How can my son be prevented from going into the forest once he has seen the face of his son' "? (pp. 20–21). But the father's deep concern and his efforts to keep his son at home were of no avail. The son, "who had stored up *karma* [ethical consequences of his actions], gave himself up to worldly pleasures so long as he had not attained rest, for this arose out of the root (of his earlier actions)" (p. 21).

Neither Siddharta nor Jean Paul Sartre experienced in his youth the formative power of work. For both, the prevenient solicitude of a wealthy familial home removed the necessity of any solicitude for self. Those who

The Basic Experience of Buddhism

have been compelled from early childhood by poverty, necessity, or education to create, maintain, and defend for themselves the scene of their own existence are thereby so steeled in their will to live that they can endure even the bitterest suffering without complaint. There is, of course, no hard and fast norm for testing the extent to which an individual has been tempered by life or is able to overcome suffering, but there are many signs that can serve as norms. A study of the problem of suicide,[7] for instance, reveals the fact, which at first seems paradoxical, that habitual poverty affords a protection against the danger of suicide. Riches, on the other hand, and a superfluity of the material necessities of life are no pledge of an attitude toward life that is happy and free from the temptation to suicide. On the contrary, as individuals amass everything that is necessary for life or that can make it happy, life becomes for them proportionately less worth living and, in an increasing number of cases, is cast off. For centuries, modern man has grown constantly richer in the material goods of this world, but his demands on life have grown so strong and have created such a hitherto unknown sensitivity to every failure to attain satisfaction therein that the level of demand and the possibility of fulfilling it have grown further apart. There is no fixed norm that states with any degree of precision what the individual person needs if he is to achieve an existence commensurate with his dignity as man. The capacity for life differs from individual to individual; it is impossible, therefore, to measure it in terms of the material goods that one possesses or does not possess. The very fact that wealth is inherited and not earned and that insufficient demands have consequently been made upon the inner resources of the individual may well lead to a satiety that turns readily into an aversion that makes life appear worthless. It is precisely this "aversion for life" that is the burden of Sartre's analysis of human existence.

Persons in relative poverty, who have had to defend their rights from an early age if they were to feed themselves and their families, learn thereby pain and sensitivity to pain, and they learn to affirm life even when it is hard. If they regard their life as the whole sum of their personal worth, which they defend by every means at their disposal, they nevertheless approach it with a certain resignation to fate. They are aware that their life has been given them as a "fact," that they possess no legal right to it. Even if they defend it to the uttermost, they are prepared to yield without much ado to "fate" when they are deprived of it. They may, indeed, remonstrate at first and complain bitterly when fate strikes harshly and summons a loved one unexpectedly from their midst, but in the end all remonstrance gives place to a gentle resignation.

The poor man approaches life with no great preconceptions; life "promises" him little. The poor man's child usually learns early in life to expend his energy on "averting need." As a result, the child is exposed to an important fundamental experience that shapes his character in maturity:

that need can be averted by persistent personal endeavor and personal achievement. The first tentative effort of the child ends in failure, but constant struggle is at last rewarded. The child "succeeds" more and more frequently in reaching the goal toward which he is striving. From life and from his elders, the poor child "learns" a more or less realistic mastery of life; that is, he acquires a basic experience that determines his entire attitude to life: that one's own competent endeavor can suffice to stave off need and that the result may be called "success" because it does not simply happen from without, but has been won by personal effort.

The will to life mastery snatches the young person from empty dreams and forces him to set his feet firmly in reality. Every "skill" that is acquired reinforces a basic human attitude that consists in an assured self-awareness, in an inner certainty that future trials can be warded off and mastered. To be psychologically sound, the individual needs the strengthening power of an innate conviction that can overcome anxiety about the future by healthy self-confidence. It is not so much the guaranteed possession of the necessities of life, but rather the firm confidence that one will always be able to provide oneself with what is necessary that makes man "happy"—in so far as it is possible to speak in these terms. Scientists who studied the pygmies in Africa were astonished to discover that their attitude to life was both affirmative and happy although they lived from hand to mouth and were never able to provide for the future. When a person has only a scant supply of what he needs, when he must work hard and constantly to obtain it, his hope is held within "realistic" bounds; it does not exceed the limits of what can be realistically expected. The person who has been tempered by life is in no danger of losing himself in illusions and unfulfillable dreams. He has learned to distinguish between what can and cannot be expected. He knows that a temporary deprivation that causes suffering, but that can be removed by one's own effort, makes what is eventually attained doubly precious and rewarding in a very different way from what has come to the individual without his effort. The person who not only has been tempered by work and become accustomed to deprivation, but who has also acquired self-certainty by virtue of his own achievements, possesses in consequence an affirmative attitude toward life that may be attributed to his own successes.

It is quite different for the "rich" boy, especially if the father is determined to shield his son from every "need" and from every shadow of "suffering," for such a youth is deprived not only of the experience of real need, but also of the "rewarding" experience that this need can be averted by his own effort. Instead, someone is always present, when such need shows itself even in the distance, to save him the trouble of striving to avert it. In his well-protected state, he is spared the experience not only of real suffering in life, but even of genuine happiness. For "happiness," in its proper and real meaning, does not depend on what happens to the individual without his own inner participation, but in the experience that emanates from the feeling that he has "succeeded" in something by his own acquired and skillful ability. On the other hand, the careful shielding from every suffering and need and the certainty that someone will always be waiting to heal the breach of approaching need or suffering deprives the young person of one of the most important basic experiences of human life. No self-acquired resistance to the storms of life can be developed in the youth who is too well protected. The formation of a sound self-confidence is hindered if he has been "spared" the necessary experience of the steeling of his powers.

In the human development of the growing individual, the formation of the erotic and sexual drives is of central importance. In the healthy individual, they create strong tensions that spread their influence even into the psychic sphere. *Eros,* as Socrates and Plato understood the term, was that force that could be detected again and again, in their highly developed civilization, in literature, art, science, and religion. In a languishing civilization, on the other hand, drives are satisfied before they are able to create effective tensions.

For real devotion to wife and family, it makes a great difference whether the young man—as happens in most princely families—is married early and more or less passively or whether there arises in him in the course of a slowly ripening inclination a strong tension that is operative in his wooing of a bride. "Happy is he who leads his bride home," says a popular proverb. The tension that is stored up during the period of wooing and is resolved into the happiness of possession and satisfaction when the bride has been brought home is of the utmost importance for the formation of a sense of duty in the husband who knows that he "belongs" to his wife just as she belongs to him. In such a case, the husband has pledged himself closely to a life task that justly makes demands on him. He is "totally committed" to his wife and family.

It is otherwise when the prince's son is "spared" the strong personal effort required to constrain his drives and is permitted to fulfill them too excessively and too soon. This was the case with the young Buddha if we can believe the Vitae. He was encouraged to trifle amorously with women. Coquettish young women tempted and overcame him with sexual crudities. But whereas erotic pleasures used sparingly are an effective device for stirring the soul, they eventually produce the opposite effect if used without restraint: disgust consumes the initial pleasure. One becomes aware of their transitory nature. In the Tibetan Life of Buddha that has come down to us we read: "And so the young (women), whose thoughts had grown arrogant through love, attempted this and that mode of behavior with the young prince. Although he was diverted by them, he had shrouded his senses with strength and was troubled by the thought: 'Man must die,' and so was without joy and fear" (*Asvaghosa,* p. 34). "I did not turn away from sensual objects. I know that they are the essence of the world. Now that I have realized that the world is not eternal, however, my spirit finds no joy in them" (p. 36). Only one who lives in "blindness" (p. 37) can set his heart entirely on the fulfillment of his sensual desires, for he who does so is like the animals, he "is like the birds and the gazelles" (p. 37). Whoever sets his heart on such things is not "true to his being" (p. 37). "Let that action be despised in which the whole being does not participate" (p. 37). Those who are consumed by passion disappoint one another. "Since this is so, it is not right to lure me with ignoble desires (or ignoble sensual pleasure), for I am liable to death and to old age and I am plagued by suffering" (p. 37).

If a prince marries young, and especially if several women are placed at his disposal, the preconditions are lacking for the personal bond between two persons that is the recognized ideal of monogamous marriage. The time for developing tension is too short. The bride is bestowed on the prince too soon, before he has exerted himself to win her. Moreover, it is hardly possible for the drives to produce any tension worthy of the name if the bride-to-be is someone closely related to him. In addition, the link with the family that should be formed under the protection of such a guardian remains a weak one. When the initial feeling has grown cold, the marriage entered into passively soon comes to be regarded as a shackle.

If we are to understand Buddha's fundamental experience, there is one further factor we must consider. A sentimental education that seeks to spare children every suffering in life not only prevents the necessary inner hardening, but permits the development of an unhealthily rampant sensibility and sensitiveness. In Asvaghosa's life of Buddha, it is reported that the young Buddha once watched the plowing of the fields and was "disturbed" (*Asvaghosa*, p. 39) by the realization that the tender living things and the worms were killed in the process and that the oxen used for plowing had to suffer. He "suffered" on their account and spoke: "In truth, this is misery" (p. 37).

"Spoiled" children, whose demands on life are all too readily fulfilled by others, tend to place too many demands on parents, environment, and servants because their limited experience conceals from them the burdensome difficulty of the work that is required to fulfill their demands. The rich young man, moreover, can cultivate his subjective needs in a way that is impossible for the poor, who are caught up in the yoke of work. The person who is bound to no intrinsically great goals, but is intent only upon himself, is always concerned about his own feelings. In contrast to the positive and complete feeling of happiness that the poor man enjoys when he achieves his goal by his own efforts, the rich man must be satisfied with a "happiness" that comes from without and finds no echo in his innermost being. No subjective feeling, however intensively it may be cultivated, can be maintained at the level at which it is first experienced. It loses in intensity with every repetition, and this, in turn, leads the individual to simulate great feelings that he does not really possess.

The Basic Experience of Buddhism

Feelings that are convulsively clutched and cherished cannot long endure; more often, they turn into their opposites. When he has reached the limit beyond which his demands on life are no longer capable of fulfillment, the dissatisfied individual refuses at last even to accept the satisfactions that life does offer him and that he regards as too insignificant. Accustomed to demand without inquiring whether his demands can be fulfilled, he has learned meanwhile from experience that obstinate protest still sometimes leads to success. In consequence, he ends by protesting stubbornly against life and explains in angry caprice: "Everything that life offers me is 'nothing.' " "Like a lion that has been pierced to the heart by a poisonous arrow, he attained no happiness and acquired no strength, this son of the king of Sakya, although he was inclined to demand those sensual objects that enjoy the utmost respect" (p. 39).

Like the young Sartre, the young Gautama may also have been the idol, the bright rising star, of his family, for whose ascent everything was done. Such young people fall victim to the presumption that they are something special, that they stand above the mass of "ordinary people," for whom, they believe, suffering, old age, and death, as well as the absence of every success, are the normal conditions of life. There is repeated mention of the "arrogance" of the young Buddha, from which he was delivered by his experience of the nothingness of the world. "The arrogance that had become himself" had "its origin in his strength, his youth, and his life" (p. 40). "The arrogance of youth," "the arrogance of good health," and the "arrogance of life" determine the rich young man's attitude toward life. His preferential position in life leads him to believe that he has a claim to it and that he is therefore "something in his own right." But the experience of nothingness revealed this arrogance for what it was: man is nothing in his own right, "absolutely nothing."

The forces that slowly arise and become alert in the young person are waiting for goals to be set toward which they can direct their efforts. It is only when they have reached such goals that life, which is initially "empty" and "worthless," is filled with content, meaning, value, and significance. But if these forces are not awakened and developed, life remains "empty," "without content," "without significance," basically "worthless." As soon as this "emptiness" and "nothingness" are strongly experienced in a particular series of events, there arises a satiety with life, a *taedium vitae*, that undermines everything. The concomitant devaluation of world and life expresses itself in a nihilism that envelopes all of life: basically, everything is nothing.

As we can deduce from Sartre's analysis of his youth, it is above all the lack of meaning and significance in life that oppresses the "happy" child. Sartre experienced "emptiness" in this regard as a "lack of substance," as "nothingness." "The anxieties of childhood," he once said, "are metaphysical" (Sartre, p. 116). Since his father had died young, the boy could not regard the continuation of his father's work as his own natural task in life. "In short, I had no soul" (p. 88). His inner unrest arose from the fact that, despite his basic conviction "that nothing exists without a reason" (p. 86), he could discern no fixed place for himself in the universe. In the presence of strongly integrated personalities, he had the feeling: "I was *nothing:* an ineffaceable transparency" (p. 90). The spoiled child was immensely bored; "a bewildered vermin . . . [without faith or precept], without reason or purpose" (p. 93).

What troubled the boy most, what created in him the strongest sense of "insipidness" (p. 109), was the feeling that his life was without a goal; for this thought, he repeatedly uses the imagery of the passenger without a ticket in a moving train. At any moment, the ticket can be demanded of him and he can be asked his destination. Such an eventuality will cause him the utmost embarrassment. Although he was "idolized by all," possessed the "conceit of a lap-dog," and had become "the Proud One" (p. 110, passim), he was nevertheless oppressed by the feeling that he had boarded the train without any real reason for doing so.

Friends might think that the child never thought of death. "They were unaware that I didn't stop living it for a single minute" (p. 197). The "sneaking feeling that I lacked substance" (p. 208), the feeling of still not being real, drove him into daydreams about his future and about the fame that would make him immortal and his work eternal. It was, in fact, to conceal from himself the image of real death that he pictured in such glowing colors the image of the fame that was to come and that would begin with his death. He sought himself, the "great dead one of the future," who had actually been able to exist or to have existed. But all these anticipatory dreams were of no avail. To draw himself out of his own meaninglessness, he gave himself a vocation. It was not his past that became a psychic force in his life; it was the future that drew him to itself (p. 237). It might be said that he fled toward it.

As long as he had no self-assigned task in life, the child felt as though he were "condemned to experience the eternal recurrence of the same [day]" (p. 231). Once he had such a task, however, his attitude to time changed completely. "Time no longer flowed back over my childhood; rather, it was I, an arrow that had been shot by order, who pierced time and went straight to the target" (Ibid.). From that time on, it was the impetus of "faith" that lent Sartre wings, although he came later to the realization that it had been only the unauthentic faith of a substitute religion that had motivated him for decades. As he looked back, he also came to the realization that his pseudofaith had thriven in the soil of disintegrating but genuine religious faith. Whether or not it was a substitute faith, it was nonetheless able at the time to extricate him from the discomfort of a life that was stagnant.

In his daydreams, the young Sartre occupied himself with his "vocation," which, he thought, some Providence had designed for him. It was "the mandate of protecting the race" (p. 169). He imagined himself in the role of a hero, of a priest, who offered himself as a "mystic offering" (p. 179) to rescue mankind from the danger that threatened it. He would defend his people and draw down the blessing of heaven upon the human race. In doing so, he would make himself immortal.

We do not know the daydreams of the young Buddha. But it would be an understandably human trait if he had been moved by similar thoughts. There are, in fact, many indications that he dreamed of a similarly messianic role for himself. In any event, he strove to escape into broader realms from the "narrowness" and insipid emptiness of a life that was rich, but meaningless; but it was not given him to learn the role of great men from literature, as did the young Sartre, who grew up in a world of books.

A young man can be delivered from his *taedium vitae* and given new "spirit" by the sudden appearance of a new goal. The outbreak of a war that the nation regards as a struggle of life and death for its own existence, for instance, can inspire young men and make them capable of sacrificing their lives. Like everyone else, Jean Paul Sartre was given a new "spirit"—was, as it were, "swept away"—by the outbreak of World War I. One clear indication of the effect that such an experience may have on young men is the sharp decrease in the suicide rate at the beginning of a great war. Research has established this fact as a norm for many countries. It was also true of Japan's last great war. Whereas the rate of suicide in Japan before the beginning of this war was very high, it fell precipitately—at a yearly rate of almost 10 percent [8]—with the outbreak of war. Collective belief, even if later disappointment reveals it to have been belief in an idol, is better able to stir men to affirmative action and to the employment of all their strength than is the belief of the individual who must struggle to maintain it against those who do not agree with it.

Once a great life goal has become a leading principle in his life, even the self-dependent young man who regards his present life as empty and meaningless will direct his plans and actions toward the future, where he hopes to be able to establish his life on a solid foundation. Even when he is burdened with the necessity of having to create it for himself, he does not regard his own efforts as pointless or meaningless. At least, he can hope to establish and support a family in his new existence. He affirms life and approaches the future with confidence. This is even more true when the urge to achieve ideal goals has been awakened in him.

The faith of the young Sartre was a secularized faith, but it was, nevertheless, a faith that strained toward and rested in goals toward which he was impelled by the spirit of his environment. The young Buddha, on the contrary, had no such incentive. The thoughts that were to determine his actions and his person were already rooted in the Brahminism of his era. Long ago, this Brahminism had produced a pessimistic attitude toward life that dominated men's thoughts. Suffering because of the finite world and its suffering had engendered the idea of redemption. Redemption was sought in renunciation of the world. The philosophy of the era bore witness to a universally accepted "negative trait: the highest good is not the active formation of the world, but the dissociation of oneself from the world" (Oldenberg, p. 54).

We are justified in doubting whether the melancholy young Sakya prince was acquainted in any detailed way with the texts of Brahmin speculation; but he would certainly have known them from hearsay. For the historian, there can be no doubt that the tone of the religious thought and feeling of Buddhism has been derived from Brahminism.

There had long been monks such as Buddha wanted to become. Even before Buddha, as we read in a Brahmin text, it was not unusual that "Brahmins should cease to desire sons and to desire material possessions and to desire heaven in this world, and should go around as beggars" (p. 38). It is possible, therefore, that a meeting with such a monk may have provided the last incentive for the young Buddha to leave home and hearth and to exchange his princely garments for the rough clothing of a monk. In the Tibetan Life we read:

> While the pure knowledge of the noble one was increasing, free from stain, a man passed by who wore the clothing of a monk. . . . "Who are you, speak!" So spoke the son of the king, and the other answered him: "I am a religious (sramana), who has gone out in search of freedom, troubled by birth and death. . . . Because I sought the place that is happy and in which there is no becoming, and because I wished to be free in this world that is [subject to] the law of decay, . . . I freed my senses from the harmfulness of sensual pleasures. I go about free of longing and without disciples in order to attain the highest goal (as an) unencumbered mendicant who finds a dwelling place in the roots of any tree, in the forest, on a mountain, or in a house of human habitation." (*Asvaghosa*, p. 40 f.)

The report of how Buddha left the world has been adorned with many legendary elements. Warned by a monk's prophetic utterances about his newborn child, the father did everything in his power to prevent his son from renouncing the world and choosing the life of an ascetic. But the father's solicitude was in vain. On his excursions outside the palace, the youth was not spared the sight of decrepit old men, of sick men, of decaying corpses, and of ascetics. Shocked by these sights, he asked the charioteer the meaning of what he saw. After every excursion, he returned home deeply moved by the explanation that he had received. As he was returning from his fourth excursion, he received the news that a son had been born to him. He was grievously troubled and cried out: "Rahula has been born to me; a shackle has been forged for me!" But even this new "shackle" was unable to bind him forever to the homely world of his family. On the contrary, he came to realize that all existence is full of pain; and the realization drove him out into strange places. We are told in full detail how

The Basic Experience of Buddhism

Gautama stood one night for the last time beside his sleeping wife and newborn son and then took silent leave of them and of the palace where the court coquettes had been overcome by sleep. Accompanied only by his trusty charioteer, he rode to the hamlet of Anuvaieya, where he dismounted, laid aside his ornaments, exchanged his silken garments for coarse ones, and sent his companion back to the palace to report to his despairing father, to his inconsolable wife and family, the step he had taken. At the time, Gautama is said to have been twenty-nine years of age.

This report is confirmed, to some extent, by a traditional teaching that has been attributed to Buddha. It reads thus: "While I was living amid riches and pomp, the thought came to me: 'If an ignorant worldling, who is himself liable to old age, sickness, and death, catches sight of a man who is old, or sick, or dead, he feels uneasiness and aversion. But if I, even though I am also liable to old age, sickness, and death, should feel uneasiness and aversion at the sight of a man who is old, or sick, or dead, this would not be right of me.' With this thought, I lost forever all the arrogance of youth, of health, and of life."[9]

Under two teachers whom Buddha later accorded much recognition, he exerted himself to practice the salvific way of yoga. But he did not find there the satisfaction he sought. For that reason, he withdrew for many years into solitude and sought divine enlightenment through strict asceticism. In a state of complete exhaustion, he realized at last that he could not reach his goal in this fashion. To alleviate the dangerous weakness he had brought upon himself, he once more partook of ample nourishment. Under a tree the Buddhists have named "Bodhi," that is, the tree of enlightenment, he at last attained the enlightenment for which he had searched so long: in all its forms, all of life is filled with suffering; the source of this suffering is human covetousness; it is, therefore, only by sublimating this covetousness into a state of passionlessness that suffering can be overcome. This enlightenment, it will be perceived, contains nothing that was not contained in Buddha's first experience. What it means, in practice, is that the originally perceived "nothingness" of human existence has been raised to a "principle" by which everything else can be explained and from which prudent conclusions can be drawn as from a source.

The "fundamental truth" of all Buddhism—that the world is made of suffering and that flight from the world is, therefore, the only proper attitude toward it—is basically neither an ontological predication nor an insight into the existential state of the world. It is rather the outward projection of an inward experience in such a way that it becomes a quasi-principle of the world in terms of which everything can be explained and evaluated. An exaggerated resentment might declare at this point: The "whole" world is made of suffering and "only" of suffering. For this reason, it is well that we should examine the psychic background of Buddha's "enlightenment" instead of assigning it at once to logical and ontological categories. Buddha's primary experience is a "disillusionment" with the world that increases into a kind of "despair" with it.

To understand this, we must understand the full meaning of the word *disillusionment (Ent-täuschung)*. It is life that "dis-illusions" the person who lives it consciously *(er-lebt)*. The word *disillusion* is related to the word "delusion." To some extent, life "deludes" the person who must live it consciously; that is, it does not give him what it has "promised." Only that person can be disillusioned who has attempted to live his life consciously on the basis of a specific preconception. The person who approaches life with no preconceptions cannot be disillusioned by it. The greater the preconception and the deeper it is rooted in the soul, the greater and deeper will be the ensuing disillusionment. The person who is so disillusioned by life that it means "absolutely nothing" to him any more must also be the person who, in the truest sense, has been most deeply disillusioned by it.

It is not enough, however, to interpret this primary experience of the young Buddha as no more than the adolescent reaction of a spoiled young prince. On the contrary, we must admit the revelation thereby of a metaphysical depth that has its own meaning. This interpretation is confirmed by the parallels to be found in the youthful experiences of Jean Paul Sartre, in whose case the fact that he was a spoiled child did not exclude the possibility that the revelations even of childhood had their source in the metaphysical depths of his being. Whatever the reason may have been, Buddha's primary experience revealed to him the metaphysical insufficiency of the world and of life and, in doing so, posed a perennial question of mankind.

Both Buddha and Sartre experienced disillusionment with life. But the circumstances were different in each instance. In the case of the young Buddha, there had been no opportunity for a liberating faith to take form; his disillusionment with life came early and was applied without exception to "everything." It was otherwise with Sartre. For decades, until the object of his faith was revealed to him as an idol, a self-made faith rooted "in the soil of Catholicism" had delivered him from his *taedium vitae* and had given impetus to his life. It is not yet clear whether he remained fixed in his disillusionment or whether the realization that his pseudofaith was but an idol inspired him to seek further for a true faith. The analysis of his youth was written precisely to clarify his disillusionment for himself.

But there is one respect in which Buddha and Sartre are in agreement: in their denial of the personal reality of man. If Buddha, on the basis of his experience of nothingness refuses to accept the personal reality of man or his possession of an immortal soul, he must have had a preconception of person and soul that transcended man's reality. Only in this way could he have experienced the disillusionment that has since been converted into a kind of doctrine in Buddhism, namely, that man is not a person; that he does not possess a soul. The young Sartre endured a similar disillusionment. He sought for a self that was true and lasting, for the eternal self that must exist behind the fleeting and constantly changing experiences of time, or—to express it in terms more familiar to the Existentialists—for the self that he could create for himself as his eternal self. The impossibility of possessing such an enduring self led him to deny the enduring personal reality of man.

The constantly changing individual—in whose consciousness one concept drives out another and nothing has permanency, in whom no emotion is enduring, but is flung aside, in the rhythmic flux of life, by its counteremotion—cannot be regarded as a person. A real person, in Buddha's unexpressed preconception, should be able to possess himself absolutely and enduringly without danger of losing this self-possession; he should be able to maintain himself constantly on the highest level of emotional intensity.

This preconception presumes an a priori knowledge of the absolute: without this, there could be no disillusionment. In the depths of the human soul there is an unrest that yearns for absolute being and self-possession. That is the norm against which the real being of man is measured and found wanting. For that reason, the existence proper to man is regarded as empty because it lacks the requisite divine likeness. Behind man's resentment-laden denial of personal reality, it is possible to glimpse the demand for an absolute being in the divine likeness. Because the empirical I is rejected as impermanent, the eternal self, the atman, is sought in its place. Union with the atman is seen as the true redemption; if it could be attained, it would afford the desired redemption.

MAN BETWEEN ALL AND NOTHING

Buddhist and Christian Experience of Nothingness

Buddha's most basic experience was of the absolute nothingness of man and of the world; in his "enlightenment" this nothingness, which is identical with the state of suffering, becomes the principle to which everything else is subordinated. Thus *nirvana* (the state of beatitude) is the last state that can be reached—although it is not clear whether this "nirvana" is to be identified with "nothingness." The experience of nothingness is also not foreign to the Christian; on the contrary, it forms an important, even a crucial, component of the Christian attitude. In response to a query, the famous Jesuit theologian Francisco Suarez is said to have replied that the most important knowledge of all is the realization of the nothingness of the world. Unlike Buddha, however, the Christian does not regard nothingness as a final beatitude; his experience of the nothingness of his own being and of the world becomes for him the springboard for a dialectical leap from "nothing" to "all," for his inner ascent to God. Thus we read in the prayer of the Mass in honor of St. Sylvester on November 26 that God, in His great mercy, "called the saint, as he stood piously before an open grave, meditating on the vanity of the world, to the life of the desert"—and, therefore, to the way of holiness.

In both the Old and the New Testaments, man is reminded again and again of his nothingness. In Psalm 38, the psalmist speaks to God: "Behold thou hast made my days but a short span, and my life is as nothing before thee: every man is nothing but a breath. Man passes like a mere shadow, his confusion is all in vain; he stores up and knows not who shall take possession of these things" (Ps. 8:6–7). Man stands like a "breath" and a "shadow" before Yahweh, the only and unique God, beside whom there are no other gods; they are as nothing (cf. Is. 2:8). Deutero-Isaias makes the vigorous statement: "All nations are before Him as if they had no being at all, and are counted as nothing and vanity" (Is. 40:17). It is Yahweh who "bringeth the searchers of secrets to nothing, who hath made the judges of the earth as vanity" (Is. 40:23). About "false gods" Isaias speaks in particularly scathing tones: "Behold, you are of nothing, and your work of that which hath no being" (Is. 41:24).

The biblical reproach of "nothingness" is a sharp arrow against the presumptuous claim of creatures to be something in their own right. It is not only in the "service of false gods" as such that creatures are guilty of such presumption, but also in every defection by which the created world fails temporarily to take God into account. Such "foolishness" gives things the appearance of godlikeness and causes those who are deceived by this appearance to fall prey to the vanity of nothingness. From this, there arises the desire for "impure" activity. Such a life is reduced to "the vain manner of life handed down from your fathers" (1 Pet. 1:18). Because of its defection, all creation has been subjected against its will to nothingness. This is apparent in the "corruption" under which creation groans, but from which it longs to be delivered (Rom. 8:19–22).

In the Epistle to the Galatians, the apostle Paul upbraids those who flatter themselves that they are "something" in order to persuade them that they are thereby deceiving themselves, for in reality they are "nothing." "For if anyone thinks himself to be something, whereas he is nothing, he deceives himself" (Gal. 6:3). Therefore, no one should seek after empty fame or encourage another to do so, nor should anyone be envious of another.

Again and again, Paul condemns ambition, for man has *nothing* of himself, nor does he possess anything that he has not received (1 Cor. 4:7). By his reproofs, Paul hopes to stem the feverish ambition of the man who struggles to make "something" of himself, to "be" something in his own right.

However sharply the apostle reproaches the greed of mankind, however clearly he tells man that he is "absolutely nothing" in himself, it would be rash to overlook the dialectical reverse of Paul's concept if we want to grasp the entire Christian teaching about man. The whole Christian answer to the question of what man is in this world is contained in Pascal's famous aphorism: "A Nothing in comparison with the Infinite, an All in comparison with the Nothing, a mean between nothing and everything . . . infinitely removed from comprehending the extremes. . . ."[1]

According to his nature, this aphorism tells us, man is to be characterized as a mean between nothing and everything. But it also tells us that man must live his life between the two abysses of nothing and everything. It is in relation to these two extremes that he must master his human "existence." Far from understanding either extreme, he is fascinated by them, at once attracted and repelled. We might say that man stands between nothing and everything as though between two millstones that threaten to crush him, or between two magnets that draw him from opposite directions.

So far as man is concerned, not only the origin of his existence, the "whence" of his life, but also its end, the "whither" of his life, lie in impenetrable darkness. He is equally incapable of seeing the nothing from which he has been drawn or the infinity by which he is mysteriously attracted. The light in which he stands is the flickering gleam of a light shining in the midst of temporary things, bright enough to arouse hope, dark enough to permit a lapse into despair.

In principle, no man who is aware of himself as man lacks a knowledge of the fundamental facts about the beginning and end of his life. Everyone knows that his life proceeds from an incomprehensible beginning to an equally incomprehensible end; even in ordinary conversation, this truth recurs again and again. No one, it would seem, remains unaware that the state in which he now lives is a temporary one that comes to an end somewhere, that it ends in a nothing that—an inner voice whispers—is not really a nothing but an all; nevertheless most men act as though they had received a silent revelation that they should exclude from their everyday lives this knowledge of the secrecy-shrouded facts of their beginning and end and should live as though the present life were the only one.

No one contests the fact that there can be no true and lasting satisfaction in this life or that our joys are basically only vanities; yet almost all men exert themselves to "pass" their time in temporary and transitory satisfactions. They do so with as much zeal and earnestness as if, by this means, they were seeking an alibi, an excuse, for the fact that they spend no time at all in the pursuit of what is essential and beyond the reach of time. This, then, is man's true misery: that he cannot keep both ends in view. This is why he clouds his vision and attempts to establish and entrench himself in the world of temporary things as firmly as though it were a permanent world.

For many persons, it is a kind of inner paralysis and confusion that prevents them from attaining a self-consciousness that would make them able and willing to consider their existential condition in the world and, from this consideration, to draw conclusions that would direct and change their lives. Their inner confusion is strengthened by what can only be called the fascination that the things of this temporary world exercise over them: they have become incapable of freeing themselves from the bonds of this fascination. For a man like Pascal, who was open to questions about the essence of life, the blindness of the many who did not pursue these questions was monstrous and shocking.

Admittedly, one should be slow to speak of "blindness." Often, it is something much simpler that is involved, namely, helpless perplexity. Men plagued in this manner stand somehow on the edge of existential discernment. Their daily remarks about the quick passage of time and the unavoidable approach of death bear witness not only to this fact, but even more to their inability to adopt a genuine, humanly meaningful and tenable attitude toward the basic questions of life. The short-lived demands of daily living are too pressing to permit them to do so, for they do not allow man to withdraw into the realm of his spiritual "interests" and so to "lose" himself in far-reaching reflections. The necessities of life compel him to act on short notice rather than to linger over time-consuming deliberations and debates. As a result, his concern for what is essential, for what is beyond the reach of time, is postponed again and again in the silent hope that someday, without his effort, a light will dawn, a way will be opened, a leader will show himself.

The psychiatrist who inquires into the motives behind the unsuccessful suicide attempts of those whose usual concern is with the success of their weekends discovers with inner perturbation how radically the perspective of the average man in the street, who has been drawn into the hectic bustle of life in a metropolis, has been narrowed to what is immediate and closed to what lies beyond. Many of these persons admit that they succumbed to the strength of a momentary emotion with no thought for the outcome. Instead of restraining the emotion and looking once more for solutions, they retreated too soon into themselves. In short-sighted bitterness of heart, they overestimated the small annoyance in their lives augmenting it into an "all," and came to the conclusion that they could no longer live in this way. If they had waited peacefully for the emotion to subside and had achieved a sense of distance from their affliction, they would have perceived that it did not "pay" to be "afflicted unto death" since what troubled them was basically "nothing."

Jealousy, which has already cost the lives of so many men, is the natural concomitant of the griefs that make life unbearable for those ensnared in their own unbridled desires. It arises when a man has linked his existence to some person or thing and that person rejects him or that thing eludes him. The man who is plagued by jealousy believes he cannot live without the object of his desire and would rather destroy it, if it has become interiorly alienated from him, than relinquish it. Once he has been healed of this fever of jealousy, however, he shakes his head in retrospect at the madness into which he had fallen.

Individual aberrations and obsessions find their natural healing in the passage of time and the inevitable alternation of interests that accompanies it; but time alone is insufficient to heal a general attitude of premature and total abandonment to values that do not "keep" what they "promise." The person whose life is consumed by such desire experiences again and again the suffering of disappointment. In this way, he may come eventually to the realization that his entire life is "nothingness."

As he reviews his life and the storms now ended, the old man, in particular, is aware of the total "nothingness" of all that is past. Thus the patriarch Jacob complained on his deathbed: "The length of my pilgrimage has been one hundred and thirty years; short and wretched has been my life, nor does it compare with the years my fathers lived during their pilgrimage" (Gen. 47:9). The "length" of a life is something very relative. Jacob's life seems long to us, for it is about twice the length of the average span of life today. But he himself measured it against the even longer life of his forefathers. In the last analysis, however, it was not the relative shortness of his life that led him to complain. Once a time is past, it makes no difference how long it has lasted. When even the longest life nears its end, a choking anxiety arises: whoever is close to death has the feeling that he has not yet begun to live properly. Until the peak of life, he did not regard as applicable to himself the common human lot of mortality. Now that death reaches out for him, all colors lose their glow. Everything that has thus far seemed important and that has served to distinguish him from others—health and strength, higher or lower station in life, happiness or unhappiness—reveals its insignificance before the common fate of all mankind. In a few brief years, the life of even the longest-lived comes to an end; what is past survives only in its consequences.

The sense of the nothingness of human life deepens when the individual becomes aware that he cannot live his talents to the fullest. Even the oldest man complains, when he nears death, about the shortness of his life. At first glance, this may seem incompatible with the boredom that lies heavy on whole periods of man's life during which life seems to stretch ahead endlessly, each hour seems to tarry, and no end is in sight. But as soon as the end approaches, the time that has passed begins to seem like a dream with no full reality of its own. As long as we are able to plan our lives, to look ahead, to use our powers; as long as we know that we are responsible for the course of events, these events acquire for us the character of a reality that we possess and shape. The present moment belongs to us; but it is fleeting. Once it has gone and we look back upon it in memory, we see our past life as it were from outside, as a time that has elapsed and in which we no longer exist. Even those events that lasted the longest are like dust and weigh nothing in comparison with that moment of life in the world that is still with us. Not without justice, a Latin proverb says of man: "Dum spirat, sperat"—"While there's breath, there's hope." The man who is alive hopes for great things from life; in virtue of this expectation, we have at every moment an inner awareness that we possess a living soul. If we look back, we are disappointed to discover how little life has thus far kept its promises. We live on these promises, but we are compelled again and again to realize that life has not kept them. In retrospect, we mourn for our days, which were "few and evil," however long our life may have lasted. If we have nothing more for which to hope, we are threatened with "desperation," hopelessness, despair.

The despair of most men is a mute resignation; they are incapable of really understanding their condition and of explaining it to themselves. Their complaint is a lament before men who do not consider themselves responsible for this fate since it does not differ from their own, and who, for that reason, pay little heed to such a complaint. Only the effort really to understand his lot can help the individual to overcome his mute despair. Both the Christian and the Buddhist regard life as full of suffering if for no other reason than that it is transitory. But they make no attempt to bolster their contention with statistics by totaling up the harsh fates of individual men. The fact that life is transitory is for them sufficient grounds for denying to every happiness that life has to offer the power to satisfy them completely. That alone is an unmistakable proof that man's earthly life promises something that it does not bestow. It promises a life that is completely immortal, but life is mortal. Death is contained in life just as eternity is contained in time. As Kierkegaard once remarked, man is a paradoxical synthesis of time and eternity.

Life on earth charms us with beginnings that have no real endings in our lifetime. Our intellectual gifts, for instance, force us, once we are aware of them, to the conviction that they will have to outlast this life if they are to be realized and perfected. For those who recognize their nature, they are, as Cardinal Newman once said, a pledge of immortality. When we consider the greatness of these gifts and the shortness of the time in which they are to be developed, they compel our spirit to think ahead and to assume, as their almost necessary counterpart and as a logical inference from the shortness of this earthly life, a life that does not come to an end. The Christian expects, as a kind of compensatory justice from a Lord of the World who did not create man for nothing, the possibility of living to the fullest, in a life without end, the potentialities that have been given him.

For most men, these thoughts are subliminal. When they hear them expressed for the first time, they feel they have been penetrated to the depths of their being, but they do not always have the courage to admit this fact even to themselves.

Newman expounded this clearly in his analysis of the Christian experience of nothingness. Man's natural longing to endure beyond the confines of this life is characteristic also of the non-Christian and of those who lived before the advent of Christianity, but with this difference: that the latter were able, even less often than the Christian, to summon the courage to admit this expectation to themselves in its more positive sense. There were two reasons for this. If the man who lives under the influence of Eastern thought does not have the positive promise of divine revelation, he has little opportunity to discover by experience what fruits can be expected from his own efforts to use his gifts to the fullest. The Buddhist is not compelled by an already awakened and repeatedly nourished inner necessity to make something of his life, to trade with the talents that have been given him for his life's journey, so he will be able, in the end, to return them with fruit and with interest.

The Christian who sees a respected fellowman of his acquaintance sink into the grave is usually overcome by the sad thought: This man has not been able to develop the gifts that were bestowed upon him to anything like their full potentiality. For that reason, even the old man, whose life has been full of activity, has the feeling that he has brought nothing at all to completion, that his life has hardly begun. Many men mature slowly and painfully; for years and even decades, they are prevented by their inhibitions from living their lives as they would like to live them. Yet, at the very moment when these inhibitions have at last been overcome, when the hurdles of their trials have all been taken, when they would like to let the whole warmth of their hearts and the clarity of their spirits shine forth, at that very moment, their life is prematurely broken off. They have never been able to show all that was in them. There are others who have spent years in physical or spiritual prisons; when they are finally released into blessed freedom, their strength has already been exhausted.

We lament the dead who bore a treasure within themselves that they were unable to use. Compared with their potentialities, their days were indeed but few and evil. In consequence, we feel ourselves driven to look to a future state in which these unrecognized gifts will emerge and be fully developed. Such experiences can lead the Christian, on the basis of his particular presuppositions, to a kind of obvious conviction that a future life does exist, to a certainty that touches and pierces the heart that is palled by the palpable imperfection of the present. For such a one, even the misery of this present life on earth is overcome by the prospect of another life that promises dignity and worth.

If all striving and experience are "vain," as he who preached the "vanity of vanities" (Ecclesiastes) complained; if this life is repeatedly designated as a kind of "dream," this is done in the simultaneous expectation that this "dream" will be followed by an "awakening," this "nothingness" by "fulfillment." In this way, the present life does not lose its value; on the contrary, its value increases, for it is a time of risk in which the other life can be won or lost. If our earthly life is no lasting part of us because our true life is immortal and our true being is permanent, it is nonetheless the stage on which our game of chance is to be played. Its purpose is to test us.

It is true that the Christian is seldom completely aware of this meaning of his life. He lives, for the most part, in a certain dependence on the world; because he has closed his eyes to the things of eternity, he needs the exhortation of Ecclesiastes or of Angelus Silesius, who urged:

> Be what you are, O Man!
> When time shall be no more
> And chance has lost its sway,
> The real will yet endure.

The exhortation is a plea for "conversion" (German: *Be-kehrung* = a total turning from or to)—not only because of man's forgetfulness in his dependence on time, but also because of that particular temptation from which not even the Christian is immune. For that reason, Paul warns the Christian against the feverish anxiety of wanting to become or to be something in order to be proud of becoming or being it.

It is precisely this striving, this wanting to be "something," combined with the nihilating experience that one can make "nothing" of oneself that we find analyzed in the works of Jean Paul Sartre. It is important to pursue his line of thought, for his philosophy is highly regarded in East Asia. Indeed, the understanding of his fundamental thesis can build a bridge between the Christian and the Buddhist experience of nothingness. For far too many Japanese, Sartre is a magician of words who utters secret words that no one really understands, but behind which one suspects the existence of an undecipherably deep meaning. Sartre's experience of "being" and of "nothingness" can lead us to the meaning of that temptation of which both the apostle Paul and the mystics have warned us and of which—when he is rightly understood—Buddha, too, would warn us.

Sartre's idiosyncratic philosophizing in his principal work *Being and Nothingness*[2] is not concerned with being as such, but with the basic problems of human existence. The problem with which he is struggling is the problem of human "nothingness" and of man's attempts to overcome it by his own efforts. Man's philosophizing begins with the fact of his consciousness. Unlike inanimate objects, which exist *in* themselves *(en soi)*, man is that which exists *for* itself *(pour soi)*. The man who has become conscious of himself suffers from his own being because it is not its own foundation of being *(causa sui)*. For that reason, he looks with envy upon the being of those creatures that exist in themselves, for they seem to him to be "being" in its purest form. Sartre regards the conscious "awareness of self" not as an increase but as a decrease of being because it seems to cause a fissure in the unity (of being) that was originally normative: he regards consciousness as something negative, as, indeed, the nothingness of being. For it is by his consciousness that man becomes aware of the nothingness, of the "original contingency," of his being.

The "in-itselfness" of being is forced from its positivity and unity into a state of "presence-to-itself," but in such a way that the "in-itselfness," although it is not lost, never matures into "the foundation of being." Thus man experiences in his consciousness his own "original contingency." This does not mean that man's "being-in-itself" is not retained in his "being-for-itself." But the nihilation of his "being-in-itself" that gives rise to his "being-for-itself" tears that "hole of being" *(trou d'être)* that Sartre calls nothingness. Because "being-for-itself" remains linked to "being-in-itself" with its contingency, man becomes conscious of his original contingency as "abandoned-ness"—as a condemnation to total responsibility for himself. In his being as known to his consciousness, man is but a "happening," a "fact," apparently without foundation.

He is suspended over nothingness. Precisely this awareness creates in man an anguish, a primitive anguish, and a striving to "found" his being. As there is apparently nothing that is a foundation of his being, man's passionate longing is to give himself a foundation. Consequently, his being-for-itself continues to do what had previously been done by his being-in-itself—and Sartre designates this as a "fall."

Sartre offers his faithful readers a unique myth of being. He allows a cosmic drama to unroll before their eyes. In the beginning, there existed being-in-itself, resting in itself and perfected in perfect positivity, but also absolutely contingent. In this being-in-itself there arose one day the wish to achieve a foundation for its being. Since nothing was present except itself, it had to make the attempt itself to found itself. But such a self-foundation, such a self-justification, was possible only if the being-in-itself established a relationship to itself; in other words, if it dissociated itself from itself and set itself into a relationship with itself. In doing so, it could not avoid assuming nothingness into itself, what Sartre calls the "ontological fall," the consequence of the hubris of being-in-itself, which was not satisfied with a paradisaic contingency. The nothingness that was assumed rent the being-in-itself and settled in the resultant fissure as a "nothing-in-itself." In consequence, however, being-in-itself fell from its peaceful perfection, was "degraded," and was marked in a certain measure with the eternal unrest that is the sign of Cain. The goal of the transformation of being-in-itself into a full being-for-itself was not reached. There is always present in being-for-itself an untransformed remnant of being-in-itself, and this is its original contingency.

Of this ontological fall is born human consciousness, the ability not only to speak of oneself as "I," but also to separate oneself from everything that is not "I." At the same time, nothingness, the basis of all negations, is thereby brought into the world. For Sartre, the absolute event is the appearance of a being-for-itself that is in the process of becoming self-conscious. It corresponds to the expulsion of being-for-itself from the paradise of the static contingency of being-in-itself and the simultaneous entrance of nothing into the world. Human reality is never simple. It is the constant compulsion of having to found oneself without being able to do so. In this connection, Sartre wrote the following sentence that shimmers with a kind of self-knowledge: "Human reality is the pure effort to become God without there being any given substratum for that effort, without there being anything that makes such an effort" (p. 664). Every human reality is a passion that has as its goal both to found being and, at the same time, to constitute that being-in-itself that is not subject to contingency because it is its own foundation, a kind of *ens causa sui*. In consequence, it is man's constant goal to make himself God; in reality, however, he destroys himself in the attempt.

Sartre's phantastic myth about the beginning of consciousness nihilates man's intellectual self-possession. Sartre does not see, in the fact that man can possess himself intellectually—or, as he expresses it, that man is "being-for-itself"—a condition of being that has positive value, but a deterioration, a fall, a *negativum,* something of which man would gladly be free again. When he explains the origin of consciousness by means of a cosmological myth that contains palpable contradictions, he gives rise to the suspicion that he has failed to recognize the positive significance of man's self-possession because he does not want to acknowledge the task that is inseparable from it. Pure being-in-itself is said to burn with the desire to found itself and to have caused, by this hubris, the fall from positive being-in-itself. The contradictions are obvious: "desire," "hubris," "fall," can exist only where consciousness is already present. Being-for-itself is a precondition for their very existence. In the world that we know from experience, there is only one place where "desire," "hubris," or "sin" could originate, namely, in the man who possesses himself. It is here that we must seek the origin of that covetousness that is, as the apostle tells us, the root of all evil (1 Tim. 6:6). So far as we know from experience, it is only man, goaded by selfishness and greed, who can do "evil" and thus, in the words of the poet, give rise to that evil that must always produce further evil. It is an all-too-human trait that man does not find the courage to admit this fact, but is concerned, instead, with "excusing" himself. For this reason, he ends by shifting the guilt from himself onto whatever uncontrollable cosmic power phantasy may suggest to him. Nor should we evaluate differently the myth of Brahminism that ascribes suffering in the world to some initial sin of Brahman himself, thereby turning the whole history of the world into a history of suffering in which Brahman does penance for his initial sin.

Because of the cosmic sin of being-in-itself, the striving to found himself and so to make himself God is rooted deeply in man. Man, Sartre says, is a useless passion, for the idea of God is contradictory and we destroy ourselves in vain. To this we might answer: Man's striving to become his own foundation does not founder because the idea of God is contradictory in itself, but because the foundation of man's own being, out of which he has sprung as a being established in fact, always lies before him; thus man, for all his compulsive striving to found himself, must always come too late because of his facticity. He will never be able to reach the foundation of his own being in such a way that he would be not only "for-himself," but also, and in addition thereto, "his own foundation."

As Sartre has shown in his great self-confession *The Words* and as we have already described briefly, both his youth and the peak of his life were ruled by the delusion that he could free himself from his contingency by virtue of the written word, could give himself a lasting foundation, a lasting name, and a lasting meaning. The great insight of the aging philosopher was his realization that such an attempt was an empty delusion, that it was "nothing," that it had deceived and blinded him to the utmost degree. In retrospect, the illusion of faith in himself has crumbled away. His atheism has become for him a long and terrible venture that rends him tragically.

Because of this second great experience of nothingness, Sartre is confronted with the necessity of making a new decision. His "faith" in himself grew in the soil of Christianity; it conjured up the idea of God in his life, and he is not able to rid himself of it. His insight into the complete nothingness of his own being informs him that this being neither is, nor can be, "its own foundation." Nevertheless, it would be precipitate and misleading to conclude therefrom that one's own being is nothing at all. It "is" without a doubt, but it is a being without a foundation in itself. In that case however—and the conclusion is ineluctable—its foundation must lie in another being, and that being must really be, as Sartre says, an *ens causa sui*. But that can only be God. If this self-evident and spontaneous inference is not drawn, it can only be because it has been deliberately and intentionally excluded. Once enkindled, the desire for "self-glorification" will not tolerate this obvious conclusion.

Sartre is the product of an intellectual world that was becoming more and more alienated from Christianity. It was from this world that he derived his knowledge of God. The attempt at self-glorification that he has thus far been making is, therefore, an unqualified atheism, a decision against God. If his great "disappointment" with life has brought him once more to a turning point in his life, it is not yet clear whether he will change the decision once made against God or whether he will become obdurate in it. Emancipated from his long delusion by disappointment and by the renewed experience of the nothingness of life, he is again free and at liberty to make a new decision.

What Sartre attempted so unsuccessfully was attempted with equal lack of success by other writers of recent years. Four in particular might be named here: Stefan Zweig, Cesare Pavese, Klaus Mann, and Ernest Hemingway. Common to all four is the fact that their great disappointment with life led them to lay violent hands on themselves. In an analysis of the self-revelations of the last three, Hans Jürgen Baden[3] has shown to what extent suicide was the logical consequence of their disappointment with life. All of them had had great expectations from their literary work: it was to make their name luminous and preserve it for posterity. It was to "justify" their existence. They were filled with the ambition of really making something "of themselves," but they understood this "something" as "something that they had produced of themselves." All of them, however, learned to their grief that ambition had led them to place too great demands on literature. Once they realized that even their literary work was transitory, that it was subject to the forgetfulness of a generation with totally different expectations about literature, they became more and more acutely and radically aware of nihilism and its logical consequence. For this reason, too, their work lost its enchantment for them. The myth of creativity, of the self-insurance of the creative man in his work, evaporated. There remained only the lonely and anguished creature at whose feet the abyss was opening.

During the war years, Klaus Mann, the son of Thomas Mann, was able to postpone the last consequence of his nihilism by means of a military "engagement" that dispelled—admittedly only for a time—his melancholy, his despair, his longing for death, and his hallucinations. After the war, however, when he was discharged from the service and had to return to the emptiness and meaninglessness of his own existence, he was lost. He did have a distant vision of the thought of God as an anchor of hope that could save him from sinking into despair. But he lacked the strength to return to a faith that had never been a living one for him. So destiny was fulfilled. At the early age of forty-three, he took his own life.

What these writers had in common was the fact that they came from an intellectual world in which the thought of God occupied a central position. It is difficult to say to what extent they themselves had been affected by their intellectual environment, but it would seem that they were at least to that extent alienated from it that only an exterior and real "conversion" could have made them open to a decision in favor of God. It is otherwise with men who as youths have been awakened in the depths of their souls by the *mysterium fascinosum* of God. An awakening like that of the young Friedrich Nietzsche cannot be obliterated. A life that has experienced it must henceforth revolve around God whether it decides for him or against him. It remains bound to God even when it strives to escape him. It cannot remain entrenched in an inner, unmoved neutrality. Personal decision must end either in the "yes" of love of God or in the "no" of hatred of him. There is no third alternative.

This is not true of Gautama Buddha. His conversion included no decision for or against God because he had never experienced a vital confrontation with the thought of God. Before we continue with our analysis of the Buddhistic experience of nothingness, however, it will be well to explain further the temptation to which Sartre was exposed.

Although we possess in Sartre's self-analysis a "model case" in which the meaning of the experience has been grasped and expressed with great awareness, even though the interpretation is faulty, it is also true that we meet with much the same attitude in daily life among those who do not, however, possess such a clear awareness and, in particular, such a broad view of its inner consequences. Even Christians, who claim to believe in the living God, merit the reproach of the apostle that they imagine themselves to be something whereas they are nothing.

The reproach is directed at those who lack adequate self-knowledge. The Christian ought to know that he possesses nothing of himself, that he has been able to achieve all that he has achieved by his own efforts only because he was possessed of an a priori talent, because he was "gifted," to bring to fruition precisely those efforts. It follows that his own achievement is not his own in any real sense of the word; of himself he possesses nothing to the degree that his willing or thinking would or could be the foundation of its being. The Christian who does not arrive at this self-knowledge, but believes that he can ascribe to himself all his being and achievement, is "blinded" by empty pride. A fundamentally foolish desire to be entirely himself prevents him from perceiving the simple fact that no man can be his own possession if this is taken to mean that he thereby possesses himself as his own foundation. Indeed, this suppressed knowledge rises again and again to deprive him of inner peace; in disappointments, he realizes anew that he does not—and never can—possess himself as his own foundation.

The attempt to possess oneself as one's own foundation, combined with the blindness that refuses to recognize the facticity of one's own talents and frustrated by the unceasing disappointments that do violence to such a presumptuous attempt, brings man finally to that state of despair that Kierkegaard describes as "the despair of willing despairingly to be oneself."[4] In this despair, the despairer expresses his disappointment about his expectations, more particularly, about his expectations of the eternal that he seeks in himself. His defiance will not admit that the existing self is not really eternal. The "eternal in man" that burns in expectation of fulfillment, but that is not purely eternal, ends in defiance, in the "despairing abuse of the eternal in the self to the point of being despairingly determined to be oneself. But just because it is despair by the aid of the eternal it lies very close to the true, and just because it lies very close to the true it is infinitely remote. The despair which is the passageway to faith is also by the aid of the eternal: by the aid of the eternal the self has courage to lose itself in order to gain itself. Here on the contrary it is not willing to begin by losing itself but wills to be itself" (p. 201).

There is a deep meaning in the paradoxical words: whoever wants to gain his self must lose it. Whoever wants to gain his self in its full reality as determined by and founded in God must give up the struggle of the separative self *(das verselbstete Selbst)* that destroys itself daily in the impossible attempt to found itself. The feeling or attitude toward life of the individual whose self is totally preoccupied with self, who refuses in his soul to accept the facticity of his self, can be regarded only as "tragic." By his attitude, such an individual has closed to himself every possible road that might have led him to the discovery of God.

The attitude toward life of many cultured Japanese who have been impregnated with Buddhism is one of sad resignation, of dissatisfaction with existence and self as they are in fact, and of regretful certainty that no change is possible. For the cultured Japanese, indeed, it is an affair of honor to have to present "a gloomy countenance" to the world. He takes pleasure in resignation. "No change is possible in this regard"—*Shikataganai*—is an expression often repeated in Japan. It expresses vexation at and a haughty acquiescence to the tragic unchangeableness of life. Although generalities are dangerous, it would seem that not a few Japanese regard it as superficial to be unruffled, to accept life as it is. It is a sign of greatness not to be satisfied with one's existence, but to disengage oneself from it, to wear a constantly pained expression. "To be pained" by "existence" and to display one's pain defiantly is a "heroic" pose that is readily assumed.

Suppressed resentment against existence, the tightly clutched mask of tragedy, leaves its corrosive mark on the individual's attitude. There is no room for humor, no liberating laughter; the most one can permit oneself is a self-satisfied smile. Humor would be interpreted as an affirmation of the sharp edges, the corners, and the insufficiencies of one's own being and of life together with others, as a sign that one did not accept these lacks as an unchangeable *brutum factum* of existence, but as a call to patience and to the effort to come to terms with them. A German professor teaching in Tokyo reports that his attempt to stage a German comedy with Japanese as actors very nearly resulted in tragedy because they were at first totally unable to relax their stiff features in liberating laughter.

Akirame is a word that is very characteristic of the Japanese attitude toward life. It has been explained as follows by one who knows Japanese life well:

> It might be possible to translate it as resignation or submission. There is hardly another word that appears so frequently in modern lyric poetry or in religious writings. In modern usage, it expresses weltschmerz or the melancholy of being, especially of human existence in an alien world. Buddhists, in their interpretation, associate the word with "akikara ni muru," that is, "to see clearly"—to see, or at least to suspect, the absolute through the veil of this world; but this is possible only for him who has renounced all unruly drives and impulses. The original meaning seems to have been that one ceased to pursue his personal wishes in order not to run counter to the wishes of one higher than himself. Since the meaning of the word is derived from three different sources, it is not surprising that it is used frequently today.[5]

Between the Christian and the Buddhist experience of nothingness, there is an essential difference that should not be overlooked. Arthur Schopenhauer once compared Buddha to Francis of Assisi: Both were deeply aware of the nothingness of life; both were "converted" and left their father's house to become mendicants. In both, there was a certain predisposition that prepared them to hear the call when it came. A band of disciples gathered around both.

According to ancient Buddhist records, Buddha quickly became a successful preacher. His success was almost certainly due to the fact that many of his contemporaries, especially among the nobility, were of a frame of mind very similar to the one that had led to his own "conversion." To a certain extent, they were ready for the leap into a new life; only the final impulse was lacking. It required no more, therefore, than a living example that compelled their imitation to bring clearly to their consciousness the insight into the "nothingness" of their former arrogant way of life.

In the "Songs of the Elders," the most renowned of Buddha's followers tell how their personal meeting with him provided the last impetus needed to make them take the step from home to homelessness. Even if these poems have only been ascribed to the disciples whose work they purport to be by later poets of the spiritual life, they may nevertheless be an accurate reflection of the experience of those called to be disciples. In these self-revelations, they tell about the happiness and sorrow of the life in the world that now lies behind them, of the time when arrogance about their exemplary birth and wealth, about beauty and alluring love held their enraptured hearts in the thrall of oppressive longing. In memory, they dwell on struggles and expectations. "Who in this world will loose my bonds? Who will let me enjoy the awakening?" To those who waited, there appeared the luminous picture of the great bringer of peace: "I looked upon Buddha, the hero, accompanied by the throng of his disciples, as he entered the royal city of the Magadha country. Thereupon, I threw off the burden that I bore and went and bowed down before him. Taking pity on me—yes, on me—he stood still, the Highest of all men. . . . Then the compassionate Master, the merciful Lord of all the earth, spoke to me: Come forward, monk! It was the consecration of a monk that I received."[6] As the text continues, it resounds like a song of triumph; memory recalls the great and decisive moment in which the struggler won his victory, in which darkness was dissipated and the soul lost its bonds.

For the circle of his disciples, Buddha's own experience of conversion was the great model that they imitated and tried to reproduce in their own lives, but that they also, in a typical way, surpassed. The "ascetics who follow the son of Sakya"—as Buddha's disciples were first called—freed themselves from family and relatives as the master had done. "Those thirsting for salvation recognized in no bond of love or duty the right to hold them back in the world; the husband who wants to follow Buddha says to his wife: 'If you cast our child to the jackals and the hounds, O wretched one, you will still not move me to return for the child's sake'" (p. 144). Gautama himself had taken tender leave of the wife who had touched his heart. Out of gentle thoughtfulness, he had been unwilling to awake his sleeping spouse and his small son. Among his disciples, however, the departure that separated them from their loved ones was harshly exaggerated and rudely and ruthlessly carried out. If Buddha's followers shared their master's experience of nothingness and rejected the arrogance that was based on life, riches, and health; if, like their master, they left their home and went into homelessness, there arose in them, nonetheless, a new arrogance that had its source in their awareness of having been saved by their renunciation of the world and of having entered into the number of the chosen.

Did Buddha, too, possess this arrogance? The reports contain unmistakable indications that he did. After his "enlightenment" under the Bodhi tree, Buddha "enjoys" and, therefore, for some time refuses to detach himself from his unique experience, to communicate it to men, and thereby to set in motion the wheel of his teaching. The "tempter" tries to entice him to enter quickly into the final nirvana and in this way to deprive men of his preaching of "salvation." In his self-enjoyment, he feels inwardly compelled not to concern himself with the salvation of others. But he lets himself be moved to pity. Brahman himself comes down from heaven to beseech him humbly and fervently. At last, therefore, he "relents" and begins the work of salvation for others.

Through his "enlightenment," Gautama rose to the status of a Buddha. It is important that we understand clearly that the dignity of Buddhahood was not bestowed upon him by someone else. No superior court has the prerogative of deciding who is to attain Buddhahood or when it is to be attained. Brahman, who was originally the God of the World, has lost his high status; his is not the highest court of justice. In his hand, he holds no scale for weighing, judging, or evaluating. He comes himself, as a lowly suppliant, to Buddha, who has achieved the highest knowledge and who, in doing so, has bestowed upon himself the dignity of Buddhahood.

In this way, he became the "Exalted One," that is, the qualitatively different one who had been raised above the ranks of ordinary men. It was he himself—and this must be emphasized again and again—who bestowed upon himself the title of the "Exalted One," although, to be sure, his disciples fawningly accepted it. In this way, they began a cult of the person of Buddha that has resulted, in many Buddhist groups, in his being placed on the throne vacated by the God of the World. This exaltation and self-exaltation are in sharp contrast to Buddha's original intention of pointing out to his disciples the unique way that was to lead them to the same enlightenment that had been his.

In itself, the great "enlightenment" of Buddha was his insight into the total nothingness of everything human. By a remarkable inconsistency, however, precisely this experience was enhanced into something that raised man into a completely different, higher, even absolute sphere.

In the community of those who believe, Buddha's "enlightenment" about the total nothingness of world and life and the consequent necessity of renouncing the world is raised to a joyous experience; they are "victors" over those who are still imprisoned in the world. Of course, it is only hinted that in reality every "victor" ought to become a "Buddha," for, in fact, only one, the first, the leader, attains to the dignity of Buddhahood. It is precisely this self-bestowed Buddhahood, or at least quasi-Buddhahood, that provides a very positive conclusion to the successful endurance of the experience of nothingness. All those who have seen through the nothingness of the world, who have freed themselves from their customary "home life," and who have gone out into the endless expanse of homelessness know that they are the "Exalted Ones." Although they consider it beneath their dignity to petition for favors, they walk in the firm confidence that ordinary people will deem it a privilege if the "Exalted Ones" accept gifts from them. The mere renunciation of the world is for these "victors" the perfection of their call "to live in holiness and to make an end of all suffering" (p. 153).

For the Buddhist convert, this "living in holiness" is something quite different from the Christian convert's life of striving for holiness. For the Christian, the experience of nothingness is not something final in which he can rest, but a step by which he ascends. The Christian convert knows that his experience is only the gateway, the transition, to a new beginning. He knows that he is "on the way"—*in via;* that he is the *viator,* the pilgrim. With his conversion there was opened to him a timeless and lasting world of values; now he is to realize these values in his life. He has been assigned a task that can be accomplished only by the unremitting effort of a whole lifetime.

It is otherwise for the Buddhist "saint." He is already in the state of holiness. He is no longer a "viator," a pilgrim, but one who has been perfected. This statement must be qualified. In many Buddhist sects, constant effort is consistently demanded and Buddhahood is regarded as something in the nature of a distant goal that is always fascinating and attractive, but not totally accessible to anyone.

As the individual's reliving of the original experience of Gautama Buddha, the Buddhist experience of nothingness does not encompass that great decision to which the Christian is brought by the experience of conversion. The danger of that "mystical self-intoxication" of which one wise expert on East Asian Buddhism has spoken (Reischauer),[7] is, in fact, a danger that the Buddhist himself prefers to deny; but it is present, for all that, and must be regarded as an obstacle on the journey to God. In Buddhism, the path of such a journey is not barred; on the contrary, it lies open to those who seek it in sincerity of heart. On the basis of his own experience and knowledge, in any event, Enomiya-Lassalle is convinced that many individual Zen Buddhists of high rank have completed this journey in their own lives, although they do not speak of it.

The Christian ascetic regards the glorification of his own experience of conversion as a serious temptation that must be overcome. Once his life has been thus changed, he presses forward constantly toward the great goal that rests in eternity. He perseveres in humility and strives always to realize the values of eternity. As long as his earthly life continues, he stands before the judgment seat where, in the end, it will be decided whether or not he has reached the state of perfection.

4

BUDDHIST VERSUS CHRISTIAN DOCTRINE OF SUFFERING

It is only since the last century that the necessary conditions for a comparison of Buddhism and Christianity can be said to exist. After a journey to the Far East, the Frenchman Anquetil Duperron (1731–1805) translated into Latin the so-called *Oupnekhat*, a Persian version of fifty Upanishads. While Arthur Schopenhauer was in Jena, it was called to his attention by the Jena Orientalist, Friedrich Majer, a disciple of Herder. This young enthusiast, who extolled the Hindus above the Greeks and Romans, was convinced that man had reached, in the Ganges valley, the highest goals of religion—nothing short of "a revelation of the eternal upon whose pure glory the dazzled eye of mortal man can hardly bear to gaze."[1] Majer's enthusiasm was transmitted to Schopenhauer, whose melancholy attitude had already caused an estrangement from his more optimistic mother, and who now found in Brahminism and Buddhism a philosophical affirmation of his own pessimism.

So far as we know, Schopenhauer was the first person in the nineteenth century to compare Buddhism with Christianity and to conclude therefrom that they were, by reason of their pessimism about the world, fundamentally identical in greatness. Indeed, he went so far as to believe that he should bestow the palm on Buddhism because it was more consistent in its view of the world's wickedness.

Genuine Christianity was, it must be admitted, something alien to Schopenhauer. He knew it only in the form of a liberal Protestantism that, with its twofold "repeal," actually "repealed" Christianity—a fact that Schopenhauer, because of his critical spirit, realized more keenly than anyone else. In 1874, when Eduard von Hartmann entitled one of his writings *The Spontaneous Decomposition of Christianity*, he was merely making use of an expression that had been in current usage for some decades.[2]

Schopenhauer directed his fierce criticism against "Hegel, the professor of philosophy," whom he accused of having invented the expression "absolute religion" to conceal his true intentions. In particular, he felt called upon to denounce the pantheism of Hegel and other theoretical philosophers. According to Schopenhauer, *pantheism* is an expression of cowardice; it identifies God with the world "for no other purpose than to be able to dispose of Him with decorum."[3] Nietzsche, who regarded Hegel as the retarder of modern atheism, which was long overdue, credited Schopenhauer with being "the *first* avowed and inflexible atheist we Germans have had."[4] Unqualified atheism was for Schopenhauer, as Nietzsche correctly added, a prerequisite of his whole philosophy. For that very reason, however, it is difficult to see in him the qualities needed by one who would make a valid comparison between Buddhism and Christianity. This is equally true of all those who accept the thesis of the "spontaneous decomposition of Christianity." The result of Schopenhauer's comparison cannot, therefore, be accepted without correction.

"For me," Schopenhauer once said,

> the fundamental difference of all religions is not, as so many would have it, whether they are monotheistic, polytheistic, pantheistic, or atheistic, but whether they are optimistic or pessimistic, that is, whether they represent the existence of this world as justified in itself and therefore praise and extol it, or whether—because they realize that pain and death cannot abide in the eternal, original, unchangeable order of things, in that which, in every respect, ought to exist—they regard it as something that can be comprehended only as a consequence of our guilt, as something that ought not, therefore, to exist at all. The power by which Christianity was able to overcome first Judaism and then the paganism of Greece and Rome rests solely in its pessimism, in the admission that our condition is at once extremely sorrowful and sinful, whereas Judaism and paganism were optimistic. That truth, experienced deeply and painfully by all, predominated and entailed the necessity of redemption.[5]

Christianity and Buddhism agree, according to Schopenhauer, in their recognition of the state of the world as one that ought not to exist. We are as we ought not to be and, as a result, we necessarily do what we ought not to do. "Therefore, we need a complete metamorphosis of our disposition and being; that is the rebirth that has redemption as its consequence."[6] The root of our guilt, Schopenhauer says, lies in our essence and existence. Our only true sin, he contends, is original sin.

> But the Christian myth has original sin appear only after man already exists and endows him besides, *per impossibile,* with a free will: but it does this simply as myth. The innermost core and spirit of Christianity is the same as that of Brahminism and Buddhism: they all teach that man's burden of guilt comes from his existence itself; but with this difference, that Christianity does not do so directly and openly as those more ancient religions do. It does not regard guilt as the inescapable concomitant of existence itself, but as caused by an act of the first two human beings. This was possible only if one accepted the fiction of the *liberum arbitrium indifferentiae;* it was necessary only because of the fundamental Jewish dogma into which this teaching was here to be grafted. For in truth the very origin of man is itself an act of his free will and consequently identical with his fall into sin; original sin, therefore, of

which all other sins are the result, had already come into the world with man's *essentia* and *existentia*. But Jewish teaching did not accept this postulate. Therefore Augustine taught in his books *De Libero Arbitrio* that it was only in Adam before the fall that man was free from sin and had a free will, but that, from that time on, he was entrapped in the necessity of sin. (Ibid.)

Schopenhauer is of the opinion that the story of man's fall into sin is the only possible place in Jewish theism where the graft of an Old Indian stem is possible. In that case, he insists, existence itself must be looked upon as an aberration, and redemption as the return from it (vol. IV, p. 625). If Schopenhauer denies the possibility of a free human will and, therefore, the possibility of sin in man, it must be the original being itself that bears guilt for the fall of the world. In fact, he says this explicitly and, in doing so, agrees with Brahminism.

> Brahma brings forth the world by a kind of fall into sin or aberration and remains in it himself to do penance until he has redeemed himself from his sin. Fine! In Buddhism, the world has its origin in an inexplicable darkening of the heavenly brightness of Nirvana, that blessed state that had been earned by penance and had endured so long; that is to say, the world has its origin through a kind of fatality, which must, however, be understood to be fundamentally moral despite the fact there is an exactly parallel image and analogue of it in the physical sphere—in the inexplicable origin of a primitive streak of mist that eventually becomes a sun. By a series of moral lapses, however, the world later becomes worse and worse even in the physical sphere until it assumes its present dreary aspect. (vol. VII, pp. 275–76)

Schopenhauer is not troubled by the contradiction that, in the absence of free will and of any inherent necessity of sinning in the physical sphere, there should still be expected another "moral" lapse that would once more be operative in the physical sphere. For him, in any event, the center and heart of Christianity is "the doctrine of the fall, of original sin, of the wretchedness of our natural state, and of the depravity of the natural man, linked with the mediation and reconciliation of the Redeemer, in which the Christian shares by belief in him. In this way, however, Christianity reveals itself as pessimism and consequently as directly opposed to the optimism of Judaism and its legitimate offspring, Islamism, and as related to Brahminism and Buddhism" (vol. VII, p. 356). Because, as Schopenhauer repeats, the basic difference of the religions lies not in their belief in God, whether it is monotheistic, polytheistic, pantheistic, or atheistic, but in their basic attitude of optimism or pessimism, he regards the Old and New Testaments as "diametrically opposed to one another"; their union, he says, creates "a strange centaur" (vol. VII, p. 357).

In their real meaning, "guilt" and "sin" are possible and significant only in a personal world. There is an inner contradiction in attributing to an originally neutral, but impersonal absolute a "fall into sin," especially if that fall is supposed to have consisted in the creation of the world—by whatever name that act is designated. Wherever the personhood of God and the creative freedom of man to decide for God or for evil have been denied, theories about the origin of evil necessarily revert to mere mythologizing. This is true also of the reflections of modern philosophers, as, for instance, in the case of Schopenhauer and Eduard von Hartmann, who believed that theirs was the age of the "spontaneous decomposition of Christianity" and who had repudiated belief in a personal God. Eduard von Hartmann's expectation of a "synthesis" of all Eastern and Western, pantheistic and monotheistic religions would have been possible only as a syncretic mythology.

Heedless of the illogic, Sartre, too, had to refer to a primeval original "fall," although there would have been no one there to be guilty of such a sinful lapse. Even though he merely proposes his myth with none of the imaginative elaboration that had characterized the myths of antiquity, he was nevertheless unable to raise it above the level of an inwardly contradictory mythology. In the Bible, on the other hand, this has been successfully achieved.

Even in the Old Testament, the level of such mythologizing has been transcended. The Creator expressly recognizes the works of His creative activity as good: "God saw that all He had made was very good" (Gen. 1:31). "For God created man incorruptible, and to the image of His own likeness He made him. But by the envy of the devil, death came into the world: and they follow him that are of his side" (Wisdom 2:23–25). If the world is corrupt, the guilt therefor falls not upon the original foundation of being, the Creator, but upon his creatures, who have misused the freedom that was theirs and have risen up against the order that was established from the beginning, drawing with them into ruin their posterity and all nature besides. If the world is corrupt, this evil does not come from the root of being itself; for that reason, it is not so permanent as being itself, but is rather a historical phenomenon of the present age, of that great world epoch in which we live. It does not, therefore, exclude the possibility of a liberation from the fall and its fateful consequences—by a God-sent redeemer, let us say, who will turn the history of the fall into the history of salvation.

By this means, the fallen world has been rescued from the clutches of that dismal hopelessness that rules wherever evil is believed to proceed directly from the root of being. A comparison of the Old Testament with the world of ancient oriental myths reveals the singular grandeur of its world view as opposed to the misty world of phantasy-born mythologies. For decades, the study of comparative religion has shown parallel traits in the *Enûma Elisch*, the Babylonian epic of creation. But if the Biblical text and the *Enûma Elisch* have certain traits in common, they also reveal definite differences. In the Babylonian text, guilt makes its appearance even among the gods.

Doctrines of Suffering

> Apsu and Mummu have been murdered and death has thereby come into being. Kingu, the leader of the divine rebels, is put in bonds. The assembly of the gods condemns him to serve in driving evil once again out of the realm of the gods. For this purpose, he is put to death and mankind is created out of his blood. Thus the guilt that had originated in the divine sphere is entrapped and perpetuated in the mortal existence of man, which is delivered over to every evil. At the same time, the gods themselves are freed of it. . . . Men serve the gods by a cult. Even before that, however, they have already served them by their very being, for they are basically nothing in themselves but the expulsion of Evil from the divine realm, which has thereby become pure and holy again.[7]

Norbert Lohfink, from whom we have borrowed this account of the Babylonian myth, calls attention to the significance of this mythological explanation for a theology of evil: "Evil already exists in man's being. It has come to him from the divine realm. The meaning of man's being is nothing other than to trap evil in his existence."

Whereas the Babylonian myth has man arise out of the guilt-poisoned blood of the gods, in the Biblical account he is formed out of the earth. In this fact, Lohfink rightly detects a kind of countertheory—one might even say a "demythologizing." In the Bible, evil makes its appearance in creation in a manner totally different from that of the myth. It is not so old as created being, but a later intrusion that is due to sin. Sin stands at the very beginning of the history of mankind; as a result of it, man was driven into exile in a land that had been cursed for him and was made a prey to death.

It is plainly misleading to turn the Buddhist doctrine of suffering into a metaphysics of suffering for the sole reason of comparing it with the Christian doctrine of original sin. For Buddha was always strongly opposed to every metaphysical speculation that inquired into the beginning or the end or that attempted to establish things in any logical context. In place of final explanatory concepts, as Hermann Beckh says,[8] Buddha inserted a dash; this dash is rooted in the deepest essence of Buddhism and has led to repeated misunderstandings. If speculation has been revived in later Buddhism and in the sects, it does not belong in genuine Buddhism, which offers its spiritual doctrine of salvation in psychological categories. For purposes of comparison in a dialogue between Christians and Buddhists, all later accretions must be disregarded and attention must be centered on the Buddhist doctrine of suffering in its original form.

It is true that Gautama had to penetrate the four "truths" to become the Buddha and that he then proclaimed them as the four basic holy truths; it is also true that ignorance of these four truths is regarded as the deepest and ultimate source in which all earthly, deceptive, transitory, and painful becoming has its beginning and by which it is constantly renewed. Nevertheless, these truths refer to something inward and psychic: suffering itself, the origin of suffering, the removal of suffering, and the ways that lead to the removal of suffering.

Urgently and solemnly, Buddha turns to his former companions:

> This, O monks, is the holy truth about suffering: birth is suffering, sickness is suffering, death is suffering. To be joined with what one does not like is suffering; not to obtain what one desires is suffering. To lose what one loves is suffering. In short: The five principal forms of clinging to one's own existence, namely, body, sensation, perception, striving [the so-called aggregates], consciousness, are all linked to suffering. They are all transitory, subject to beginning and end, and unable to obtain or retain what they desire. Everything composite, my brothers, is doomed to corruption. Whatever begins and ends in this fashion without attaining a fixed goal or any satisfaction is full of suffering. Yet it cannot attain thereto because there is nothing lasting, nothing enduring, no self to be found in any of the five principal areas of life that we have just named. The body is not the "I" or the lasting self, nor are the sensations. Neither are the changing perceptions, or the willing and striving, or the state of consciousness that accompanies all of them. In these, there is nothing lasting, nothing essential, nothing enduring. Of none of them can one say: "That belongs to me, that is my self." These five principal components or areas of life have come together only as a result of conditions that continue to exist, and they remain together only so long as the effective and persisting power of these conditions does not fail. As a result, man's coming and going through this world, like that of all other created things, is due to the coincidence of the conditions of his existence. So it is also with the chariot. For the wheel is not the chariot; nor is the axle or the shaft. It is only the combination of necessary parts that constitutes a chariot. In consequence, the marks of impermanence, suffering, and unreality are imprinted on all the things of this world. And so long as man continues, in this ceaseless state of flux, to compare, differentiate, and contrast; so long as he continues to regard things erroneously as permanent and real, just so long will he be entrapped in delusion and suffering. For in none of them is anything absolute or final, any escape or redemption to be found. They contain nothing on which man can rely. Enmeshed in this world we have wept more tears than there are drops of water in all the four oceans of the world.

In the preceding paragraph, we have reproduced the first holy truth as Günther Schulemann has reconstructed it, in his own translation and in the style of Buddha, from many places in the Pali Canon.[9] Unfortunately, Schulemann's translation has received little recognition although, by reason of its comprehensiveness, it is the first work to convey the full impression of Buddha's doctrine—an impression that cannot be gained from the short sentences that have had to suffice in other accounts. In what follows, we will again make use of this translation, but will omit the accompanying Sanskrit terminology.

> This now, O monks, is the holy truth about the origin of suffering. What, in fact, is the root of all suffering? It is the craving that leads from rebirth to rebirth, the thirst for pleasures, the thirst for becoming, the thirst for transi-

Doctrines of Suffering

tory things. It is the inordinate striving for happiness that seeks to satisfy itself now in this form, now in that. It is sensual pleasure, covetousness, selfishness; it is ambition and craving for one's own existence and one's own affirmation and gratification in this or another world. It is the clinging to this world of delusion and the egoistic attachment to one's own individual existence. "Like a creeping vine, thirst grows in the thoughtless. Just as apes in the forest seek for fruit, so desire drives the thoughtless endlessly from rebirth to rebirth." But how does this thirst bring about the cycle of rebirth? The question is answered in the likewise very ancient doctrine of the twelve-fold chain of causation that applies to everything that exists. The doctrine is as follows: Delusion, sometimes identified simply as ignorance of the four truths, gives rise to (material) forms, acts, strivings. This is not immediately to be understood as temporal or cosmic, but rather in this manner: when there are stirrings in the originally blind and unconscious forces of existence and life, these forces at once seek to establish themselves as unconquerable energy in existence and in a definite direction of development. These strivings, tendencies, and forms evoke an increasing separateness, an ever sharper individuation. When the opposites and differences are very marked, the state of consciousness arises. When this occurs, the world is divided into subject and object. Differentiations of name and form, spirituality and corporality arise. These, in turn, give rise to the six provinces of knowledge, viz., the customary five senses and the mind, which then come into contact with their proper ends or objects. From contact proceeds the sensation of pleasantness and unpleasantness, and so on. The pleasant is sought after. When this occurs, thirst arises and the desire to achieve one's own happiness and satisfaction. This leads to the development of an inordinate attachment to existence. But existence, seeking its own pleasure and continuing to be active as an unconquerable energy laden with wishes and guilt, hopes and fears, belongs to the factors that determine a new becoming, a new individual existence, which it causes to appear not as the transmigration of a soul, but as an inherited tendency to a new birth. Thus new birth and, finally, old age and death are the last effect. Yet that does not mean an end to existence, but, on the contrary, only another beginning. According to the inexorable law of cause and effect, birth and old age and death, lamentation, suffering, misery, and despair recur again and again since they are inseparably joined to all life. Just as when the flame of one candle is lighted from that of another, so the will to live keeps the glow alive without there being anything permanent in the flames that live on fuel. Man's path and pilgrimage go upwards and downwards through the heavens of the gods, through the regions of the demons, through the world of men and animals, through the kingdom of restless spirits, through painful hells. Nowhere in the realms of air, in the depths of the sea, in the caves of the mountains, nowhere in the world is there a place where man can be freed of his evil deeds. "For all our being is the fruit of our disposition. In it are rooted thoughts, words, and actions. If it leads to evil, then suffering follows us as the wheel follows the foot of the beast of burden." This is the law of the compensation of actions (karma) that have not been brought to an end, that reach out with their tendencies to determine the new form of existence. Its continued existence is the constant thread on which individual existences are strung like pearls. There will be a time, O monks, when the great ocean of the world will be emptied, will dry up, and will be no more; when the mighty earth will be destroyed by fire, will be annihilated, and will be no more. But I tell you, O monks, that there will be no end to suffering for the individual sunk in delusion. The bustle of this world, O monks, is a wild sea, without beginning or end. And our life upon it is like a bubble, like a bit of foam. Indiscernible is the beginning of those deluded existences, victims of thirst, who are led from birth to birth and pass through the endless cycle of rebirth.

This now, O monks, is the holy truth about the removal and destruction of suffering. When ignorance is removed, forms, conscious knowledge, and even the whole gamut of constantly renewed sufferings are also removed and brought to silence. It is the cessation of thirst, the complete destruction of desire by the total absence of passion, by the rejection of it, by the deliverance, emancipation, and separation from it. "Whoever vanquishes this thirst that burns and is not easily overcome in this world is no longer troubled by suffering, just as water never penetrates the lotus leaf." Just as the great ocean, O monks, has only one taste, the taste of salt, so this doctrine and order has only one taste, the taste of redemption. And what, now, is the goal of redemption? It is the extinction of delusion (nirvana), O monks, and is attainable even in this existence, not just in a future one. It is inviting and attractive, and the wise man knows it. It is nothing other than the true and the highest, the removal and the end of all differences and strivings. It is the opposite of the world and the bustle of the world of suffering, of impermanence, of unreality. But it cannot be compared with anything in the world, so that it would be possible to say: "This is it" or "This is not it." And of the wise man who has reached the state of nirvana, it cannot be said: "He is" or "He is not." "Those who have reached the end of their pilgrimage, who have attained the cessation of thirst, delusion, and suffering, are no longer touched by pain. All their bonds have fallen away. They are free on all sides." For there exists, O monks, an unborn, an unoriginated, an unbecome, an unformed. If this were not so, you would find no end of suffering, no possibility of escape from the world of the born, the originated, the become, the formed. But to ask for more, O monks, would be as if a man who had been pierced by a poisonous arrow would not allow it to be withdrawn, but first asked and insisted on knowing who had wounded him, where he came from, what he was like, and what the arrow was made of. And yet, he would not be able to learn all that he wished to learn, for death would too quickly overtake him.

This now, O monks, is the holy truth about the path that leads to the cessation of suffering. It is the noble middle path that avoids extremes, just as a string that is drawn neither too tightly nor too loosely yields the proper tone. There are two extremes that ought not to be pursued. What are they? One is a life devoted to the enjoyment of sensual pleasures; it is degrading, vulgar, common, fleeting, vain, purposeless. The other is a life devoted to self-mortification; it is sinful, unworthy, weakening to mind and spirit, and equally purposeless. Avoiding these extremes, the released person has found the noble middle path, the way of seeing and knowing, the way that leads to peace, to enlightenment, and to the cessation of every delusion. "If you

Doctrines of Suffering

follow this way, you will find an end of suffering. It is the path that I pointed out when I perceived how to remove the thorns." "You must exert yourselves. Only to teach is the vocation of the 'thus-gone' [the released ones: *Tathagata*]. Whoever pursues this way of thoughtful meditation will be freed from the slavery of evil." It is the noble eightfold path that consists of the following stages: 1) Right Views about the world and life by insight into the four truths; 2) Right Disposition and Right Resolve; 3) Right Speech; 4) Right Conduct; 5) Right Livelihood; 6) Right and Proper Effort and Endeavor; 7) Right Recollection; 8) Right Concentration and Contemplation. Of these eight stages, the first two may be summarized as wisdom, the next three as morality, and the last three as meditation. On the threefold vehicle of wisdom, morality, and meditation, the ocean of samsara (the cycle of rebirth in the world) is crossed. To wisdom and enlightenment belong the aversion taught by the four holy truths and the resolve to live thereby. To morality belong the observation of the principal virtues and the avoidance of the ten principal sins. In particular, there are five commands that are binding on all; not to kill, not to steal, not to lie, not to act unchastely; not to enjoy intoxicants. To meditation belong reflection on the nothingness, transitoriness, and frailty of the body, of the senses, of the thoughts, and of the conditions of existence, and the regular practice of love, compassion, sympathetic joy, realization of the vanity of all that exists, and equanimity of spirit. On the basis of these meditations undertaken on one's own initiative, it can happen that one rises to the four stages of higher contemplation: serenely relaxed reflection in solitude; quietly happy, unreflecting concentration on one truth; calm and blessed tranquillity of all one's spiritual powers; and perfect, painless peace of mind.

As the fruit and companion of these higher degrees of contemplation might be mentioned loftier gifts and insights into the nature of the universe. But, even in this instance, nothing should be sought out of egoism, curiosity, or ambition, for the conquest of one's own unruly will is the principal task. "To compel one's own self is better than to bend the world to the yoke." "To avoid every kind of sin, to do good wherever you can, to strive for the purification of the heart—this is the teaching of everyone who has been awakened." "Calling nothing our own, so let us seek to be happy in life. We will be like the brightest gods, whose food is bliss." "Therefore avoid having a preference for anything whose loss will always be painful. Only he who knows neither preference nor hatred is without bonds." "I call him truly a man of the spirit who shows himself patient, calm, mild with those who are ruled by hardness, impatience, passion." "For it has been known for a long time that hatred does not yield to hatred. Only love sets a limit for hatred." Just as unruly attachment is a hindrance, so the universal, tranquil kindness that is born of compassion is a virtue and a great means of advancing toward perfection. In daily contemplation, therefore, every pious person should radiate this love into all parts of the world and should thus captivate even the animals. "Just as the light of all the stars, O monks, is not worth the sixteenth part of the light of the moon, but the light of the moon absorbs it into itself and outshines it with its radiance and glow, so all means of gaining religious merit in this life, O monks, are not worth the sixteenth part of love, of the redemption of the heart." This kindness that is born of compassion leads him who possesses it to proclaim salvation to all beings without passion or violence and thereby to fulfill the highest of all tasks; for the highest gift is the gift of the law. It is the opening of the noble eightfold path to deliverance and salvation.

If conditions are favorable, it might be possible even in a life in the world for someone to reach this goal. Usually, however, there are too many fetters, and the path is trodden most securely by those who follow Buddha's teaching as hermits or as members of a community of monks. "Joined for spiritual purposes, they take their departure, because household life suffices for them no longer; like swans that move away from the sea, they abandon home and hearth." If you follow this way, O monks, you will find an end of suffering, dead to all delusion, separated from all sorrow, safely landed on the opposite shore.

This presentation of the four holy truths of Buddha, which Schulemann reconstructed out of many mosaic stones taken from the Pali Canon, is surely unique in its inner unity and its linguistic formulation. It obviates the necessity of a long commentary and the discussion of details. We need only emphasize some of its unmistakable trends.

Contrary to Christian belief, which affirms passing suffering as an important and necessary ingredient of our pilgrimage, "suffering" is here, in every respect, a *negativum,* something worthless. The source of suffering is all human craving. No distinction is made between the objectively justifiable drives of life to which no exception can be taken and those passionately exaggerated ones that must be cut off. Every craving leads to suffering and is therefore worthless, must therefore be quieted and removed. That which survives death is, on the one hand, the inordinate craving for existence and, on the other, karma—the fruit of man's deeds. It is these two that constitute the connection between various existences and lead, soon after death, to a new reincarnation. Nevertheless, this teaching remains in the background; it is accepted and allowed to survive only because it stems from tradition and is, therefore, not to be questioned. For the rest, the primary concern is always the human subject and his desire to be free from suffering. If craving for existence is the origin of a painful existence, the removal of existence, which is regarded as identical with suffering, is to be achieved by the removal of craving.

Schulemann has aptly translated *nirvana*—the goal of Buddhist asceticism—as "the extinction of delusion." Here, too, the primary emphasis is on something subjective. Any inquiry into the ontological aspect is expressly excluded. It matters not at all whether the perfect one "is" or "is not." What matters is that he has reached an end of suffering. Because this suffering arises from the separateness of conscious subject and corresponding object, consciousness is thereby extinguished; the "I" is buried once more in the unconscious.

There can be no question about Buddhism's complete devaluation of world and life or its demand to avoid world and life; for this reason only

Doctrines of Suffering

monks can attain perfection. Naturally, however, the laity cannot be barred from participation in the striving for nirvana.

It is obvious that the negativism and the limitation to the human subject are not consistently held. A positive absolute is dimly perceptible. There is reasonable doubt, also, whether the words about the "unborn, unoriginated, and unbecome" stem from Buddha himself. In any case, they transcend the other, agnostic formulation to an astonishing degree. It is idle to speculate whether this further advance into the positive had already taken place in Buddha's time or is a later development. What is certain is that the turn to the positive is unmistakable in the later forms of Buddhism.

This is especially true of the Buddhist ethic, which in its first and basic aspect was negativistic, but which has acquired more and more positive characteristics. This ethic was also centered at first only around the subject and his efforts to free himself of suffering, but it gradually developed independent precepts that were valuable in their own right. The very fact that an ethic should have been developed at all is in itself a kind of affirmation of life, even if that ethic is inwardly inconsistent. Buddha required neither a complete denial of the will to life nor a total suppression of all affirmations of life. On the contrary, he spoke of a middle path that provided a kind of ordering of life between two extremes. The one extreme is a life that is devoted to pleasure, the other a life of strict, life-negating asceticism. Buddha condemned both extremes as one-sided. He rejected excessive penitential exercises; he regarded them as "vulgar, unworthy, and worthless."

What he himself required and what he understands as "right conduct" and "right life" can be learned from the "ten commandments," of which the first five are binding on all Buddhists, the last five only on monks. Here, too, the negativistic character is clearly evident; they are not really "commandments," but "prohibitions."

In his life, the Buddhist should be just, gentle, and kind. His kindness should extend to all creatures, even to those without reason. This approximates a retraction of the radical denial of life. Nevertheless, the basic character of the Buddhist devotion to man and world is an inconsistent one. Negativism prevents a complete devotion, for it contains no demand for positive action. As a result, there is no positive formative goal even in the Buddhist ideal of monkhood. There is no stimulus to the work of formation that leads to culture. Granted that meditation and, to some extent, study claim a large proportion of the horarium of the monastery, there is nevertheless lacking that active impulse that characterizes the monasteries of the West.

From the Christian affirmation of the world, there arises an actively positive, affirming love of all other men because they have come into existence by the will and the love of God. Such a loving affirmation approaches active *caritas*. The "caritas" of inner love finds its expression in external deeds of "caritas." Love of this kind is foreign to Buddhism in its original form; its kindness is basically passive—it consists in harming no one. Buddhism "awakens and fosters the attitude of kindly goodness and mercy toward the whole world, but it never forgets that every clinging of one's own heart to another being is an enmeshment in the joy, and therefore in the suffering, of what is transitory. All pains and complaints, all the many forms of suffering in the world, come from what one holds dear; where nothing is held dear, they do not arise. Therefore let him who is striving to be where there is no pain or sadness regard nothing in the world as dear to him."[10] Because of its own attitude toward love, it belongs to the innermost nature of primitive Buddhism to strive to prevent the positive activity of love. For every deed, even the best, is a chain that binds the individual to life and contains the nucleus of a new reincarnation, of a life of suffering, in the future.

The later forms of Buddhism have clearly detached themselves both from the historical Buddha and from the negativity of his attitude toward life. This is especially true of Ngarjuna and his doctrine of the "Great Pass." In it, he teaches:

> It is not only the perverse craving and clinging to deceitful sensual pleasures that is to be avoided, but also the attitude of him who is concerned only for his own deliverance and redemption. It is not enough to renounce and flee; one must also accomplish exemplary deeds in his devoted service of others. The ideal is not the ascetic who lives only for himself, who has escaped all struggle and effort by means of peaceful contemplation, but the individual who, while he rightly comprehends the nature of the universe and strives for the state of highest enlightenment, at the same time renounces his own well-being for the sake of those who suffer and are in error. Such a wise man (bodhisatva) constantly postpones his own rest in order to serve others. He is ready to come again and again, as helper and redeemer, into the world of suffering, perversity, and deceit so that he may lead others along the right path. To this task he directs his exceptional and self-forgetful exercise of the virtues by which he has already reached the state of bliss: beneficence, morality, patience, and, above all, meditation that rises to contemplation and knowledge. (Schulemann, p. 52)

Buddha's goal was a practical one: to teach man how to draw out, before he dies, the painful "arrow" of suffering that resides in his flesh. To reach this short-termed goal, he must disregard everything extraneous, including the inquiry into who has shot the arrow and what it consists of. Now that it has become clear, however, that Buddhism, in the course of its own development, has turned aside from this simple goal and, especially, now that it seems questionable whether it has reached its great goal, it is imperative that we take up the question that was suppressed—that we ask

Doctrines of Suffering 59

who actually did shoot the arrow and what is its nature. This question cannot be left unanswered if only for the reason that Christianity possesses a positive doctrine of suffering. We find ourselves compelled, therefore, to make some basic inquiries into the nature of suffering.

5

"FREEDOM FROM SUFFERING" BY MEANS OF SELF-REDEMPTION?

Buddhism and the Stoa

With respect to the problem of suffering, there is a unique middle position between Buddhism and Christianity that might easily be confused with either of them. Its chief representative is the Stoa, which has persisted even to the present day as the spiritual rival of Christianity. It shares with Christianity the belief in the basic goodness of the world and in a divine providence that turns everything, even every suffering, into good. With Buddhism, on the other hand, the Stoa shares the will to self-redemption through suffering. The principal goal of Stoic striving is to deliver mankind from the troublesome whirlpool of life, to help him attain a godlike imperturbability that is strongly reminiscent of the Buddhist nirvana as a deliverance from delusion. Yet the Stoa differs in characteristic ways from both Buddhism and Christianity. As a result, reflection on the Stoic doctrine of suffering sheds clarification and light on that of the other two.

The primitive will to achieve a happy life, which has its source in the depths of our spiritual nature, has never failed to stimulate man to reflect on how such a life is to be achieved. Seneca, for instance, begins his reflections on the "happy life" ("De Vita Beata") with this basic assumption, which he expresses in the pithy sentence: *"Vivere omnes beate volunt"* ("All desire to live happily"). The words sound the whole chord of man's longing for a life that is fundamentally complete and happy. It must be admitted, however, that their full tone very quickly fades into the plaintive question of how man can rid himself of suffering. However clear and unambiguous the first goal may be, Seneca, when faced with the inevitable next question about the *way* to the goal, came to the logical conclusion that men grope in darkness and therefore seek the light.

It is not only because man is oppressed by suffering that he strives for a great and full happiness, but also because there lies concealed in his very nature a unique promise of happiness. But the goal toward which he strives is all too quickly brought one step nearer. Instead of the great positive goal (on which he had originally set his sights), he contents himself with one that is negatively formulated—with "deliverance from suffering" in a state of "freedom from suffering" (=*apatheia*). His attitude betrays his unexpressed willingness to sacrifice his hopes of full and positive happiness if only he can rid himself of the perpetual misery of suffering. However ardently the hopes of inexperienced youth may rest on the first of these

"Freedom from Suffering"

goals, man resigns himself, on sober second thought, to the mere removal of suffering. If, indeed, the first is beyond his powers of achievement, he is not, for that reason, ready to renounce the second.

It is precisely this advancing of the original goal that places the Stoa in an inner proximity to Buddhism. "Apathy" is the mark of both, although a subliminal hope of happiness lets itself be heard again and again in the teachings of the Stoa. Also common to both Buddhism and the Stoa is the attempt to reach their goal of "freedom from suffering" by means of self-redemption, thereby distinguishing themselves from Christianity, which does not recognize a self-redemption.

Buddhism derived its first explicitly pessimistic basic "truth" from the wisdom teachings of ancient India: In all its forms, all life is suffering; the source of suffering is the desire that is inherent in every life and that spreads like a consuming fire to everything around it; for this reason, suffering can be removed only by the total extinction of this fire. Although the human heart has never been completely satisfied by it and man's longing has filled nirvana with positive traits, the true goal of "freedom from suffering" in "nirvana" is the "nihilation" of all life.

The Stoics, on the other hand, belong in the mainstream of Greek thought. The longing and speculation of the Greeks were directed, in a positive sense, to "happiness" *(eudaimonia);* their philosophers strove constantly to define this *"eudaimonia"* and to find the way to it. In this basic frame of mind, the Stoics showed themselves to be true Greeks, even when they resorted, with a certain resignation, to the lesser goal of deliverance from suffering. In sharp contrast to the explicitly pessimistic tendency of Buddhism, the Stoics took their stand on the generally positive and affirmative level of the Greek attitude toward life. They strove for "happiness" as such, even though they perceived it, at first, as no more than an imperturbable peace of mind.

This was what the Greeks demanded of the Stoic teachers of wisdom: Show us how that man must be constituted who is sure of his happiness whatever the fate of the world may have in store for him. What the Stoics did was to advance the image of "the capable man," of the "master of life," of "the virtuous man"—not allowing the word *virtue* to be weakened, in the process, by the anemia of later moralistic ideals, but equating it, instead, with "manliness" and "effectiveness." That this virtuous man owes his virtue to his understanding of the nature of things and that he must, therefore, also be a "wise man," can be deduced from the generally accepted Socratic proposition that virtue is fundamentally knowledge. Even this teaching represents a very optimistic view of human nature—the conviction, namely, that he who knows the good cannot fail to practice it. In consequence, all the Stoics exerted themselves to depict the ideal of the wise man, that is, of the man whose understanding makes him at once virtuous and happy. In this respect, they do not differ from others who taught wisdom to the Greeks. The most outstanding element in their definition of the wise man is the inner imperturbability that must characterize the man who has freed himself from the pressure and favor of the world and who knows how to find his happiness in himself alone. "The happy man," says Seneca, "is the one who is freed from both fear and desire because of the gift of reason."[1]

If the Stoic is deeply convinced of the possibility of being happy, he is, at the same time, fortified by a fundamental confidence that his own nature will provide him with the guide to its development and perfection. He is confident that he will attain true wisdom, which for him is identical with the state of happiness, if he does not deviate from his own nature, but forms himself according to its law and model. The fruit of this wisdom is the peaceful composure and inner freedom that result from the exclusion of everything that might disturb one's inner equilibrium. The desire for sensual pleasure deprives man of his freedom by making him dependent; it makes him as insignificant and mean as the object of his desire. It is replaced in the wise man by "a boundless joy that is firm and unalterable, then [by] peace and harmony of the soul and true greatness coupled with kindliness. . . ."(bk. III, sec. 4).

The autarkic wise man seeks within himself for "the highest good," which is this: that the spirit is entirely in possession of itself, that it has repudiated everything that happens merely by chance, and that it rejoices only in its own virtuous attitude. Seneca finds innumerable ways of expressing the one concept that man's happiness stems from a basic attitude of the heart. For him, happiness is "to have a mind that is free, lofty, fearless and steadfast—a mind that is placed beyond the reach of fear, beyond the reach of desire. . . ." (bk. IV, sec. 3). Happy in his possession of self, serene in the depths of his soul, steeped in a joy that has its source in the highest values, the wise man no longer seeks to satisfy his base, vapid, and impermanent desires, to attain that gratification of the senses whose only reward is slavery and suffering.

Man sees himself obliged not by any outward circumstance, but by his own nature, to struggle for freedom. Once he has achieved wisdom, and hence freedom, he has abandoned the misty and crowded world of average men and has ascended to the qualitatively different level of an existence that is divine. Just as man, in the wisdom teachings of the East, strives for an immanent union with the divine, with Atman, which is basically identical with Brahman, so the Stoic, when he seeks to become wise, seeks in reality to become godlike, for his concept of the world is also monistic. Men call the All and the One, that which is the foundation of all that exists whether of world or men, by various names: "God," "nature," "reason," "providence." In the foundation of its being, all is one and the same. Since this fundamental being is the guiding principle of the whole world, the world must be good in essence, even perhaps the best of all possible worlds.

The Stoics see in everything an expression of the divine World-Reason; therefore, they conclude, the world must be organized in the best possible way.

Whatever their fundamental and radical optimism about existence, the Stoics had to cope, nonetheless, with the presence of real evils in the world; they found themselves compelled, therefore, to answer the difficult question of how this evil was compatible with the goodness of a divine providence and reason. If the fact of manifold evil is not to be disputed and if, at the same time, the world is to be looked upon as the admirable work of a divine world architect who is good, then something counterdivine must be at work to cause disturbance in the world. Where is the scapegoat to be sought? Plato attempted to explain the existence of evil by means of a *theodicy,* that is, by a vindication of God notwithstanding the evil in the world. He believed that obdurate matter, which existed independently of God and would not allow itself to be thoroughly penetrated by the divine work of formation, was responsible for evil. The task of vindicating God was assumed by Stoic philosophy and made the object of special consideration. If the solution that it offers is not quite satisfactory, it nevertheless contains valuable insights that have earned the respect of many later attempts at a theodicy.

Any attempt to vindicate the existence of evil is impossible without some differentiation of the far too general collective term *evil* as well as of the various levels of human existence, so manifestations that are evil on a lower plane can be regarded as values on a higher plane. Thus the Stoics attempted to show that physical evils, such as pain and sickness, are by no means evil in themselves; that they are rather the inevitable consequences of natural laws that can be shown to be purposeful and that they can therefore—and this is the essential point—possess a high ethical value for man. In this way, their innate lack of value is relativized and overcome.

It is far more difficult to explain the existence of moral than of physical evil. In the eyes of the Stoic, it is the only real evil. On this higher plane, only a very partial and limited relativization and refinement are possible. Why does God permit it to happen? The Stoic would answer: because even moral evil serves the good. It is only in contrast to evil that the good acquires its luminous meaning. Yes, the light of virtue has need of the shadow of evil. Only the innocence that has proven itself against the tempter, only the conviction that has withstood the pressure of a strong opponent, has full value. ". . . the greater [the] torture is, the greater shall be [the] glory." "Without an adversary, prowess shrivels. We see how great and how efficient it really is, only when it shows by endurance what it is capable of." [2] Even what is evil in itself can be transformed by the divine *pronoia* that plans the world into an instrument that serves the larger whole. Such a transformation is possible only with reference to something else: the absolute worthlessness of moral evil remains unchanged in itself.

So long as the framework of a strongly monistic world system is preserved, the thought that even moral evil serves a purpose can lead to a disastrous relativization of good and evil. This relativization is most clearly stated in the familiar words of the poet who referred to the evil that always wills to do evil, but always does good.[3] The utter reprehensibility of moral evil must be affirmed even while it is being accorded a certain justification by reason of its secondary and side effects, which are governed by a God-determined world order. Even if moral evil possesses a certain importance, in our world as it is, as a stimulus for awakening healthy powers of resistance, nevertheless this is not to be interpreted as an absolute justification. In a monistic system, contradictions are all too easily transformed and reduced to mere differences.

In the Easter vigil of Holy Saturday night, the Christian church ventures to express the jubilant rapture of its Easter joy in the bold words of the "Exultet": *"O certe necessarium Adae peccatum, quod Christi morte deletum est! O felix culpa, quae talem ac tantum meruit habere Redemptorem"* ("O truly necessary sin of Adam, which was blotted out by the death of Christ. O happy fault, which merited such and so great a Redeemer"). Such bold words have their real meaning in a philosophy of the world in which the differences that are so glaringly apparent within the world find their counterbalance in the infinite, which is qualitatively different from this world. Solely within the world, it is impossible to achieve such a *coincidentia oppositorum*.

In an immanent and monistic philosophy of the world like that of the Stoics, the "quasi-necessity" of moral evil becomes an absolute necessity in view of the coming redemption. As a result, however, the effort to construct a theodicy is undermined by an insoluble antinomy: differences become contradictions and rupture the envisioned oneness of the world.

For the Stoic who remained true to the concept of an immanent God, the antinomy was unavoidable, so unavoidable, in fact, that as a result he found himself exposed to considerable ridicule. The Stoic who believed that he had made the transition to the wise man's qualitatively higher level of existence was convinced that he had thereby become not only like, but equal to, God. He had entered, or so he believed, into the cosmic city of those gods who were led by *Logos* (reason)—an illusionary supposition that is belied by every painful experience of daily life.

Unlike the Buddhist, the Stoic regards intellectual self-awareness as something positive and godlike. He does not endeavor, therefore, to free himself of self-awareness, as though it were a burden, in order to arrive at a foreknown union with the absolute. What is not spiritual can never have a share in the truth. But possession of the truth seems to the Stoic to be the highest value. He ascends to it by the continual spiritualization of the reason that he is coming to possess. The cross-currents of passion are, for him, a disruption of the control of reason. "Apathy" and "freedom from suffering," on the contrary, signify freedom from every stirring of passion, calm repose, and inner equanimity. Whereas the passions and affections are still evaluated positively in the classical philosophy of Plato and Aristotle and as something to be restrained, but not suppressed, the Stoic, with his strong conviction of the domination of the spirit, would place them squarely in the realm of the negative. His ideal is the complete absence of passion, which he equates with the absence of suffering.

In his determination to free himself unconditionally of every passionate desire, the Stoic is like the Buddhist. Both fear the inner bondage that comes from yielding to the affections, whether the yielding is to love or to pity (i.e., sym-pathy—a suffering *with* someone). Both demand that the wise man set his heart on nothing lest he become inwardly dependent on it and be reduced to sadness at the loss of a beloved possession. The compulsion to be totally free leads even to the hardness of heart that refuses to share the sufferings of a friend. Epictetus gives this strange advise: "So far as words then, do not be unwilling to show him sympathy, and even, if it happens so, to lament with him. But take care that you do not lament internally also."[4]

The most radical development of the Stoic principle of reason is to be found in the severely monistic psychology of Chrysippus. Pure reason is, for him, more than just the central organ of the soul. He will concede no value to any independent impulse that exists apart from it. The affections, he says, are nothing but the weaknesses of a reason that is not yet fully aware of itself. In themselves, they are the foolishness of him who has not yet discovered wherein true good and evil lie. All fools are like men drowning in the waters of vacillating opinions. But the wise man has safely reached the firm land and the pure air of knowledge of the truth, which he also recognizes as life itself.

The Stoics never wearied of emphasizing that there was not just a difference of degree between the foolish man and the wise one, but a difference of essence. Equal to the other gods, the wise man takes his place in the *polis* of rational beings. But whereas earthly nations are protected and guided by national laws, the great city of godlike beings is guided only by the law of reason itself. Awareness of his membership in this *polis* was the Stoic's greatest religious experience; it was the foundation of his claim to a unique place among other men.

The wise man imagines himself to be in possession of perfection, not just on the road to it. He has reached his goal. In the absolute knowledge of good and evil, which is identified with virtue, the wise man also possesses inner peace and harmony of soul as a precious good. As a result, he is sufficient unto himself. He incorporates in himself both autarky and autonomy. Through knowledge, he has grasped the only true good that a rational being can possess. "And this possession makes him like the godhead. He himself is a godlike man."[5]

Precisely on this account, the wise man, whose autonomy is based on reason, has the right to decide, in case of necessity, whether his own life is to continue. If life no longer seems to him to be worth living, he may choose to commit suicide. There can be no doubt of it, the wise man has become reason incarnate; he is the ideal man, the absolute model that is raised above all human weaknesses. The Stoa clung unflinchingly to this "myth of the wise man" (p. 158); consequently, it claimed for man a likeness to God that drew the ridicule of its opponents upon this "wonder" whose likeness to Zeus could be laid low by a head cold. It is impossible to detect, in the writings of Zeno and Chrysippus, that "Zeus" was anything but a name to them. Here man has become a God in his own eyes. The wise man has freed himself—has redeemed himself—from the world of suffering by no other means than by comprehending himself intellectually. In principle, this way is open to all men.

Nevertheless, the Stoics were not able, in the end, to conceal from themselves the fact that the wise man's delusion of godlikeness is a presumption, that the state of final perfection can never belong to man in this lifetime. He cannot confer perfection upon himself. He can never escape totally from the state of fallibility or exchange it for the qualitatively different state of infallibility. His human and weak freedom is always threatened by error and abuse and, therefore, by the punishments due them. From this point of view, his proud and individualistic self-certainty must be deflated as a presumptuous pose and he must stretch out his arm to the redeeming hand that is extended to him from above. This is what Cleanthes does in his hymn to Zeus. Before the divine majesty, man's proud self-awareness loses its power. Oppressed by the intellectual and moral necessity with which man is burdened, he utters his ardent prayer to Zeus, the Giver of all good, the gracious Father—something that Zeno and Chrysippus would never have been capable of doing.

But this is to sacrifice the "myth of the wise man" who has himself become God. Man is never able by his own efforts to change into a totally different mode of existence and to prepare for himself the fullness of *eudaimonia*. If he were able to do so, he would also be able to raise himself above those sufferings that can lead him to choose his own death. Even the so-called perfect man cannot avoid those marginal situations in which his suffering is so great that he prefers not to continue in existence. On the one hand, the right to suicide is the logical consequence of the "autonomy" of the wise man who is one with the Logos. On the other hand, it is the insuperable proof that *eudaimonia* is not attainable in man's always fragile existence. Self-redemption is likewise an unattainable phantom.

6

ON THE MEANING OF SUFFERING

At first glance, the theses of pessimism and optimism seem to be mutually exclusive. Either the world and human life consist entirely of suffering, or they are intrinsically good, even perhaps the best that are possible. There is no third alternative. In the psychic circumstances from which both opposites arise, however, a dialectical connection makes itself visible. This is indicated, in fact, by the affective undertone that is clearly to be heard in the attempts of both positions to provide themselves with a rationale. However self-assured they may usually be in presenting their positions, the reasons that they advance are meaningful only to one who has already made a "prejudging" choice that corresponds to the basic temperament by which he is governed. A choice made from feelings that are not clear or are only half clear—even if it is later justified on "objective" grounds—is constantly threatened by the possibility of a subsequent change of mood, to which we humans are never totally immune.

Such changes of mood take place on many different psychic levels. We know from daily experience the change of mood that occurs on the easily moved surface of our minds. This is particularly true of sanguine young people, whose feelings alternate quickly between *Himmelhoch jauchzend* (to heaven rejoicing) and *Zu Tode betrübt* (sad unto death);[1] among adults, on the contrary, the pendulum swings more slowly and considerably less widely. On a deeper level, many persons are so conditioned by nature that they experience regular changes of mood from the manic to the depressive and back. Depending on the state in which they find themselves, they see the experiences of their whole lives as either bathed in a brilliant light or buried in gloom.

Finally, there are enduring states of mind that persist for a long time in the depths of the soul and that are usually slow to reveal modification or change. It is on this level that we must seek the affective root from which pessimism and optimism grow. In the history of their origins, optimism is the original, natural attitude. It is only when excessive optimism has experienced repeated disappointments that there is formed a core of permanent frustration that can be turned by the basic temperament into a lasting pessimism. A paradigmatic case is that of Hegesias of the Cyrenaic school, who began his philosophizing with exuberant optimism, but in his later disappointment became *peisithanatos* (death's advocate).

In the intellectual maturation whether of individuals or of whole cultural communities, perceptions formed earlier in the twilight of unilluminated emotions are exposed to the light of critical awareness. In the process, even those things that had always been taken for granted are again placed in doubt. If we are to establish our original attitude on a deeper and conscious foundation or—should that seem desirable—if we are to relinquish it entirely, even those things that have long since grown familiar to us, that we have accepted unquestioningly, must be questioned in the light of new reflection and of confrontation with a thesis that runs counter to them. The Greek philosophers had already attempted to achieve just such progress, which is to be distinguished from mere "opinions" *(doxai)*, and had striven to gain insights of their own. But it is impossible to arrive at decisions that are human in the full sense of the term, for which we accept all the responsibility, and that rest on objective grounds, until we have had the discernment to free ourselves from all "prejudgments."

In much the same manner, the incipient dialogue between Buddhism and Christianity cannot ignore the necessity of rethinking the whole question of the validity of a pessimistic or optimistic evaluation of human existence and of the world. To decide between Buddhism and Christianity is, of course, not simply, although it is essentially, to decide between a basic pessimism, at least in regard to primitive Buddhism, and a basic optimism—here, too, with the understanding that reference is made only to primitive Christianity and that the Christian teaching does not in the least minimize the terrible reality of suffering even while it bestows on it a positive and redeeming significance.

In the following discussion, we must begin with the rudiments of the problem, that is, we must reflect first on those aspects that have heretofore been taken for granted. We must ask what "suffering" really is, how far it extends, where its roots are, and how it is to be evaluated.

In its most general meaning, suffering *(Leiden)* as passive endurance *(Er-Leiden)* may be regarded as the opposite of active doing, behaving, and making. Both suffering and doing are primeval factors in our experience of self. Yet, although it is true that we can clarify them for ourselves by a kind of phenomenological self-reflection, we have not yet been able to discover their rudiments.

It is by such self-reflection that we reach our first basic insight, namely, that, in our state of being, suffering is an earlier and more primitive experience than doing. Before we can engage in activity that is fully human, we must be masters of ourselves. Conscious possession of self is the precondition for every activity. In our existence, there is no possession of self that has been natural to us from the beginning. On the contrary, we passively endure *(er-leiden)*, in the beginning, the stimuli of certain life experiences that awaken our unconscious and slumbering ego and stir us to self-comprehension. It does not matter whether these stimuli arise from experiences that press upon us from without or from tensions formed by experiences within us. What matters is the fundamental fact that our human existence as such begins with suffering and that no human consciousness or human actions would be possible without the endurance of suffering. What we are has already been determined before we are in a condition to determine anything for ourselves. We remain as we have been made until we reach the point at which we can take an active part in reshaping our life and the world. In so far as our being is concerned, then, we are primarily those who undergo suffering until we can bestir ourselves and engage in some activity of our own; even then, we cannot exceed the possibilities opened to us by our natural potentialities. However impatiently the man of action may tear at the chains that bind him to his preordained finite nature, he cannot free himself of them. His impatient struggle often has the very opposite effect of disturbing, if not actually destroying, the foundation of his activity.

If a man is in conscious possession of himself, it is because he has become conscious, inspired by that power that is not the conscious ego, but antecedent to it. Only because he has been awakened by nature can man be defined as one who has found himself, who has become aware, one after another, of the potentialities that are inherent in his nature and that he can realize by his own activity.

For short periods, the potential of man's basic nature makes it possible for him to possess himself, but only in such a manner that the energy thus placed at his disposal is quickly consumed; when he has been exhausted by his span of alert activity, he is drawn back into the bosom of nature so his spent powers may be renewed in sleep.

By its monotonous insistence, this constant rhythm of sleeping and waking convinces man, as no other experience can, that his own acceptance of the suffering that he must endure has to precede every manifestation of activity on his part. The rhythmic alternation of sleeping and waking has its source in man's inner nature. But just as falling asleep is not to be attributed to the mere absence of stimuli, so natural awakening is not to be attributed to a renewal of stimuli. Instinctive awakening is a spontaneous manifestation of that life that precedes all conscious activity and that, for this very reason, is "nature." Only because nature has been relieved of tension in sleep can man, in his waking hours, assume new tensions and use them to carry out the task on which he is engaged until the tension relaxes and incipient weariness forces him once more to shed his tension in sleep.[2]

The daily awakening reminds us that we are about to enter into the world. When we opened our eyes for the first time to the light of the world, we were not able to cross the threshold of a dim stirring of consciousness. As we developed and matured in the years of childhood and adolescence, the strength of our self-possession was nurtured by the manifold incentives and sufferings that we experienced until it reached that magnitude that a "creative man" is able to reach—yet never to the extent that he becomes a "creator" by his own power, but only by the preordained capacity of his nature and within the framework of the potentialities it reveals as proper to his being.

For man, self-consciousness as a perception of one's own "self" exists only in confrontation with the "other," with something that is not the self. Man becomes aware of his own ego only when his ego-self comes in contact with an environment that is largely a social one, an environment of other selves. More specifically, the maturation of human consciousness requires many years of influence, awakening, and formation by human society. For that reason, human consciousness cannot unfold fully in those children who do not experience a constant awakening by others, especially by adults. In this connection, we might think, for instance, of the "wolf children." They were children who had been reared by animals until, after many years of such a life, men drove the animals away. But it was too late to train them to a completely human way of life. Once the most favorable conditions for the child's development have passed, later efforts to awaken fully his latent potentialities are of no avail.[3]

But even adults cannot simply plot a course of direct activity that is intended to educate, awaken, and form another's consciousness; man as a spiritual being cannot come into direct contact with another spiritual being like himself and influence him spiritually. On the contrary, he can accomplish this only through the medium that is provided for us by the material world as it exists in time and space. Since we cannot convey our thoughts and feelings directly to others, we are limited, in our attempts to communicate and understand, to systems of signs that are linked to the material world. The most important of these is the speaking and hearing of language. Even when the adult uses this means, however, he is to some extent unable to do more than knock at the doors of the consciousness of the one to be formed, can only challenge him to apprehend and comprehend for himself the meaning that is inseparable from the sign; he can never penetrate into the interior of the other. When a too eager educator will not observe these limitations and prefers to force rather than inspire the pupil, he usually discovers to his sorrow that the pupil resists such obstinate pressure and turns a deaf ear to his importunities.

During childhood and youth, there is formed, by gradual experience, a clear distinction between one's own inner world and the world of the other and of others. If it were possible to implant thoughts and feelings directly in the consciousness of others, man would never be able to distinguish his own thoughts and feelings from those of others.

The whole material world around us is the medium that both separates men and binds them together. To fulfill its task, the material world needs firm inner laws as well as a firm independence; to these must be added a certain plasticity within the framework of its own inner laws, but not

On the Meaning of Suffering

enough to expose it to the absolute arbitrariness of men. On the one hand, the limitation that the material world sets upon human activity is necessary for man in his own particular state of being; on the other hand, it is a source of manifold trials and sufferings because man can never take possession of the material world to the extent that he might like to and, in consequence of the unexpected obdurateness of things material, must often endure its painful eruptions into his own world.

By innumerable and varied influences that can never be completely resolved into individual stimuli, those primary and secondary natural impulses are awakened in man that increase his tensions and influence him to choose a sex partner, for instance, and to traverse many tangled paths to realize certain life goals. If years of training and self-training have created enough "ambition" in him, such a secondary urge can maintain a man in a state of tension until difficulties have been overcome and the desired goal has been reached. Years of practice enabled Demosthenes to overcome a congenital speech defect and to become a celebrated orator.

So far as our human existence is concerned, the endurance of suffering is the first thing we learn to control, but never in such a way that we can later attribute our success entirely to our own activity. Let us examine one of mankind's typical experiences. In a given biological emergency, whether it arises from too much heat or cold, from fire, or from some other similar cause, I am awakened from sleep; "I" am inspired and compelled to bestir myself to get help in "averting the emergency" and so to save my life. I arouse myself from empty reveries; I do not let myself be carried away by wild panic; on the contrary, I check the onrush of feelings so I can consider calmly how I am to save myself. If someone is so confused and surprised that he can only stare at the approaching danger, he cannot fix his thoughts on the means of saving himself. But if he succeeds in letting those thoughts that a long experience has stored in his memory rise to the surface, it may be that there will be among them one thought that will show him the way out of the danger in which he finds himself. In thus helping myself, I am by no means always active; I cannot summon up the saving thought out of my memory, I must rely on "sudden inspirations." The proverb "necessity is the mother of invention" is true in only a very limited sense. However great the suffering that an emergency may force upon us, there is little possibility that it will be able to point the way to its own alleviation. In times of famine, whole populations have been known to starve to death although they lived near bodies of water that were filled with fish, and the "invention" of fishing would have alleviated all their misery. Even if the sufferer must depend on "inspirations," however, it is nevertheless expected of him that he will not remain entirely passive, but that he will listen "keenly" in case some saving idea may occur to him that he can put into operation. What I do, then, is always secondary—the echo of a voice that has been heard, the grasping of an inspiration that has come to me.

If I have grasped the lifeline of the assistance offered to save me from danger, if I have transformed into action the plan that occurred to me for helping myself, I can later breathe freely in the conviction that I have "succeeded" in saving myself from danger although I am aware that the attempt might well have foundered at certain danger points. At the same time, I feel a certain pride that I was "successful" in this endeavor and that I am indebted to no one but myself for my rescue.

This simple example has an important universal validity. It is true that I know myself in my active role as one who has set in motion a new chain of circumstances, but I am likewise aware that I do not owe my possession of self to myself and that I cannot act as I please. Just as it was on the first occasion in my life when I was fully conscious of myself, so it is on every later occasion. As a prelude to everything else, I must be jolted out of my passivity by the necessity of enduring suffering. A painful present necessity or an alluring promise of pleasure urges or attracts me until I pass dead center and begin to be active. Alert self-possession and, with it, the ability to become the origin and initiator of a new chain of circumstances are not possessions that arise out of conscious action; they are capabilities that nature has bestowed upon me and that she withdraws again and again in rhythmic waves only to fill them with new strength and restore them to me.

Thus far, we have spoken of suffering in a general sense. Let us turn our attention now to the "pain" that a careless use of language often identifies with suffering, but that is something quite different from it. Pain, in the first and proper meaning of the word, is a sensation that, like other sensations, is experienced by the sense organs. The human organism is equipped with sense perceptors for pain that are linked to certain nerves. It is true, of course, that even the simple "sensation" of pain has a distinctive and special place among the other sensations. All the other sensations call attention to objects outside of us; they construct bridges to the world around us; light and colors, sounds and tones, smell and taste, touch and pressure, make us aware of objects that stand "apart" from us. They have meaning for us only when we refer the messages they convey "intentionally" to objects that are distinct from ourselves. Pain, on the contrary, conveys information not about objects "apart" from us, but about conditions "present" to our own persons. This is true even when the pain is caused by an object outside of us—if we prick ourselves with a needle, for instance, we are aware of more than just the pressure on our skin. Pain informs us that the skin has been injured. We are aware, at the same time, both of our own condition and the object that causes us pain. As a result, pain achieves a closeness to the self that the other sense perceptions can never achieve. It is classified, therefore, not only among the sensations, but also among the feelings.

It is pain that first makes us aware of our bodies. If it is a "painful" master, it is also an indispensable one for teaching the child the difference between the body sphere proper to himself and that other world that is not proper to him and, consequently, for teaching him the distinction between his "I" and every "not I." It is only through painful experiences that the child learns from the resistance of the other that his own "I" is separate from the "not I" of the other. That this separateness must be learned becomes clear to us when we hear that children and primitive peoples, when they are examined by a doctor, are not always able to indicate the exact location of their pains. It is not even unusual for children to insist that their pains are located outside their own bodies. The healthy man, who is never ill, knows his own organs only from hearsay; it is only through the pain of a painful illness that he becomes painfully aware of them.

Bodily pain has an eminent significance for maintaining the healthy good order of our bodies. It is the alarm bell that sounds whenever the body is threatened. Pain tells the "I" that something is not as it should be and urges it to take heed and provide a remedy. Often the pain is not simply diffuse, but has very pregnant qualities that demand a particular course of action. Attention to these particular demands and the conscious fulfillment of them led to the beginnings of the human science of healing. This is not to say, however, that there does not exist, along with the fundamental and positive meaning of pain as the organism's sentinel, the further fact that pain may begin too late in some instances or that pains of the worst kind can still torment us when it is too late to remedy them. Along with the primary and positive value of pain, then, we must acknowledge a secondary, negative effect of which we shall speak later.

The labor pains associated with birth offer a paradigmatic proof that pain is nature's great means of arousing man's sleeping consciousness of self to a humanly conscious existence. They obviously have very special powers of arousing. An observation of animals for purposes of comparison makes this clear. Experiments with animals have demonstrated the important significance of labor pains; they are not pathological, but natural. To discover the meaning of labor pains, the African naturalist E. N. Marais carried out a series of conclusive experiments on a herd of sixty half-wild Kafir sheep in South Africa. After he had determined that there had not been a single occasion in the last fifteen years when a ewe had refused, under normal conditions, to accept her young, he used a narcotic to render several of the ewes unconscious during parturition to eliminate labor pains. The unambivalent result was startling: the ewes that had had a full dose of the narcotic refused to accept their young after birth. The result was otherwise if the narcotic was not administered until after parturition or if the quantity administered was insufficient to produce total unconsciousness. From his series of experiments, which are here described only briefly, Marais was convinced that mother love is first awakened by labor pains. If the animals did not experience labor pains, they later experienced no motherly concern for their offspring. If the birth is accomplished without hindrance, the ewe is not interested afterwards in her young. Obviously, the root of mother love is something latently natural in the case of human beings, too; like the animals, they also need a psychic awakening.

These experiments confirm an important rule: labor pains open the door to mother love; if they are absent, mother love is absent; if they are slight, the resultant mother love is also slight. Medical observations in the last decades have shown that the attitude of the mother-to-be to the coming birth of her child is of decisive importance for the course of the birth itself and for the result. As we have already noted in another connection (chapter 2), many primitive peoples regard birth as something completely natural. The expectant mothers often go alone into the bush and are able to care for themselves soon after parturition without endangering either themselves or the newborn child. It must be regarded as an alienation of nature in civilized life that birth has so often come to be an event that requires more and more medical assistance. Preventive training based on the practice of primitive peoples would be immensely helpful today for the civilized mother who bears her children with such excessive danger and pain.[4]

What takes place on an elementary level in the pains of biological birth takes place on a higher level in the process by which man becomes human. In consequence, "birth" and "labor pains" have become concepts that are frequently applied in a figurative sense. "Delivery" of the latent depths of the human spirit requires the passage through "labor pains." Only in this way can the awakening to new levels of spiritual wisdom take place. "Labor pains" accompany the carrying out and maturing of great ideas, plans, and works. This is especially true of the last and highest maturing of man in his awakening to mystical life. It cannot occur without the passage through the "night of the senses," as the great mystics have described it from their own experience. This experience is often rooted in the circumstances of a "rebirth" to new life.

It is an ancient human concept that pain and suffering are indispensable stages on the great man's road to maturity. It is significant that the Romans used the word *pati* (to suffer) also in the meaning of *pati posse,* that is, to describe one whose power of enduring suffering and pain had been tried and proven. It was considered high "virtue" (= *virtus* in the sense of manliness) for the individual to stand firm and upright in the face of suffering without allowing himself to be inwardly crushed or made powerless by it. There is a question here of far more than just a passive laissez-faire. The individual who maintains a long and often apparently hopeless struggle against the assault of suffering until it has abated wins the proud knowledge that he is, in an exceptional way, a man "tried by suffering."

Thus far we have pursued the problem of pain to discover its meaning and place in the world in which man finds himself. In the discussion between pessimists and optimists, however, the main emphasis is usually on a secondary meaning that is often treated as a principal one. This secondary

On the Meaning of Suffering

meaning refers to the characteristic effect that suffering usually has on human feelings. What sufferers complain about is the mark of unpleasantness, painfulness, and embarrassment that is inseparably linked to the essence of suffering. In the emotional echo of suffering, its painfulness is easily exaggerated. In his bitterness of heart, the complainer becomes the accuser who rejects the world with the statement that all life is basically only suffering.

It is possible today, on the basis of our biological knowledge and understanding, to differentiate and concretize the universal complaint about the painful sufferings of this world. We know that a high percentage of animals—some say one-third—live parasitically, that is, by invading and feeding upon other animals. Nor do they hesitate to invade the human species. Particularly in the tropics, which Northern man, in his dreams, likes to idealize into a kind of paradise, men are plagued by parasites to an extent that it is hard to depict. The well-known European biologist, Adolf Portmann, was deeply shaken by the impressions gained on an expedition that was supposed to give doctors and biologists a vivid awareness of tropical diseases. His impressions were, in truth, of a kind to shock anyone who contemplated them. "All the skin diseases, the diseases of the eye, the disfigured limbs, the feet crippled by parasites, the rows of waiting children who had been attacked by the dread sleeping sickness. No," he said,

> words can hardly picture them.... All this suffering has a common base: parasites are the direct cause of such severe illnesses—some of them so small that they are invisible even with the microscope; then bacteria, one-celled animals, worms, crustaceans, insects, spiders, even vegetable forms, like mushrooms, that cause serious harm, especially to the skin, with their filaceous growths. We are acquainted, it is true, with many of these threats even in our lives here at home: even in our climate, infantile paralysis is caused by invisible viral agents, tuberculosis by bacteria.... But in the tropics the number of such possibilities is particularly high. How many varieties of worms can thrive there in the intestines; can nest in the blood stream, in the brain, in the liver, under the skin; can cause severe sufferings in the eye; can destroy organisms. A large army of insects is perfectly adapted for a parasitic life in men and higher animals: fleas and flies, bugs and lice, a variety of spiderlike ticks—and all of them feed on blood.... Severe sufferings, dangerous parasites, exist in our climate also—but in the tropics there is an almost inconceivable number of these sicknesses that are caused by other living agents. A world of suffering and horror opens up before everyone who has anything to do with this side of life.

For one who knows this aspect of its life, the "land of laughter" becomes the "land of suffering."

What is especially shocking in all this is that it is not just an open "struggle for existence of all against all" that causes the death of so many living things, but that the parasites have developed an ingenious technique for causing suffering. Portmann continues:

> The ascent into the land of suffering and sickness leads to an area of life in which there is high perfection, where the techniques are as meaningful as any of those that we admire in the bright domain of a flowering meadow, in a rose arbor. In the workroom of suffering we find contrivances so subtle that human phantasy seems poor and obtuse beside them. How many appliances for sucking, for pricking, for spraying, for poisoning; what pills, whose dangerous components have been timed so that they can be released at a favorable moment! What cunning devices for making the very sweat of the victim a veritable hotbed for these parasites! What artful instincts allow the blood-suckers to find their way so surely and certainly to the blood vessels under the skin and to infect them! The result is an *instrumentarium* that is best described as "devilish."[5]

The very fact that from this point of view "suffering" is more than just a hard and passive necessity, that a large percentage of these parasites have been able to perfect a highly developed technique for actively inflicting suffering, makes man prone to doubt the existence of a meaningful and divine guidance of world events and to yield to the deadly surmise that some evil demon stands behind the world and finds satanic pleasure in tormenting his creatures. Before complaining too quickly about the way the world is, however, it would be well to reflect that all biologists are convinced that parasites did not belong to the original state of nature, but invaded it later. Even today, it is sometimes possible to observe that certain forms of life that had hitherto found food normally have turned into parasites.

No one would deny, of course, that nature as it is today is not all good but has an evil side as well. But we must assume that its original goodness was later clouded by evil. This leads us to ask when and how this occurred.

Before answering, however, we must pose the question on the level of man. If, on the lower levels of existence, the preying upon one another leads only to death, there exists on the higher levels a consciousness that experiences pain; in the case of man, there exists a spiritual consciousness that not only experiences pain, but that suffers from this life in a way that only man can suffer.

Let us turn our attention now to the typical complaint and accusation formulated by C. S. Lewis:

> The creatures cause pain by being born, and live by inflicting pain, and in pain they mostly die. In the most complex of all the creatures, Man, yet another quality appears, which we call reason, whereby he is enabled to foresee his own pain which henceforth is preceded with acute mental suffering, and to foresee his own death while keenly desiring permanence. It also enables men by a hundred ingenious contrivances to inflict a great deal more pain than they

otherwise could have done on one another and on the irrational creatures. This power they have exploited to the full. Their history is largely a record of crime, war, disease, and terror, with just sufficient happiness interposed to give them, while it lasts, an agonised apprehension of losing it, and, when it is lost, the poignant misery of remembering. Every now and then they improve their condition a little and what we call a civilisation appears. But all civilisations pass away and, even while they remain, inflict peculiar sufferings of their own probably sufficient to outweigh what alleviations they may have brought to the normal pains of man. That our own civilisation has done so, no one will dispute; that it will pass away like all its predecessors is surely probable. Even if it should not, what then? The race is doomed. Every race that comes into being in any part of the universe is doomed; for the universe, they tell us, is running down, and will sometime be a uniform infinity of homogeneous matter at a low temperature. All stories will come to nothing: all life will turn out in the end to have been a transitory and senseless contortion upon the idiotic face of infinite matter.[6]

Such a wholesale condemnation of the world and of human life must be attributed to a viewpoint that is narrowly one-sided. Generalizations are just as indicative of the man who has been internally injured by suffering as is the frustrated contention that behind everything lies only nothingness. For Lewis himself, the complaint thus formulated is only the background against which he established his own argument for a world that, in the last analysis, he regarded optimistically. Emotional upsets must not be allowed to lead us to rash prejudgments. Rather, we must postpone our judgments until we are once more in full possession of ourselves and can pursue our line of thought without frustration or annoyance.

What is true of living organisms below man is obviously true in some way of the individual man and of the whole human species. Whatever it is that causes evil, that causes distressful pain, did not belong to man's original state; on the contrary, it must be attributed to a later corruption of something that was initially good. Here too, however, we must raise the question that is no longer purely metaphysical, but also historical: When, where, and how did this deterioration occur?

Whoever restrains his rash, emotionally tinged complaints and accusations and looks instead at the list of the most common human sufferings will discover at once that by far the majority of these sufferings stems from man himself. It was not Brahman or God who invented torture, whips, prison, slavery, cannons, bayonets, and bombs. Hunger, poverty, and misery do not have their source in the parsimony of nature, but in the greed, wickedness, and stupidity of man. If the source of the primeval goodness of the world and of life is to be sought in the nature of the world before man existed there, we must look to man himself as the proximate cause of the cessation of this goodness.

To understand how man can be the source of suffering, let us take one example—the case in which man fails to use his human faculties to avert a pressing need. We have already noted that the proverb "necessity is the mother of invention" is true, but not always applicable. In any event, necessity has not made that man inventive who, instead of seeking ways to avert need, begins to lament and complain as soon as it begins to show itself. For the active man, "consciousness" and "reason" are the preconditions for finding ways of averting need, of successfully putting them into practice, and of being able, afterwards, to assert proudly that he has "succeeded" by his own efforts. A man who has been matured by the experiences of life, who is intellectually alert, will not fall into the mistake of consciously allowing an additional new burden of suffering to be imposed upon man by the living organisms below him. Here, indeed, the failure to use one's human capacities would be at least an added source of suffering and pain.

Just as man's failure to act in the measure required of him by a given circumstance can be a source of suffering, so can his expenditure of too much activity. Anyone, moreover, who has succeeded in an undertaking has made the important discovery that it is not only the reaching of a goal that makes an undertaking pleasing, but also one's own active engagement in it from the very beginning. If a person has been prevented for a long time from engaging personally in an action, he regards it as a kind of redemption when he can at last begin to be active. The bright alertness, the ability to do and dare, the conceiving and working out of plans, is just as welcome to him as the later carrying out of the plans that he has made. In the process, he evaluates unreflecting, natural consciousness and reason as positive assets; he rejects every dispiriting pessimism.

It must be admitted here that the individual who has learned from happy experience that his youthful alertness can rule with easy certainty over the potentialities of a situation, that his creative effort can shape things anew, may be so fascinated thereby that he will begin to exaggerate the personal freedom that is his by nature and to make of it a "self-glorification" that tries to set aside all limitations on his activity. The man who is fascinated by the success of his own creative ability will not admit that his potentiality for action is strongly limited by reason of his nature and the quality of his existence, that his effectiveness is circumscribed both by the limits of the means that are at his disposal and by the exigencies and ordinances of his own nature. He falls prey to the delusion of wanting to base his existence on his own activity.

Only the person who strives compulsively to do everything by his own effort and who wants to be the foundation of his own being will experience the limitations that nature has imposed upon him as a suffering from which he really "suffers" and is wounded. The person who is satisfied with the nature that he has received does not suffer because there are limits to what he can do; he rather rejoices in the realization of those potentialities that his nature makes available to him. Only the person who is possessed by the ambition of gaining everything unconditionally by his own efforts experiences his metaphysical limitedness as a real "suffering." Such striving found its mythological defeat in the persons of the Titans. Prometheus scoffed at the First Maker and set about redoing the work in a better way. But he was as unsuccessful in his undertaking as was Sisyphus, who pushed a heavy rock with unutterable strain to the peak of the mountain only to have it roll back down again and again. The Titans possessed the defiant ambition of wanting to be "like God." This, according to the Bible, is the primal sin that enmeshed mankind in an unbreakable chain of misery. From this point of view, "suffering" also emanates from man's excessive desires and demands. If man did not expect too much of himself and his nature, he would be able to find pleasure in the positive potentialities for personal activity that his nature affords him.

We have reached the point at which man must make a kind of fundamental decision: Either he must willingly accept and abide by the order (that his nature has imposed upon him) or he must burn with the unruly desire of relying autonomously upon himself alone, in which case, he will call down upon himself as an inevitable nemesis the constant suffering of inner conflict. It is only in Christianity that the place of this initial and primal decision has been comprehended in all its breadth and moved into the light. That is the deeper meaning of the doctrine of primal and hereditary (original) sin.

Precisely because it does have a clear view of the breadth of human freedom and of primal and original sin, Christian doctrine can claim to be not just the wisdom of man, but the revelation of God. For even man's first attempt to owe himself only to himself, to possess himself of himself, was more than an offense against the limits established for human nature; it also led to an overtaxing of nature that is harmful. Every further attempt confirmed this. Instead of reaching the state of superalertness for which it strove, human self-consciousness sank into a state of subalertness, of spiritual darkness and murkiness. Conscious alertness is possible only if nature is so empowered and then only to the extent to which it is so empowered. But as soon as man refuses to recognize the limitations imposed by nature and tries to exceed the measure of his self-possession, he actually harms nature; instead of reaching a higher state of consciousness, his bright clarity is dimmed; the certainty of his judgment about the basic facts of his own actions and the consequences thereof is lost. As a result, he succumbs to the phantasies of a mythology that seeks to excuse the breadth of his sinfulness. In non-Christian religions and ideologies, the sense of sin is not precisely dead, but it is more and more frequently ignored or distorted to the point of being unrecognizable. If, on the contrary, a sense of sin has been preserved in Christianity, it is clear that this fact must be attributed to a divine revelation.

Today we are in a position to study the excessive demands made on human activity in terms of a single concrete example. At the turn of the century, death from heart disease ranked in about seventh place; now it has moved into first place. The frequency of such deaths in the present is not to be attributed to the heavy blows of fate, for in the years of the last war and in the difficult postwar years death from heart disease was much rarer than it is today. In fact, it was only in direct proportion to the rate of economic reconstruction that death from heart disease increased to such a frightening extent. After 1948 the number of such deaths was tripled within seven years. But the increase in heart disease is not limited to the years of economic reconstruction; it is rather a symptom of our times. Since the beginning of the century, it has moved steadily forward to head the list of causes of death. This occurred first in the United States and then in all "Americanized" nations. Medical analysis of the so-called executive syndrome has revealed that there is no somatically comprehensible cause for the frequency of such deaths. They are rather to be attributed to excessive tension, immoderate ambition, the constant anxiety caused by competition or the fear of losing one's own ability to achieve, an unregulated way of life, continual use of stimulants, too rich food, and the lack of physical exercise. Heart disease, which is presently on the increase especially among males, is not a biological fate that befalls man, but a typical consequence of the prevailing mood of the age and of the characteristically hectic activity that disregards the limits of man's nature and wants to be and do by its own efforts more than human nature is capable of being or doing. The individual who has succumbed to this mood is unaware of its cause or its whole range. The more he has allowed himself to become identified with it, the less he is able to achieve inward distance from it and to perceive relationships. His suffering is tragic, for he eventually becomes aware of the fatal consequences of his attitude, but he does not have the strength consciously to oppose it, to come to terms with it, and to retreat from unsalutary excess into the salutary moderation of nature. In this instance, we have a model of the way in which a first "basic" sin can become a "hereditary [original] sin."[7]

The basic sin was, in truth, the opening of a Pandora's box from which, once it was opened, there issued an unending stream of further suffering. Undoubtedly the most regrettable consequence is the decrease in alert vigilance, the implication of the individual in the downward trend of the masses, the inability to account to oneself for what has happened. The final result is the disappearance of a clear concept and awareness of sin. Even when these have not been totally lost, it is nevertheless possible, in view of the clouding of man's vision and his all too natural inclination to excuse himself, for him to lay the blame on some world cause.

It is characteristic of the situation in which man makes his basic decision that it can be understood without special training. It is as easy for the child to understand it as for the scholar, just as it is equally easy for either of them to allow his view of it to become clouded by emotion. It is a question of deciding between an unconditional state of "being one's own" and a willing submission to the commands and demands of an order that has been imposed from without. It may be that the outlines of a divine being whose function it is to impose such order are only faintly discernible behind the order emerging in one's own self-consciousness (Mit-Wissen = *conscientia* [cf. Scholastic *synteresis*]). Nevertheless, at the very moment when there arises in him the temptation to follow his own will unconditionally, the individual who has suddenly become conscious of his own condition does in fact have at least a presentiment that there *is* a divine being who establishes order in all that exists. Man's consciousness of his own dependence implies a vision, however dark it may be, of God. In the temptation to establish oneself as the foundation of one's own existence, although existence has no roots in self, and so to be able to exist for and of oneself, man becomes so directly aware of the basic human condition of his existence that he needs no special prerequisites for understanding it, no long drawn-out experience, no intellectual and cultural training, no social rank.

From the moment when man comprehends himself as self and becomes aware both of the order that has been imposed upon him from without and of the incomprehensible being who has imposed it, he must make the primal decision that is, in the last analysis, a decision for or against the God who is making his presence felt. There opens before him "the terrible alternative of choosing God or self for the centre. . . . This sin [that is, the choosing of self] is committed daily by young children and ignorant peasants as well as by sophisticated persons, by solitaries no less than by those who live in society: it is the fall in every individual life, and in each day of each individual life, the basic sin behind all particular sins. . . ."[8]

One experience recurs constantly in man's life. In the beginning, he is grateful in his greeting of whatever befalls him and accepts it with reverence; after a while, however, he comes to regard it as something that has become so much a part of him that he defends it even at knife-point as his own self. Once man, in his primal decision, has exalted self as the exclusive center of human existence, everything that he touches becomes more and more infected with the poison of self-seeking. This rampant self-seeking allows nothing that is not the self to exist independently of the self, but regards it only in its relationship to the self, as one of the many "means" to its own satisfaction. It is precisely this increased self-seeking that turns every love potion into a fatal poison. The poisoning begins where the natural impulse of love should and would bind two people together if self-seeking did not drive its poisonous wedge between them. Even if, in a first transport of emotion, they inwardly affirm each other's independent existence, it can still happen that in a second encounter, in which sexual desire has also been aroused, the beloved will be regarded as a means of sexual satisfaction and will consequently be humiliated in his status as a human being. Without being totally aware of the significance of what has occurred, an aroused desire has deceitfully undertaken to change love into something pleasing to the self and, in doing so, has taken a first step out of the order that has actually been established and into a divisive disorder that brings with it the pain of schism; this schism, in turn, often manifests itself as an unutterably long and, for the man who must endure it, painful suffering in the depths of the soul because of a relationship that has arisen out of the ties of blood, out of social obligations, or out of natural impulse, but that brings no satisfaction because one of the partners to it, although he is inwardly awake and striving for satisfaction, sees that he is not fully accepted in his status as a human being and, in consequence, feels himself humiliated and degraded.

It is understandable that, once it has been embarked upon, the devious route that leads from the corruption of fascination with self to a desire for absolute possession of self should terminate in a self-glorification that eventually sees everything solely from the viewpoint of this one basic drive. Not "being," but "seeming," is the goal of all striving. Not those achievements that have been carried out for their own objective value are considered important, but only those that are a "means" of calling attention to the self, of enhancing it, of making an impression on others. If the divine being whose function it is to establish order stands behind all objective order as the ultimate, although only dimly surmised, point of reference, the human self in its waywardness has appropriated this place to itself. The gentle attraction of a "restlessness until we rest in God" that draws man to God from the very depths of his soul is hindered in its effectiveness by a counterweight that forces him onto a steep slope where there is no stopping. The first sin, whether of the individual or of mankind, becomes a centrifugal force that moves faster and faster. Yet even "fallen man" cannot change the basic tendencies of the nature that has been bestowed upon him. As a consequence of sin, therefore, he experiences an increasing tension whose meaning he cannot interpret, but of which he is made aware by the pain and suffering of an enduring inner schism.

The history of the individual's fall into sin is repeated in the history of the fall into sin of all the generations of men. The consequences of sin shape themselves into a traditional process that stretches from generation to generation, drawing the individual with it in such a way that it is impossible for him, without a special enlightenment, to change his ways and "be converted." Just as in the personal history of the individual, so it is possible in the spiritual history of a group for certain habitual modes of action to harden into a "second nature" whose tendencies run counter to the basic tendencies of his first nature and, in the process, cause continual inner suffering.

This direction that runs counter to man's real self is so consolidated with

On the Meaning of Suffering

his "second nature" that a reversal to his original direction cannot take place without painful effort, without the "conquest of self." The man who has fallen into sin fears such a "confrontation" with his original self; but he is equally unable to remove from himself the nagging suffering caused by his own fallen condition.

Under the pressure of inward suffering, whose cause cannot be discovered because of the limitations inherent in man's nature, there develops an emotional disturbance, a resentment, that short-sightedly exaggerates the suffering and seeks a "scapegoat" that can be blamed for it. Every form of "pessimism" is ultimately a poisonous plant that thrives in the soil of irritation caused by suffering. Indian pessimism heaps the blame for the suffering of the world on Brahman himself; the guilt once incurred by Brahman must be expiated by perpetual suffering. Schopenhauer also attributed the origin of the world to an original sin. In their lamentations, the pessimists refer only to the dark aspects of the world and exaggerate suffering so they can pose the rhetorical question: can a God who is good have created such a world? They overlook the direct causes of most human suffering. We can do no better than to repeat here: God did not invent torture, whips, prison, slavery, bayonets, cannons, and bombs; it is man who, in his boundless self-seeking, has destroyed the original moderation of nature. Poverty and hunger do not have their source in the parsimony of nature, but in the greed, wickedness, and stupidity of man.

To prove the correctness of their thesis, the pessimists have attempted again and again to balance the actual weight of man's pleasure against that of his pain, to make a kind of inventory of all those things that give man pleasure and of all those other things that are a painful burden to him, in order then to balance one group against the other and to establish the expected "minus" of the result as the foundation of their pessimism. The "optimists" have also made this attempt in order to justify *their* stand by the resultant "plus."

But every attempt to counterbalance pleasure and pain suffers from the inherent weaknesses that condemn it to failure. There is lacking, in the first place, a usable, objective norm against which the comparison can be made. Nor is subjective sensibility to pain a suitable measuring rod, for it varies considerably from person to person. Moreover, the selection of test cases is never accomplished without some prejudging *(vor-urteilend)* arbitrariness. Finally, there are many experiences that cannot be labeled as unambivalently positive or negative. In looking back upon many a painful experience, the individual is inclined, in retrospect, to place it on the positive side and to regard it as a value that he would not willingly have missed.

Furthermore, there is a contradiction implicit in the very question. For peaceful order is more essentially a part of man's original state than any painful disorder. The pessimists' assertion that human existence in this world consists "solely" of suffering is refuted by the fact that suffering as a deprivation, as something that should not be, presumes order as the sine qua non of its existence.

Of its nature, order belongs at the beginning of things, together with those natural gifts that man is expected to develop and whose development comes about through his own efforts. This fact has nothing to do with the historical question about the sources of disorder in our own present world. There are reasons—and history can shed light on them—why suffering in all its forms plays so predominant a role in our world; why sickness, poverty, need, deprivation of freedom oppress so many and make impossible for them the full unfolding of their human gifts. We do not need to side with the optimists and depreciate, or even deny, the sufferings that actually exist. Millions of small children do, in fact, die of hunger; other millions suffer from contagious diseases; countless human beings are deprived of the freedom that is indispensable for a life that is fully human. All these facts can and must be regarded with sober realism. Far from justifying a fundamental pessimism, however, they should spur us on to discover their causes and to search for remedies.

Anyone who has not allowed his heart to grow hardened and who is aware of the sufferings that oppress individual men as well as whole nations will feel compelled to take remedial action. He will not follow the easy course of condemning world causes, nor will he content himself with just bemoaning the sufferings of others; on the contrary, he will be concerned to discover the causes of these sufferings so he will be able to alleviate them. If the impulse to render active assistance is lacking to Buddhism, at least in its original form, this fact is due, in some part, to its basic agnosticism. It has been noted again and again that Buddha silenced his disciples whenever they inquired about ultimate causes; but to do this is to ignore the question about the causes of suffering as well. The answer to this latter question is admittedly incapable of shedding light on ultimate causes, but it cannot fail to show the misuse of human freedom as the proximate cause of many of the sufferings of this world. This insight is not totally wanting to Buddhism. It knows that "self-seeking" and self-seeking "desire" are responsible for suffering. For this reason, it demands the mortification of the selfish covetousness that causes so many sufferings. But because Buddhism holds itself aloof from every form of critical reflection, it is unable to draw basic distinctions. It does not distinguish between the natural impulses of the human being, which are to be affirmed and whose development bestows upon the individual a certain natural happiness, and the misuse of freedom through selfish desire, which destroys order and leads to the misery of numerous schisms. Because Buddhism does not comprehend this distinction in all its clarity, it equates all striving with covetousness, regards it as valueless, condemns it as a source of suffering, and requires its followers to renounce all covetousness in order to close off every source from which suffering might flow.

A premature resentment prevents the Buddhist from being fully aware that even man's condition as man imposes upon him the necessity of making moral judgments. Because man does not possess himself absolutely, the Buddhist rejects the individuation of the person. In doing so, however, he fails to recognize that man, as a doer of good and evil, has been constituted the guardian of the order that is in the world, that it is man who, by his evildoing, opens the floodgates through which unhappiness flows ceaselessly into the world of men.

Because Buddhism fails to appreciate the human person and the responsibility that is laid upon him, it also fails to appreciate the real meaning of suffering. The Buddhist endures complainingly the setbacks that his sufferings inflict upon him without being thereby stirred to that comprehension of self that is the intrinsic purpose behind all suffering. Just as birth pangs are intended to raise to consciousness the latent motherliness that lies hidden in the depths of the mother-to-be, so every suffering is intended to impinge upon man's consciousness, to stimulate him to a new comprehension of self, to allow the latent person to mature into a self-conscious individual. No suffering, not even the physical suffering of bodily pain, is confined to the level of active life; it is able, in many ways, to permeate the whole human being, to awaken the still-sleeping spirit to a higher degree of self-comprehension.

Even purely bodily pain, as we have already noted, has a biological meaning that it is important to accept, to understand, and to take into account. It belongs to the maturing of the human person that he should progress steadily from the mere bemoaning of his suffering to the mastery of his feelings and to self-emancipation. A small child complains about every slightest suffering that befalls him; he does not attempt to restrain his cries of woe. Not until he has been instructed by adults that it is unworthy of man to greet every pain with tears and cries does the child gradually learn not to be overcome by every suffering, but to develop a steadfastness of his own. Through this learning experience he comes to know himself as a person, to have an experiential awareness of himself as the active initiator of a long series of actions and happenings.

One is inclined to link the Buddhist's denial of man's personhood to a lack of personal maturity. Just as the spiteful child, who does not immediately receive all that he demands, but only that part that adults deem fitting, promptly rejects the part because it is not the whole, so the Buddhist rejects man's relatively limited personhood because it excludes the absolute possession of self and is therefore "nothing" in his eyes. In reality, however, this limited personhood and the freedom it entails are of immeasurable significance for man's world and for the suffering or lack of it that are manifest there. Even if man is not the *causa prima,* the absolute originator, of events, he nonetheless possesses a certain secondary capacity for doing or omitting that is completely adequate for his role as protector of the preordained order of the world. It is only by his correct assessment of his task of caring for this order and of protecting it against the poisonous evil of self-seeking that he becomes aware of the meaning of "sin." Significantly enough, the Buddhist has no adequate notion of what sin is. The premature cessation of reflection on his own being has also deprived him of an understanding of the fact that there must have been a first, original sin, a sin of pride and disobedience, that sometime and somewhere paved the way for the first entrance into human history of an evil that continued thereafter to pursue its catastrophic course. Even a purely natural contemplation of the human condition reveals the factual situation that finds its explanation in the Christian doctrine of original sin.

Every pain poses a question to man. The immature person merely complains; he neither hears nor heeds the question. But the person who is approaching or has attained maturity takes the question seriously and seeks to answer it. He wonders if perhaps he himself is to some extent responsible for his suffering and what he can do to alleviate it. If he is honest with himself, he is often compelled to admit that the painful suffering could have been avoided if his own "negligent" behavior had not paved the way for it.

Another poisonous plant that flourishes in the soil of man's rampant self-seeking is the will to unconditional autocracy. The man who has attained such autocracy is no longer willing to hear the word *sin*. It imparts a meaning to his actions and sufferings that he resists because, in the basic orientation of his life, he has turned away from whatever reproaches him in this manner through his conscience. As a result, the concept of sin is suppressed among "Christians" just as it is among Buddhists, for whom such a concept is meaningless.

An understanding of sin does not debase the individual. On the contrary, it is the counterpart of his understanding of that royally free personhood that is man's prerogative and by virtue of which he has been set to guard the order of his world, of that understanding that includes a similar understanding of the unalienable individual oneness of the man who guides his own destiny, of that primarily unified being that conducts itself in a morally responsible manner. But Buddhism has no clear understanding of the fundamental oneness of man's being. It has adopted from Brahminism the concept that the human organism is composed of many elements. The usual belief is that it is composed, on the one hand, of material and spiritual elements; on the other hand, of an eternal and personal element.

Instead of making an intellectual study of the metaphysical and moral claims of the human mind and heart and arriving thereby at a positive concept of the human person, Buddhism has leaped to the conclusion that man's inborn belief in his own ego as an independent reality is the principal cause of all suffering; that a false concept of the human "ego" keeps man imprisoned in the painful course of the world, in *samsara,* the cycle of rebirth. But this is a false interpretation of a correct principle. For it is not man's belief in his selfhood that is the cause of suffering, but that excessive self-seeking that so deceives the man who is fascinated by self that he makes his self the center of his world. Buddhism is incapable of this differentiated thinking because it equates "reality" with "absolute reality" and thus denies the reality of the human ego. "Only by extinguishing his belief in his own ego can man be freed once and for all from the sufferings that belong to his transitory existence."[9]

But the cause in which Buddhism erroneously seeks the "root" of suffering results logically in a radical withdrawal from the world. From this standpoint, moreover, every attempt to realize one's intellectual and moral propensities is condemned as self-seeking. For that reason, Buddhism has no understanding of the "happiness" toward which every man is oriented and that he can achieve by his own "successful" effort. Yet man is preordained to develop his potentialities to the fullest and thus to attain the "happiness" that results therefrom.

But if the individuality of the human person comes to be regarded as pure illusion, the free human ego as the source of moral decisions also becomes an illusion and, as a logical consequence, there can be no understanding of sin and its catastrophic effects. Nothing remains thereof but fantastic distortions. The true nature of moral evil as the only absolute evil remains unrecognized. Yet even the ancient Greeks were aware that the only evil that is absolute evil is not the suffering of wrong, but the doing of wrong. All the vanity of moral evil and its consequences lies in the evildoer, who is a reality to be taken with utmost seriousness. For, in the sphere of moral evil, there is no evil that does not become absolutely evil through the evildoer, with the evildoer, and in the action of the evildoer.

To the extent that it gives any consideration to the problem of moral evil, Buddhism removes guilt as such from man and, like Brahminism, attributes it to primeval being. In time, there are added to this originally primeval guilt the sins of man's first existences, but without any attempt to identify an actually guilty evildoer. Because Buddhism fails to understand the "I-ness" of man, it places sin in earlier existences of which no memory has been retained. The Buddhist doctrines of *karma*, the retribution of man's deeds, and of reincarnation admit of no satisfactory relationship between guilt and destiny. No ego that is either conscious or capable of becoming conscious links together in memory the various forms of existence that are affirmed by Buddhism. In any event, so long as Buddhism adheres to the view that man has no lasting existence and, consequently, that the evildoer, even if caught, is not the same person that he was when he committed the evil deed, it is senseless to punish an ego that has its existence only moment by moment. The former consciousness of self has been extinguished and a new one has taken its place; but there is no continuity of the person. The one who is punished and suffers expiation is, therefore, a totally different person from the one who committed the sin. It is not merely that the evildoer has forgotten his evil deed; he has actually not committed it—not even in an earlier existence—for he is no longer the same person as the person who existed at that time. It follows, then, that the whole problem of guilt is solved neither by Brahminism nor by Buddhism; it is set aside and ignored.

If Brahman was originally a neutral absolute without consciousness, how was it possible for him to acquire guilt? Before what court did he become guilty? Against whose commandments did he sin? Who is in a position to pass judgment on his guilt? How could he transfer to others the expiatory penitential sufferings for a guilt of which they had no part? How can the unhappy sufferer be branded and burdened with the undeserved fate of appearing before the world as the guilty one? Alleged recollections of earlier existences are so improbable that they afford no proof. Even if it were possible to verify them, Buddhist doctrine would not admit that the dreamer is identical with the one of whose guilt he dreams.

The imposition of world guilt upon the absolute, therefore, is faced with an insuperable difficulty. If the absolute is rightly comprehended in its absoluteness, it must also be absolute in its moral integrity. In other words, it must be the absolutely holy, for the absolute cannot be regarded as something neutral. By virtue of its own being, the absolute must be sinless. It is otherwise with man who, because he is not an absolute being, has the freedom to choose whether he will do good or evil. His fallibility is grounded in the contingency of his intellectual and moral nature. Only a created being can sin in the proper meaning of the term because only a created being can misuse the freedom that has been given him. The prerequisite for sinning is the shortsighted self-seeking that conceals the real state of affairs from itself by means of a semblance of reality. Again, such a blinding of self is conceivable only in the case of a creature endowed with finite intelligence, because only such a one can allow vision to be obscured by instinct.

Unlike the doctrine of Buddhism, that of Christianity regards sin seriously as guilt attributable to man. For this reason, it admits of no automatic removal of guilt, but only of a personal conversion born of sorrow for sin that accepts the punitive suffering and strives to escape from the faulty attitude of sin. Whoever persists in his faulty attitude, however, and refuses to abandon his sin brings upon himself, by his stubbornness, the fate of eternal damnation.

Just as bodily pain warns that the integrity of the organism is being threatened and presses for help, so every pang of guilt seeks to inspire man to return into himself, to ask himself if and how he may have caused his own suffering by his own guilt. Many individual features of Buddhism bear witness to the fact that even here there is operative in man a subliminal consciousness of guilt that never quite achieves the status of a bright and

On the Meaning of Suffering

clear possession of self. Once the stimulus of suffering has been permitted to arouse conscious self-reflection, however, the question of personal guilt can no longer be ignored. Every humanly existential suffering is intended to instruct man, to encourage him to intellectual reflection, to lead him to ever greater heights of a self-consciousness that is aware of its responsibilities. Thus every suffering that must be borne has the meaning, as it were, of intellectual birth pains. In this way, the negative sign is blotted out and replaced by a positive one.

The biographies of great men frequently reveal a break, a change in their whole existential attitude, that has been evoked and conditioned by a suffering that has unexpectedly overtaken them on the very course that their lives had hitherto been following. As a result, they recognized the need for a reflection directed inwards upon themselves that would lead them to turn aside from their present attitude toward life and to struggle upward to a higher level of human existence. In particular, the suffering attached to punishment can produce this effect. For the English author Oscar Wilde, the dandified product of an artificial life of luxury, such an experience brought to a sudden stop the satisfaction of his perverted sensual instincts. In jail, where he had to endure a long sentence, he struggled, in inward shock, to find a meaning for his suffering. In the harsh birth pains of psychic suffering, he found his "better self," as he expressed it in his confessions, where we read: "Sorrow is the most sensitive of all created things . . . Where there is sorrow there is holy ground. . . . It is really a revelation." [10]

We should like, now, to add to what we have already said about suffering a few words about the four special sufferings that Buddhism adduces as the basis of its pessimism. It was the images of "sickness," "anxiety," "old age," and "death" that impressed the young Gautama Buddha so deeply that he believed himself justified in regarding all life as empty and worthless, in leaving homeland and family to live in isolation. In all of these sufferings, there is question primarily of a deterioration in the vitality of existence. "Sickness" is a disturbance of the inner harmony of physical and psychic existence; "anxiety"—above all, in the form of poverty—is a suffering that stems from lack of the necessary means of existence, particularly of the means of physical existence. In the actual order of life as we know it, there corresponds to the rise in the vitality of existence in childhood and adolescence and even to the height of adulthood an equally natural decline that is known as "aging." An ever-increasing retardation in the life processes results in signs of fatigue and aging that lead ultimately to the natural extinction of life in death. Even if the "necessity of dying" is not a primordial biological law, death is nonetheless, in the present order of our lives, the inevitable end of physical life. Admittedly, men have never accepted readily their lot of mortality. They have always looked upon death as something unnatural and have sought means of postponing and eventually of overcoming it. But all efforts to achieve a genuine rejuvenation have thus far been fruitless.

But are the four principal sufferings sufficient justification for the Buddhist devaluation of human life as though it were nothing but suffering? We must admit that they are not—if for no other reason than that every suffering is a summons to man, a warning that his life is in danger, just as every physical pain is intended to alert man so he will cry for help.

Let us look more closely at "poverty" and its stigma of "anxiety." There exists a whole series of statistically supported facts that belie a negative evaluation of poverty as an absolute evil. For poverty can, in fact, make a significant contribution to man's effort to comprehend himself, to strengthen his character, and to avert necessity. It is a striking and noteworthy fact that nations in which poverty is the norm are least inclined to the desperate act of suicide. In like manner, research into the problem of suicide[11] shows that instances of suicide are by no means more frequent in times of severe economic need. It is a fact, also, that suicide is reported less frequently in the poor sections of large cities than in the rich ones. "Poverty," then, is not regarded as an absolute evil by mankind, nor can it be described as such. On the contrary, "rich" men have less inner strength; they are "more sensitive"; they have greater needs, are more dependent on others—or on another; they possess less perseverance and are more easily prone to resignation and despair. Poverty, indeed, as a necessity experienced by one's self, awakens the sleeping spirit and has the capacity to activate man's powers according to the proverb "necessity is the mother of invention."

It is true, of course, that no necessity can compel the one who suffers it to a spiritual understanding of himself or to the averting of necessity by his own efforts. Even in his greatest need, man can remain sluggish, can resist every impulse to help himself. But that is precisely the risk that is implicit in man's freedom, namely, that he can answer his own cry for help, but that he does not have to do so. If man's freedom to make his own decisions in our world represents a positive value, this risk must not be foregone. Any avoidance of it would make human freedom illusory. An achievement becomes meritorious only when it has been done by one's own effort even though it would have been permissible to omit doing it. It is only the suppression of human freedom and all that it entails that converts any necessity into an absolute evil for which some anonymous world cause must bear the blame. But there is question here of a metaphysical failure, to the correction of which much serious consideration should be given.

No one who hopes to come to a new appreciation of the meaning of suffering should overlook the fact that, in times of great catastrophes, the acute suffering of those most seriously affected gives spontaneous rise to a sense of and a will to community that does not occur under ordinary

On the Meaning of Suffering

circumstances. This will to community arouses each one individually and encourages a mutual search for and undertaking of remedial action.

Thus the first three evils decried by Buddhism acquire a positive meaning in relation to the awakening and maturing of man's character. But the fourth, death, puts a definite end to human life. This is the Buddhist's main lament: All life is painful because it is passing; death puts an end to everything. Is death, then, the absolute evil? It is true that man shares with the other animals his subjection to death; but of them all he alone knows that his life is ordered toward death as an end. Life has value in itself even if it is a life that is finite. The necessity of dying becomes a negative value for man only because his drive to live cannot accept his finiteness, because an impulse that arises out of his inmost being seeks a life that is absolute and forever. But man's seeking must resign itself intellectually to his fate of mortality. As we know from our own experience of life and from the lives of others, it is precisely the knowledge of coming death that awakens man, as nothing else does, out of his metaphysical slumber. This knowledge rescues him from the vague feeling that he is carried along like a particle amid the streaming masses; it makes him rely on himself; it separates him from the masses; it encourages him to inquire what his end may be.

Even in this instance it remains true that man is not forced, even by his innermost compulsion, to make this ultimate choice. Yet, throughout man's history, the experiencing of his inevitable lot of mortality has always been the strongest force for arousing him from his metaphysical lethargy. From the core of his spiritual being, there arises in man a natural conviction that he has been made for a happiness that transcends time. This is evidenced by the fact that the negative concept of the dogma of *nirvana* (freedom from rebirth) has never become entrenched in Buddhism. Again and again, human longing has transformed nirvana into a heaven. No untimely agnosticism should be allowed to cut short man's pondering of this natural conviction. For only the man who ponders and affirms his reasons can turn his natural conviction into a conviction that is factually grounded and consciously accepted, namely, the conviction that the sufferings of this time are stimulating tests that man must endure in order to achieve, by this means, a happiness that is supreme and everlasting.

BUDDHIST AND CHRISTIAN CONCEPTS OF THE "SOUL"

Among the basic truths on which Christianity and Buddhism differ is the doctrine of the immortal soul. According to the preaching of Jesus Christ and the doctrine of Christianity, the *soul* is man's most precious possession, the basis of all his worth; its eternal salvation is the center of his striving. Official Buddhism, on the contrary, denies the existence of a true spiritual soul.

If the concept of the soul is one of the primordial concepts of mankind, which has always pondered its own existence and expressed its thoughts in concepts, there have, nevertheless, been long periods in which ideas and concepts about the soul have been vague and lacking in clarity. Even the Old Testament is marked, as was so often the case in the ancient world, by the absence of extended, clearly defined concepts. Only gradually do the vague notions achieve clarity; no clear concept of an independent spiritual soul that lives after death can be said to have existed before the period of late Judaism—probably under the influence of Greek thought.

Although Christianity and Buddhism seem, at first glance, to represent diametrically opposed views, a consideration of the historical development of the concept of the soul makes that difference more comprehensible. Ideas and thoughts about the "soul" as a supernatural life-giving principle in man are to be found among nations of every form of culture, even in ancient India. Indeed, the existence of several souls was often taken for granted in India, although it is impossible to determine whether this fact was due to an improper use of language, with the reference being merely to different functions of one and the same soul, or whether there really did exist a belief in many souls that differed among themselves. As a principle of vitality and of life, the soul is repeatedly identified with a gentle breeze or with a breath and is located in a certain organ, such as the heart, the liver, or the blood. If this vital principle leaves man for a time, he dies. A distinction is often made between this soul and a personal soul that serves as the center of thinking, willing, and feeling and that is frequently regarded as an independent being that lives in the body. In it, conscience has its roots; it is thought to dwell in the head or in the heart. After death, it continues to live on in the next world in a new mode of existence. Mention is often made, too, of an unencumbered soul that can leave the body in sleep or ecstasy and have new experiences in far-distant places. It is only in later reflections that these notions about the soul are referred to a single soul that functions in a variety of activities and events.

There is probably no one who has not had, in his acting as in his suffering, the inner experience of his own "oneness"; of himself as a single, although certainly not as a simple, being; rather as a being torn in two directions so there is opposed to his ego, to the most integral part of himself in which he consciously possesses his own life, a purely material part—his hair, for instance, or his finger nails—which, in the last analysis, is hardly to be distinguished from nonliving matter. More remote from the conscious experience of reflecting, deciding, and willing at the center of his ego are those more or less conscious processes that can be influenced only indirectly by the conscious ego or that are completely independent of it. Above all, the experiences of dreams and, even more pertinently, the puzzling act of dying, which man observes again and again among his fellowmen as a "departing," justify his assumption of a single principle of psychic and intellectual activities and his distinction, in man at least, of two realities that oppose one another as body and soul or—in even sharper contrast—as matter and spirit, but that nevertheless form, in living man, an inseparable unity.

Corresponding to this distinction, there are two sciences that deal with human life, of which one—*physiology*—is chiefly concerned with the life of the body, while the other—*psychology*—is oriented toward the life of the soul. Nevertheless, man knows that, despite all physical and psychic change, it is one and the same person who exists throughout a lifetime; and that it is a human *in-dividual* (i.e., one who is not divisible) who begins life as an infant, matures from child to adult by way of adolescence, has his own uniquely personal experiences of life, receives the reward of his good deeds while his evil ones are imputed to him as guilt even decades later. This knowledge has brought man to the realization that "soul" cannot be just a name for the totality of his psychic activities and abilities, as so-called empirical psychology has been affirming from Hume to the present. A certain fundamental positivism has evoked an unmistakable aversion to metaphysics—a reluctance to search out the actual reasons for existence behind the directly determinable facts; to deduce, from qualitatively unique psychic activities that are of a supernatural kind even when their course is linked to material conditions, the existence of a real and substantial something that is essentially different from everything material. Only when metaphysical thought has been pursued to its logical conclusion is there any possibility of forming an unambivalent concept of the soul that regards it as an immaterial, indivisible, and nondimensional something that is simple and that cannot, therefore, be subject to the deterioration that continually threatens those substances that are composed of material elements. Even though the soul is, by its very nature, linked to the body in all its activities, there are, nonetheless, different degrees of imprisonment within the body. Intellectual acts are the most free, for although they are accompanied by material activity, they are not produced by it.

It is important, moreover, to realize that the "concept" of the soul cannot proceed from the imagination; it can be achieved only by thought that has been emancipated from a too-heavy dependence on visual images. A thinker like Augustine achieved this only after years of effort. The controversy that still centers around the concept of the soul is evidence that it is a problem for the philosopher even today. The objection to the concept is, in fact, based on the mistaken belief that *substance* always refers to a "lump of material reality." But the true notion of substance is the general ontological concept of being that refers to the self-sufficiency of a being that exists in its own right, rather than as an act or manifestation of another being. Such a self-sufficient and self-reliant being can exist as readily in the spiritual as in the material sphere.

Precisely the misunderstandings of the concept of the soul that exist in many modern philosophies and especially in positivistic "psychologies," which are, for the most part, "psychology without a soul," are best qualified to engender understanding for the Buddhist denial of the soul as a substance. For the real concern of Eastern thought is not with the metaphysical quest for the foundations of being, but with the attainment of salvation. In fact, Eastern thought, with its unilateral soteriological bias, is more than likely to regard reflection on the foundation of existing objects as a worthless speculation that, because it makes no contribution to the purification of the soul, leads away from rather than to what is essential.

If Buddhism, as it is reflected in Western thought, denies the existence of a soul, this denial is, nonetheless, entirely distinct, in its foundation, from every materialistic denial of the soul and has a totally different meaning. Materialism seeks to deny the existence of a spiritually unique and independent soul and to explain spiritual experiences in terms of material causes. Such a purpose is entirely foreign to Buddhism. Otherwise, it would be equally correct to say that Buddhism denies the existence of the body, for the Buddhist regards neither soul nor body as self-sufficient, independent substances that retain their identity despite the changes they endure, but rather as complex substances with no existence outside an unending process of birth and death.

The concept that gradually developed in Old Testament thought of the soul as the life-giving principle through which the human body becomes a living entity has its roots in Genesis in the very graphic picture of the creation of man.

There, it is the Creator-God himself who breathes the breath of life into the body he has formed from the dust of the earth. In this interpretation, individual man is composed of two essential principles—an actively life-giving principle, which is the soul, and a material body, which the soul quickens and animates.

In the speech habits of earlier times, the word *soul* had a special meaning. It was not unusual for it to be identified simply as "man." Probably in imitation of Biblical usage, a master referred to his indentured servants of either sex as the "souls" who belonged to him. Even in earlier times, the word *soul* meant "living being," "person," and—in the plural—"people." The designation was especially common for domestic servants and their children. The Russian estate owner had absolute power over his "souls" and could sell or even gamble them away as he chose. Even today, we say that a parish contains so and so many "souls."

Building on the conceptual clarity of Greek philosophy and further influenced by the scholasticism of the Middle Ages, Christian philosophy at last succeeded in formulating a remarkably refined doctrine of the soul, according to which the spiritual soul, as an incomplete substance (without the body), informs the body and fashions it into a consubstantial living instrument so body and soul work together in inner unity to form a single human being.

Even in the classical Greek philosophy of Socrates and Plato, but more especially in Christian philosophy, the "soul" came to be regarded as the "primal good" and its salvation as man's principal concern. Jesus Christ enjoined: "What does it profit a man if he gain the whole world, but suffer the loss of his own soul? Or what will a man give in exchange for his soul?" (Mk. 8:36–37) ". . . Do not be afraid of those who kill the body but cannot kill the soul. But rather be afraid of him who is able to destroy both soul and body in hell" (Mt. 10:28).

Thus the admonition to "save your soul!" has become the most important, although not always the most correctly interpreted, call of the Christian "ministry." It is characteristic of Friedrich Nietzsche, as an "anti-Christian," that he mocks this call, explaining that he no longer sets any value on the "salvation of his soul." Like Nietzsche, dialectical materialism sees, in the Christian doctrine of the soul, a bastion that has been razed by the materialistic physiology of a Setschenov or a Pavlov.[1] Agnostic positivism affirms this view of dialectical materialism: *Soul* is a definitively outmoded concept, rendered superfluous by contemporary research into reflexes, which attributes to the activity of the material brain those functions formerly attributed to the soul.

It would be totally misleading to ascribe such tendencies to the Buddhist denial of the soul. On the contrary, it is more correct to say that Buddhism places so much emphasis on the salvation of the soul that, as a result, all speculative attempts to confirm the existence of the soul or to explain its nature appear secondary to it and are consequently rejected as an aberration and deflection from what is more important, namely, the direct seeking after salvation.

But even this explanation does not adequately reflect the Buddhist position. Whoever engages today in a discussion with learned Buddhists about the human person and soul discovers at once what Francis Xavier also discovered in his conversations with Buddhist abbots. In the beginning, the Buddhist doctrine is stated clearly and unequivocally: man is not a person; he possesses no independent spiritual and immortal soul. Man's spiritual life is compared to a ball of fire that throws off sparks but has no independent existence of its own. This proposition, which is advanced initially with great confidence, soon shows signs of weakening once attention is called to the illogicalities that it entails. The Buddhist denial of the soul cannot, for instance, be reconciled with the ceremonies of the Japanese Festival of the Dead, which treats the dead as though they were alive—unless perhaps one were to see in it no more than a mythical fantasy to which there attaches no value in the realm of reality. The Buddhist meets this objection with the evasive and embarrassed response that "there is something immortal in man!"

At first glance, there actually does exist an obvious contradiction between the Buddhist denial of the soul and the state of mind reflected in the Festival of the Dead. But however much we of the West may be aware of, and even disturbed by, this contradiction on the rational level, which concerns itself with existence, the Buddhist, for his part, is totally undisturbed by it. Questions about existence have no relevance for him. His concern is for something that is not easily raised to the rational level and that, in the opinion of many, should not be raised to that level. Nevertheless, no dialogue can begin by ignoring such contradictions, but must press toward a thoughtfully objective investigation of them.

Let us append here a short description of the Festival of the Dead as it is celebrated every summer in Japan. Admittedly, the "Urabon" (or, in its shortened form, the "Bon") Festival of the Dead has its origin in Buddhism. The experience of a disciple of Buddha is said to have provided the incentive for its introduction. In the rules for the Festival of the Dead in the Buddhist Scriptures, it is written:

> Buddha's disciple Mokuren (Mu liän), who had the power to commune with spirits, wanted to repay the kindnesses of his father and mother and, as he awakened from meditation, he saw that his mother had to endure terrible hunger and thirst under the devils of hunger. Therefore, he put food onto a plate and presented it to his mother. But before she could raise the food to her mouth, it burst into flames and was consumed. Mokuren, then, was unable to help his mother by his own power and asked Buddha for help. Since Mokuren's mother was now compelled to do penance for many sins and could not be freed by the power of one man, Buddha commanded him to hold a memorial service for the dead together with many priests on the fifteenth day of the seventh month. Mokuren did as Buddha had commanded him, and his mother, by this means, escaped the pains of hell and was reborn in a beautiful locality.[2]

Concepts of the "Soul"

It is difficult to say how old the Festival of the Dead is. It is said to have been observed even before the year 1300, in the time of the Empress Suiko (593–628 A.D.). There seems, moreover, to be only a broad framework of prescribed rules, within which regional customs often differ widely in individual details. In any event, the basic concept is as follows: The deceased revisit their former homes. Everything possible is done to receive them courteously, to treat them considerately, and, at their departure, to bid them farewell in the same manner. On the evenings preceding their visit, torches are lit, in anticipation, before the doors of the houses. This so-called fire of welcome is intended as an invitation to the "Exalted Souls of the Deceased" to return to their homes from the lower world; it is intended to bid them welcome. At the same time, the souls are urged to accept the objects prepared for them on the altar. On the festival days proper, the "shrine of the departed soul" is erected, before which the souls of the deceased are honored. Eating utensils are placed beside the edibles. Priests are also invited and are requested to present to the deceased the Buddhist Scriptures, the so-called Shrine Scriptures. After the Festival of the Dead, a "guiding fire" of torches is once more lit before the doors of the houses. Just as the "fire of welcome" was intended as a greeting, so the "guiding fire" is intended as a farewell to the souls as they return whence they came. Wherever there is still or flowing water in the vicinity, burning candles are placed in small "soul boats" during the Festival of the Dead to serve as transportation for the souls.

Several short poems in Japanese reflect the atmosphere of the Festival of the Dead. Two of them are reproduced here.

> *The Soul's Shrine*
> Over the cakes
> upon the soul's shrine
> blows the cool autumn wind. (Taidi)

> *The Shrine Scriptures*
> Gratefully we host
> the priest
> who brings the sacred Scriptures. (Dadudo)

The dead are honored not only at home, but also in the cemeteries where the urns of the deceased, who are almost universally cremated in Japan, are buried in family graves. Before the Festival of the Dead, there is a "Grass Fair" or a "Bon Fair"; there are "Bon dances" every evening and night for weeks after it. Today these dances are no more than popular merrymaking. No one is aware any longer of their intrinsic connection with the Festival of the Dead.

Like all the festivals associated with Buddhism, the Festival of the Dead does, in fact, lack a fixed liturgical rite and a clear philosophical explanation of its significance. Nevertheless, in its fundamental concept, it provides eloquent proof of the fact that the religious inclination of the people has revived many things that are in actual contradiction to official Buddhism.

In the philosophy of contemporary Buddhism with the festivals that it celebrates, a number of religious doctrines that were actually rejected by Buddhism in its original form have found new life. These are—to give them their Christian designations—the concepts of *purgatory* as a place of temporary purification and penance; of *intercessory prayer,* which can benefit the deceased and assist them to attain their final redemption and bliss. Even the concept of an eternal "hell" is in no way foreign to Buddhistic tales.

The—for the most part unexpressed—presupposition in this whole philosophical complex is the assumption that it is the same person who has burdened himself with guilt in his earthly life who must afterwards do penance for it beyond the grave or who must be eternally damned for it. Occasionally, the personal identity of him who is punished and him who has sinned is quite clearly and unambiguously expressed in Buddhist reports. The guardians of hell bring the evildoer before the throne of Yama, who questions him about the works and deeds he has performed during his life. If the evildoer excuses himself that he was unable to do good, King Yama answers him: "It was not your mother, not your father, not your brother, not your sister, not your friends and relations, not the ascetics, not the Brahmins, not the gods who performed these your evil deeds. It was you alone who performed these evil deeds; you alone shall reap their fruit."[3] The guardians of hell then drag him down into the place of torment.

If the Buddhist denies the existence of the soul, it is because spiritual acts have no permanent continuity for him; he regards them as permanent acts without a doer, somewhat as they are regarded in the West by actualism. Perceptions, ideas, and other spiritual occurrences interfuse; at the center of this shifting multiplicity stands knowledge. But even knowledge is subject to coming and going; it is changeable and without substance. Oddly enough, Buddhism overlooks the fact that it is possible to speak of constant change only because it is the same person who experiences this change and draws his conclusions from it. But Buddhism never thinks ontologically. "Here as everywhere it rejects the stability that we are able to confer on the bustling experiences that come and go around us through the concept of a substance by or in which these experiences take place. A seeing, a hearing, a knowing, or, more especially, a suffering takes place; but Buddhist doctrine recognizes no substance that is the see-er, the hearer, the knower, the sufferer" (Oldenberg, p. 238).

It would seem to be essentially due to its contact with Greek thought that later Buddhism entered into the discussion about the soul. A unique document in this regard is a dialogue bearing the title "Questions of Milinda." After Alexander the Great's excursion into India, in an era from which we

Concepts of the "Soul"

have Greek coins struck in India, there obviously occurred an intellectual contact between Buddhist monks and the wise men of Greece. The above-mentioned dialogue bears the name of Milinda, King of Yavana, that is, of the Ionian or Greek King Menander, who lived about 100 B.C.

Milinda's dialogue with the ascetic Nagasena is quite clearly concerned with the problem of the substantive ego. Asked his name, Nagasena explains: "I am called Nagasena, O great king; but Nagasena, great king, is but a name, a form of address, a sign, an expression, a mere word; a subject cannot be deduced from it" (p. 238). Milinda replies:

> If a subject cannot be deduced from it, who is it then who bestows on you what you need—clothing and food, dwelling places, and medicines for the sick? Who is it that enjoys all these things? Who walks in virtue? Who struggles with himself? Who reaches the path and the fruit of holiness? Who achieves *nirvana*? Who murders? Who walks in lust? Who lies? Who commits the five deadly sins? Then there is no good and no evil; there is no doer and no originator of good and bad deeds; noble deeds and ignoble deeds bring no reward and bear no fruit. Even if someone kills you, noble Nagasena, he commits no murder.

In the course of the dialogue, the king insists that there would be no Nagasena if there were no substantive bearer (of the name). The Buddhist replies that a chariot is likewise not a subject, but merely a collection of individual parts. "But a subject in the strict sense of the word cannot be conceived here." In the scholastically rigorous philosophical system of Buddhism, the "common opinion" that "a person is present there" is rejected by a simple reference to the master and with no thought of logic. The "Exalted One spoke: 'This question is not permissible'" (p. 242). "*Ipse dixit*"—this resort to authority is no genuine solution. The Buddhists did experience difficulty in reconciling the doctrine of the nonexistence of a subject that is man proper with their belief in the moral retribution of man's actions. But sophistic hairsplitting that claimed that he who received the reward or punishment would not be the same person as he who performed the deed was never able to silence man's sound common sense. Even in ancient Buddhism, we come everywhere upon the ineradicable belief that reward and punishment come to the doer himself; this belief has not been extinguished by any theoretical denial of the identity of the subject. "If, in our present existence, this or that befalls us, it is because, in a previous existence, we did this or that; in this simple, completely comprehensible belief there is contained, without regard for theoretical difficulties, the philosophy that he who commits an evil deed and he who bears the punishment for it are one and the same person" (p. 243).

Although every real questioning about the foundations of being has been cut short in Buddhism, it is equally true that Buddhism is unable to offer any satisfactory evidential basis for the nonexistence of a lasting personhood. Instead, recourse is always had to two perceptual images that are supposed to show psychic activity as a simple matter of process: the image of swiftly moving water and the image of the self-consuming flame. Both images are to be found not only in the wise sayings of Buddha, but also in the works of the Greek philosopher Heraclitus, who closely resembles Buddha in this conception. "Everything is in flux"—this maxim of Heraclitus has become a household word. The universe is, for him, "an eternally living fire." The difference between his thought and that of Buddhism is, of course, that Heraclitus used his images to affirm a metaphysical thesis, the thesis of the world as a state of pure and constant becoming, whereas Buddhism, because of its agnosticism, has no a priori moral proposition into whose existential background it is not permitted to inquire.

In Buddhism, the stereotyped emphasis on care for one's own salvation has become, one might say, a fixed idea. To this end, however, it requires images that—if they are carefully analyzed—demand a reinstatement of the identity of being that was originally denied. So it is with the image of the four great floodwaters that break destructively over the world of men:

> the floodwater of lust, the floodwater of becoming, the floodwater of error, the floodwater of ignorance. "The sea, the sea. Thus, my disciples, speaks a child of this world, who has not accepted the doctrine. But it is not this, my disciples, that is called the sea in the ordinances of the Holy One; this is merely a large body of water, a great flood of water. The eye of man is the sea, my disciples; visible things are the raging of this sea. Whoever has overcome the raging of the sea of visible things, of him it is said, my disciples: This is a Brahmin, who in his inmost being has sailed the sea of the eye with its waves, its vortexes, its deeps, its monsters; he has reached the shore; he stands on firm ground." (There follow similar descriptions of hearing and of the other senses.) "Thus spoke the Exalted One; when the Perfect One had thus spoken, the master spoke again in this fashion:
>
> If you have sailed this sea with its whirlpools
> Of water, its waves, its deeps, its monsters,
> Then wisdom and holiness are your portion;
> You have reached the land, you have attained the goal of the
>   universe." (p. 244)

The whole parable assumes that the sailor is always identical with the person who experiences the dangers of the sea, overcomes them, and brings himself safely out of all danger onto dry land.

In much the same way, fire is used in Buddhist sermons as a symbol of the unbridled desire and seeking after sensual pleasure that man ought to overcome. The image of the flame that gives the appearance of total unchangeability although, in fact, it is but a self-generation and a self-destruction is indeed an apt symbol of the power of man's tormenting, consuming, and ever-recurring concupiscence for the immediate, superficial satisfaction of the senses. Nevertheless, it is just as inadequate as the other image of the sea for providing an understanding of the existence of the soul. In all its moral teachings, however, Buddhist teaching reverts again and again to the fact that a "no" must be opposed to every short-termed earthly desire for sensual pleasure if one is to save the real and enduring self, the mystical ego, that belongs to a transcendental order.

Viewed objectively, the Christian and Buddhist interpretations are much closer to one another than the Buddhist denial of human personhood, which was stated so categorically at the beginning, would lead us to believe. As we have noted earlier, the Buddhist denial of the soul can be understood only in terms of what we have called the "original experience of Buddhism," which stands at the beginning of and is always present in every form of Buddhism. Only a return to this original experience reveals the great pertinacity with which the Buddhist clings to the conclusions yielded by the further elaboration of the Buddhist original experience into a kind of doctrine, which, however, has never been firmly and officially established. What shocked the Hindu prince's son Gautama most deeply and never afterwards lost its influence over him was his insight into the frailty and nothingness of human existence. Man is fundamentally "nothing." He is not a person; his life is like a wheel of fire that scatters sparks, but has no real substance. If the Buddhist denies man's personhood and soul, it is only because human existence is deceptive; because man is not the person that an expectation rooted deeply within him has secretly promised him that he was; because man has no permanently ensured existence of his own, but only one that is balanced between being and nothingness. In a word, it is because human existence is not divine, because it is not self-sufficient, self-guaranteed, and permanent that it is denied with resignation, and that the explanation is given that man is not a person at all; man has no soul at all. Man's expectation can in no way be satisfied by the concept of a created soul with a temporal existence, but rejects it, with deep-rooted disappointment, as nothingness.

A practical sense of reality that takes reality as it is and is untroubled by expectations and disappointments will likewise have to accept the conclusions that man's sound common sense has formulated again and again even in the realm of Buddhism.

8

THE PERFECT MAN

For the person who inquires into the Buddhist and Christian views of the ideal of the perfect man, the problems begin with the very mention of the ideal of self-perfection. Indeed, if we understand the concept in the full and proper meaning that has accrued to it in the intellectual world of the West, the most prudent comment to make of it is that it is not a major concept of Buddhism.

What do we mean by the *ideal of self-perfection*? The determination to bring something to perfection assumes that there exists, over and above what has been begun, a basic concept—at least as an ideal standard—that reveals the full potentiality of what has been initiated. To bring to perfection means, then, to realize a potentiality that has been present from the outset and, in so doing, to fulfill one's task in its entirety. The bringing of a work to perfection is something that man knows from his own experience, whether from the carrying out of architectural plans, the installation of technical machinery, or the inner ripening and gradual production of a work of art.

When that which man knows from his artistic creativity is applied to his own life, it acquires a peculiar significance for him. He experiences himself not as a static being, but as a becoming. Rooted in the nature that was bestowed upon him without his knowledge or cooperation, there is a beginning that he feels compelled to develop and bring to perfection. From ancient times, Western man has given verbal expression to this basic content of his own existence in the words "become what you are!" At the same time, man's universal determination to develop his own nature has made him aware of individual differences and depths. The intellectual maturing of a man makes him more and more aware of an entirely unique goal that has meaning only for himself, that he recognizes as his duty, as his life's "mission," to which he wants to "do justice" by "perfecting himself." Here, for the first time, we have used the word *justice*. It will recur again and again as we proceed.

Despite his "unbelief," Jean Paul Sartre was, as we have seen, a man so steeped in the religious tradition of the Western world that he was positively driven by his belief in man's uniquely personal mission. The great disappointment of his life was his belated realization that he had fallen prey to a false belief, had set himself, as it were, on a false course. He was released from his vain meandering through a barren time by the great magnet of a life goal, although he afterwards discovered that he had followed a comet that was quickly extinguished rather than the star that ruled his life. This bitter "disappointment" deprived him, at the same time, of that which he, like every other man, desired most deeply—the "happiness" that consists essentially in the liberating and satisfying discovery that he has "had the good fortune" to fulfill his mission. The person who has not yet perceived the meaning of his own self-perfection seeks "happiness" among his possessions, from which he expects the fulfillment of his desires.

Among Buddhists, there is, as yet, no such sense of a mission in life. The Buddhist has no conception of any such inner obligation to "do justice" to a life task. His first concern is subjective: to free himself from the misery of his own suffering. Although this goal seems, at first, to be purely negative, there shines through it, nonetheless, the image of the individual who has attained positive perfection, who has "had the good fortune" to achieve "redemption," as he himself understands the term, and who, in so doing, has overcome an inner dichotomy and found an inner peace.

Among the things for which Buddha's agnosticism expressly refused any explanation was the ideal of perfect redemption. "The doctrine accepted by the early community expressly demanded of its adherents the renunciation of every effort to solve the problem of the being or not-being of one who had achieved perfect redemption."[1] For that reason, too, it is impossible to give an unambiguous answer to the question so often raised about the meaning of *nirvana*. The Buddhist belief in *nirvana* rests, according to Hermann Oldenberg (p. 265), on the knife's edge between really absolute nothingness and the absolute all. Buddha's teaching about the ultimate goal of a redemption that is reached by denying the will to live is totally negative in its insistence on the extinction of the passions, the removal of karma, and the cessation of blindness. He expressly refuses to explain whether the redeemed person ceases to exist after death when his striving for release from suffering is at an end.

Yet *nirvana* is more than just a state that one reaches after death. The term is also used to designate the state of the redeemed even in this earthly life. Those who have reached perfection are referred to as "the holy ones" who have achieved the "highest happiness." "Happiness is *nirvana;* happiness is *nirvana*," exclaimed Sariputta, the noblest of all the disciples. When he was asked: "How can there be happiness, Sariputta, when feelings no longer exist here?" he answered: "When feelings no longer exist, my friend, that is happiness indeed" (p. 248).

In any event, mention is made in the Buddhist Scriptures of a "happiness" that falls to the lot of the perfect, who are likewise the victorious, even here on earth. Although his earthly life is still in bondage to the world of suffering, the perfect one is already assured that he cannot be touched by the coming and going of this world. Again and again, Buddhist proverbs emphatically ascribe to the holy one who still walks the earth the possession of *nirvana,* as, for instance, in the proverb: "He who has escaped the impassable, toilsome, and deceptive paths of *samsara* (transmigration), he who has passed over and has reached the shore, he who is absorbed into himself without wavering or doubt, he who has been freed from the bonds of earth and has attained *nirvana,* he it is whom I call a true Brahmin" (p. 248).

The "holy one" who is still in the world not only experiences, as it were in anticipation, the perfection of the next world, he actually enjoys his full share of *nirvana* without having to look to the next world for it. He has extinguished in himself all that needed to be extinguished; the consuming fire of covetousness, of hate, of blindness, has truly been quenched. He is no longer stirred by hope or expectation. Like the man who has cast aside the foolish desires of childhood, he has separated himself from every human desire for missions, goals, and hopes.

Nevertheless, it must not be assumed that the Buddhist "holy one" simply yields himself up to resignation and melancholy. Whatever nirvana may be, the Buddhist is not in the least inclined to "bemoan as a misfortune or an injustice the order of things that gives to existence precisely this and only this goal or to surrender himself to it in gloomy resignation as one would to an unchangeable fate. He strives to meet *nirvana* with the same joy in victory with which the Christian looks to his goal, to eternal life" (p. 209).

The positive mood of blissful rest, for which the very gods envy the perfect one, finds its clearest expression in the maxims of the *Dhammapada* (The Way of Truth—one of the Buddhist Scriptures), where we read:

> Let us live happily, without enemies in a world of enmity; let us dwell without enmity among men who are filled with enmity.
>
> Let us live happily, unsickened among the sick; let us dwell without sickness among sick men.
>
> Let us live happily, without aspirations among those who aspire; let us dwell aspirationless among aspiring men.
>
> Let us live happily, we who possess nothing. Like the shining gods, we feast on happiness.

The monk who dwells in an empty cell, whose soul is full of peace, enjoys superhuman happiness, for he contemplates truth in its entirety. (Oldenberg, p. 209)

The Perfect Man

Despite his objective resignation, the monk striving for nirvana is filled with inner joy. It is impossible for man to continue to regard a pure negative as the ideal of his life.

In similar fashion, historical Buddhism has given a more or less positive meaning to the nirvana of the next world, which the redeemed enters after death. But not even this "parinirvana" represents, as one might have expected, the cessation of existence in every form. It is impossible to give here a detailed account of the vacillation of meaning that marks this concept, but it can be said that *parinirvana* is often regarded as the epitome of the true life.[2]

Nevertheless, the Buddhist ideal of perfection is plainly distinguishable from the Christian one by the fact that Buddhism lacks the concept of an objective mission to which man must do "justice" and the achievement of which brings positive happiness. Because of its negative principle, Buddhist morality offers very little incentive to positive action. The ideal of the monk, for instance, is linked to no really intensive cultural undertaking, to neither handwork nor study, unless it is the study of the Buddhist Scripture. No positive goals are presented to the layman. Love for the Buddhist is primarily a passive well-wishing and a tolerance that harms no one, although the later forms of Buddhism have gone beyond these limits.

Buddhist morality serves a goal that is predominantly negative. For that reason, it lacks the impulse to any positive commitment to the world and the people in it. The Buddhist regards every positive deed, even the best, as a fetter that binds him to the world, to life, and, therefore, to the wheel of reincarnation. In this view, moral behavior has no value in itself; there is no deed that is worth doing for its own sake, whose value has been formed and determined by an objective order. Rather, "proper action" is regarded as a preparation for "proper absorption into oneself," which is centered on the human ego and occupies the most important place in the life of the monk. The various schools of Buddhism have developed the system of meditation into a fine art, but the techniques they use differ widely among themselves and even the goal is defined differently. If the proper absorption into oneself assumes, in the beginning, a certain renunciation of the world, it leads, in the teaching of early Buddhism, to the same enlightenment that Buddha himself enjoyed. It consists in the overwhelming realization of the complete nothingness of all things and thus leads to the complete and final extinction of all earthly desire.

In fact, only the monk can achieve perfection as the Buddhist defines it; only the monk can fulfill all the demands of a life lived in retirement from the world. Indeed, Buddha actually taught, in the beginning, that only the monk could reach the goal of redemption. In the beginning, moreover, he admitted only men to the life of the monk, although later, under protest since he shared the ancient Hindu disdain of the female sex, he admitted women as well. He did not believe that women had been called to redemption and feared that they would bring harm to his work.

According to Buddha's earliest teaching, lay people, so long as they remain in that state, cannot attain redemption. But they can be received as guests and thereby win the privilege of being permitted, in a later existence, to win redemption as monks. Occasionally, even in earlier times, the opinion was expressed that pious lay people might win salvation at least at the hour of death if they directed to it their last choice and their last thought, renouncing even the will to live. Thus it was said at one time: "I tell you that there exists between a lay disciple whose soul has attained this stage of redemption and a monk whose soul has been freed from all corruption no difference that affects the fact of their redemption" (Oldenberg, p. 298).

There are very obvious points of difference between the Western, Christian ideal of perfection and that of Buddhism. In the Old and New Testaments and in the intellectual world of the Greeks, it is the "just man" who is regarded as the ideal of human perfection. The fullness of meaning that is contained in the word *just* extends beyond the designation of mere moral or juridical "justice" and into the realm of the metaphysical. The concept is completely divorced from any subjective experience that would indicate its relevance to a systematized order. The man who is just before God is not merely the man who, in a negative sense, does not need to be reproved, but also, in a positive sense, the man who fulfills the ideal of what it means to be man. He is the holy one. The longing for this full achievement of what it means to be man, of what it means to be the just one par excellence, is never absent from human history. In the history of Israel, it is inseparable from the longing for the Messiah. From the suffering in man's restless heart arises mankind's poignant cry: "Ye heavens open and let the just one descend; ye clouds, rain down the just one." The words are but a slight adaptation of a passage in Isaiah that reads: "Drop down dew, ye heavens, from above, and let the clouds rain the just; let the earth be opened and bud forth a savior: and let justice spring up together: I, the Lord, have created him" (Is. 45:8).

Added to this is the further thought that the just one is a constant source of reproof to the unjust one; in consequence, the unjust are determined to remove the just one from the land of the living. Yet even the evil that is done him by the unjust proves again the justice of the just one and causes it to shine forth brilliantly. The hatred of the godless against the just one leads them to plot his destruction:

> Let us therefore lie in wait for the just, because he is not for our turn, and he is contrary to our doings, and upbraideth us with transgressions of the law, and divulgeth against us the sin of our way of life.
>
> He boasteth that he hath the knowledge of God, and calleth himself the son of God.

The Perfect Man

He is become a censurer of our thoughts.

He is grievous unto us, even to behold: for his life is not like other men's, and his ways are very different.

We are esteemed by him as triflers, and he abstaineth from our ways as from filthiness, and he preferreth the latter end of the just, and glorieth that he hath God for his father.

Let us see then if his words be true, and let us prove what shall happen to him, and we shall know what his end shall be.

For if he be the true son of God, he will defend him and will deliver him from the hands of his enemies.

Let us examine him by outrages and tortures, that we may know his meekness and try his patience.

Let us condemn him to a most shameful death: for there shall be respect had unto him by his words. (Wis. 2:12–20)

Just as the picture of the "just one" acquires graphic reality in the Old Testament, so there occurs in the Greek world—although this fact is seldom recognized—a very similar phenomenon, the meaning of which converges, in a manner that is nothing short of amazing, with the thought of the Old Testament and the historical realization of the "just one" in the person of Jesus Christ.[3] In a moment that was historically significant—although it aroused no immediate acclaim—the human spirit reached its highest comprehension of what it means to be man. The whole weight of the question in the Greek world was directed to "man" as he ought to be, to the man who incorporates the fullness of man's potential and who thus becomes a model for the rest of mankind in their efforts to realize their potential both as individuals and as members of the human community.

In the intellectual history of the ancient world, it was Plato who, in a flash of brilliant enlightenment, crowned the philosophical efforts of centuries to bring clarity to the dimly perceived image of the perfect man. In his efforts to describe and define the nature of the perfect man as the truly just one, Plato, too, proceeded not only from an ethical, but also from a metaphysical, point of view. For, according to Plato, all possible earthly qualities have no independent existence of their own, but are only temporal likenesses of eternal ideas; thus human righteousness is but the reflection in time of the eternal idea of justice itself.

In the second book of the *Republic,* which he wrote at the height of his philosophical career, Plato attempted to define justice and the just man.[4] The starting point of his dialectical philosophy was the commonly expressed opinion that the doing of injustice is, of its very nature, a good, whereas the suffering of injustice is a grievous evil. The strong accomplish the former; the weak endure the latter. After long and painful experience, so runs the popular view, men sought by way of contract to escape from the narrow straits into which they had been driven; to avoid suffering further injustice, they agreed to commit no further injustice. Laws are derived from this and similar agreements to which men have obligated themselves and the observance of which they have raised to a duty for the sake of justice. In secret, however, men still long for power, and in particular for that power that will allow them with impunity to inflict injustice upon others. But since the actual conditions of power are readily subject to change, even those presently in power must take into account the possibility of having to bear, at some future date, the consequences of their present actions. For that reason, they refrain from doing injustice even when it might be possible for them to do so. "Justice," therefore, is but a grudgingly accepted compromise. From *this* point of view, the "just one" is basically no more than a coward who, however, does not admit his cowardice either to himself or to others, but rather surrounds himself with the aura of virtue. If they were free to do as they pleased, the strong would do whatever they wished and, in the process, would trample upon the rights of others. The fiction of the total freedom of the evildoer who is not observed and is therefore not caught in his evildoing leads to the pessimistic conclusion that "no just man will ever be so unyieldingly firm that he will remain just and can bring himself to keep his hands from the goods of another." Basically, or so man popularly believes, both "just" and "unjust" are brothers under the skin. In this cynical view, "justice" is not a positive good with an independent existence of its own. What value it possesses accrues to it from man's lack of integrity. All the world praises the "just man" even while silently despising the "coward" in him.

Yet this superficial, popular judgment is contradicted by man's innermost conviction that, despite all appearances to the contrary, injustice remains injustice and justice remains justice. The very contempt in which the world holds the "just" coward bears witness to this conviction. If man is to comprehend the ideal of the perfect man, the true picture of the man perfected in justice must be opposed to this false one.

> For the height of injustice is to seem just without being so. To the perfectly unjust man, then, let us assign perfect injustice and withhold nothing of it, but we must allow him, while committing the greatest wrongs, to have secured for himself the greatest reputation for justice; and if he does happen to trip, we must concede to him the power to correct his mistakes by his ability to speak persuasively if any of his misdeeds come to light, and when force is needed, to employ force by reason of his manly spirit and vigor and his provision of friends and money; and when we have set up an unjust man of this character, our theory must set the just man at his side—a simple and noble man, who, in the phrase of Aeschylus, does not wish to seem but be good. Then we must

deprive him of the seeming. For if he is going to be thought just he will have honours and gifts because of that esteem. We cannot be sure in that case whether he is just for justice' sake or for the sake of the gifts and honours. So we must strip him bare of everything but justice and make his state the opposite of his imagined counterpart. Though doing no wrong he must have the repute of the greatest injustice, so that he may be put to the test as regards justice though not softening because of ill repute and the consequences thereof. But let him hold on his course unchangeable even unto death, seeming all his life to be unjust though being just, that so, both men attaining to the limit, the one of injustice, the other of justice, we may pass judgement which of the two is the happier. (*The Republic,* bk. II, sec. 361 A–D)

The thoughtful elaboration of these extreme opposites makes the problem absolutely clear. The just man, relying upon himself alone and without the aura of popular opinion, is the "simple, noble man" who wants to be just for justice's sake alone. To place this determination to be just in as clear a light as possible, the just man is transported into a situation where his righteousness goes unrecognized, where his commitment to righteousness is regarded as stubbornness. Indeed, for the sake of his righteousness, he has the courage to accept before his contemporaries the appearance of total unrighteousness. He preserves his righteousness even while an insensitive rabble condemns him.

In this extreme conflict, the man perfected in injustice acquires the contours of a popular folk hero who conceals his true nature with the cloak of outward appearance, whereas the really just man acquires the stature of the lone warrior, abandoned by all and surrounded by enemies as he battles for unconditional justice. "Ecce homo, indeed!" "Behold the man!" The contrast that exists in the Platonic dialogue reaches a staggering height when the fate that awaits the just man is depicted there. The speaker excuses himself for speaking so crassly. Yet he must venture to depict the final outcome: "The just man—as we have depicted him—is beaten, persecuted, bound in fetters, blindfolded, and, after all these sufferings, crucified."

In this final consequence, "at a moment when pre-Christian Hellenic man penetrates to the deepest awareness of his condition as man, when the highest ideal of man makes its entry into Greek philosophy, demanding from man the realization of justice for its own sake and at any price, there appears the image of the crucified one; the truly just man appears in a panorama of suffering that extends from scourging to torture, to binding in fetters, to the blindfolding of both eyes, and finally to crucifixion" (Benz, p. 8).

In his depiction of the man who is perfectly just, Plato stands clearly in the tradition of Socrates, who remained true to his principles in spite of the hostility they aroused, and who had the courage to die for them. But Plato goes much further. Socrates, at least, did not die like a slave the shameful death of the cross; on the contrary, he met death as a free citizen—after an ordered trial and in privacy except for the presence of his closest friends. A way of escape was left open for him. Perhaps, indeed, his accusers would not have been unhappy if he had actually escaped his execution by flight. According to Plato's presentation of it, Socrates's death was a scene of tremendous solemnity. No human indignities were forced upon him. He was not mocked. He was neither tortured nor scourged. He was not blindfolded. Above all, he did not suffer the excruciating torment of the cross.

Jesus, on the contrary, was spared none of these things—not the experience of rebellion in his own being, which protested against the "chalice" of suffering on the cross; not the total loneliness of a suffering in which his disciples could not follow him; not the fear of death in all its bitterness; not the anger of the mob that rose up against him; not the helplessness before a soldiery who exercised their coarse brutality against him with no restraint; not the stripping of his garments before all the people; above all, not the slow bleeding to death before the eyes of those who rejoiced in his death; not the scorn of his enemies. Jesus was exposed to enemies who saw him stripped of everything he possessed. For him, there was no closed prison cell to shield him from the gaze of the pack of "dogs" and "bullocks," as they are called in Psalm 21, which is the prayer of the dying Christ: Like a pack of dogs they surround him; the crowd of evildoers closes in upon him. They have pierced his hands and his feet and can number all his bones. They divide his garments among them and cast lots for his raiment. Unlike the condemned Socrates, the dying Jesus cannot resort to supercilious sarcasm against his enemies. Above all, he is not spared that which lends to his death the most extreme anguish: the feeling of abandonment by God. Does not this abandonment complete the triumph of his enemies? Is it not a proof that he is at last crushed? Yet the dying Jesus prays for his enemies and surrenders his spirit, at last, into his Father's hands.

If Plato, in depicting the truly just one, overstates his account of the actual death of his master, exaggerating it into "the road of martyrdom through all the gruesome abysses of man's pain and violation," it is, nonetheless, "only in a fleeting moment that he has surmised all this as a last fearful and terrible possibility, as an ideal addition to all martyrdoms that can confront the truly just one in his conflict with the world around him" (p. 15). The very fact that Socrates's death did not take place in the uttermost sphere of despair, in the abandonment of a cruel and helpless pain in which the sufferer writhes like a worm, justifies us in speaking here of a presentiment—or, if we prefer, of a "prophecy"—of the cross of Jesus Christ. It is exactly as if the cross of Christ cast its shadow before it; as if mankind trembled inwardly before it for the first time because here, for the first time in a world where no one else lays it to heart, a man considers how the just man perishes (Is. 57:1).

The Perfect Man

Indeed, the magnitude of such a death for the truly just man is too great to be understood by little souls. There are those who have regarded it as impossible and have expressed the opinion that Jesus succumbed to violence against his will. Certain sayings of Jesus, however, are crucial for deciding whether the historical Jesus, together with his gospel, "perished" on the cross against his will and against all his expectations or whether he consciously accepted death, and especially death on the cross, as a sacrifice. We can and must discover in the teaching of the earlier church what Jesus was and what he wanted to be. "Every verse of the gospel convinces us that the origin of Christianity is not the kerygma or the Easter experiences of the apostles or a concept of Christ, but a historical event, viz., the emergence of the man Jesus Christ, Who was nailed to the cross under Pontius Pilate, and of His gospel."[5]

According to the gospels, Jesus foretold his violent death in every important detail. The abundance of such texts proves that the predictions of the passion played an important role in the early church. They bear witness to the fact that Jesus was not surprised by death. In the eyes of the faithful, his divine foreknowledge and conscious acceptance of the sufferings associated with his death outbalanced the scandal of the cross. They made it clear that Jesus entered consciously and willingly upon the path of suffering, which he regarded as a mission from his Father.

The wording of the first prediction of the passion, in Mark, is worthy of note. Jesus "began to teach [his disciples] that the Son of Man must suffer many things, and be rejected by the elders and chief priests and Scribes, and be put to death, and after three days rise again. And what he said he spoke openly. And Peter, taking him aside, began to chide him. But he, turning and seeing his disciples, rebuked Peter, saying, 'Get behind me, satan, for thou dost not mind the things of God, but those of men'" (Mk. 8:31–33). This is obviously not a passing and hardly comprehensible allusion, but a very solid prediction that provokes Peter's protest. Jesus rebukes him sharply—a fact that cannot be regarded as a later invention. The objection has been raised that this prediction of the passion does not mention death on the cross. But the "cross" is clearly mentioned in the immediate context, for the passage continues with the words: "And calling the crowd together with his disciples, he said to them, 'If anyone wishes to come after me, let him deny himself, and take up his cross, and follow me.'" (Mk. 8:34). The expression "take up his cross" is unambiguous. The person condemned to death on the cross usually had the crossbar bound to his back and so carried "his cross" to the place of execution. If Jesus summons his disciples to follow him by carrying their cross, it must be presumed that he himself went to his death bearing his own cross.

The individual details of the third prediction of the passion in Mark's gospel reveal astounding parallels with the Platonic prediction. Thus we read: "Behold, we are going up to Jerusalem, and the Son of Man will be betrayed to the chief priests and the Scribes; and they will condemn him to death, and will deliver him to the Gentiles; and they will mock him, and spit upon him, and scourge him, and put him to death; and on the third day he will rise again" (Mk. 10:33–34). In addition to the explicit predictions of the passion, there are a number of allusions that all tend to prove the same thing, namely, that Jesus faced his own death knowingly and fully prepared to be sacrificed. In several parables, Jesus accused his opponents of plotting against his life. They understood full well what he meant. His reproach to the Scribes and Pharisees that their fathers had murdered the prophets and that they are filling up the measure of their fathers (Mt. 23:32) is unambivalent. As the Good Shepherd, Jesus has been sent by the Father to lay down his life for his sheep (Jo. 10:11).

In the Christian view, the greatness of a man's love is the measure of his human greatness. If we accept Jesus' word that no one has greater love than he who lays down his life for his friends, we must also accept the fact that the word has been fulfilled in him in a manner so exemplary that he can designate it as "his own commandment" that men love one another as he has loved them (Jo. 15:12–17). This love is so active as to include a love for one's enemies that is prepared even to sacrifice itself for these enemies and to pray for them. It cannot be surpassed among men. It stands worlds apart from the purely passive permissiveness and tolerance of Buddhist well-wishing to the world. Or, to express it differently, it is the perfection of the well-wishing that manifests itself in Buddhism because it "wishes" actively, at whatever cost to itself, for the "well-being" of the other.

By virtue of its own luminosity, the ideal for mankind that is incarnate in Jesus Christ produces its effects by its power wherever it is known. For that reason, the factual contact of Christianity and Buddhism has already had the effect of arousing in Buddhist circles the cry for an active *caritas*.

GOD OR ATMAN

No less a person than Carl Gustav Jung complained that there is nothing in our culture, "not even the Church, the custodian of religious goods,"[1] that attempts to satisfy man's craving for primal religious experience. A deep bitterness makes itself heard when he continues: "It is in fact her function to oppose all such extreme experiences, for these can only be heterodox" (Ibid.). The only movement in our culture that he will credit with any understanding of this craving is psychotherapy. As a psychotherapist disappointed by the Christian religion, he here attempts to pave the way for the entrance of Eastern wisdom into the Western world. For him, the Zen monks are individuals prepared to make any sacrifice for the sake of truth, whereas the psychotherapist deals with "the most stubborn of all Europeans" (Ibid.). Indeed, by reason of this very stubbornness, it is impossible to transmit Zen directly to Western society. "The psychotherapist, however, who is seriously concerned with the question of the aims of his therapy cannot be unmoved when he sees what ultimate result an oriental method of spiritual 'healing' . . . is striving for" (p. 26). According to Jung, there have been developing in the East for the last two thousand years methodologies and philosophical teachings "which simply put all Western attempts in the same line into the shade" (Ibid.). The Western attempts have either "stopped short at magic," like Christianity, or "at the intellectual," like philosophy. The beginnings of a mode of healing through total experience Jung finds only in Goethe's *Faust* and Nietzsche's *Zarathustra*. "If the psychotherapist finds time from his helpful activities for a little reflection" (p. 27) and if, in the process, he sees through the illusions of Western rationalism, he will soon come to realize what it means "to tear open those doors which everyone would gladly slink past" (Ibid.). That is what Jung hopes to accomplish with his commendatory foreword to the text of the Zen philosopher Suzuki.

The English author Aldous Huxley goes a step further than Jung. He, too, complains that innumerable men long for self-transcendence and would be happy to find it in the church. But "the hungry sheep look up and are not fed."[2] Even when they take part in church ceremonies, listen to sermons, repeat prayers, their thirst remains unassuaged. The mystical experience for which all of them yearn is not granted them. If the Christian church offers only stones, however, Huxley is prepared to offer "bread"—the "bread" of the narcotic mescalin, derived from the Indian cactus known as peyote. After testing it on himself, Huxley believes he can recommend mescalin as a means of "chemical openings of doors into the Other World" (p. 71). In the ecstasy that he experienced, he believes he actually arrived at that enlightenment *(satori)* that Zen Buddhism regards as the great goal of its meditation exercises. In his report on his experiences, Huxley says: "The Beatific Vision, *Sat Chit Ananda,* Being-Awareness-Bliss—for the first time I understood, not on the verbal level, not by inchoate hints or at a distance, but precisely and completely what those prodigious syllables referred to" (p. 18). Then he recalled a passage that he had read in a work by the Zen philosopher Suzuki in which a Zen novice inquires about the dharma body of the Buddha (the *dharma* body of the Buddha is another expression for spirit, suchness, the great emptiness, the Godhead) and is told, by way of answer, "the hedge at the bottom of the garden." The irrelevance of the answer, Huxley found, was eliminated by the ecstasy. "Now it was all as clear as day, as evident as Euclid" (p. 19). For in the ecstasy he had discovered what he calls "the sacramental vision of reality" (p. 22), in which everything is illuminated by an inner light and is infinite in its meaningfulness. It is, at the same time, the experience that the personal self has flowed out and the monistic identity of all in all is directly perceived.

On the basis of this experience, Huxley believed he knew from within himself the language of the visionary, the medium, and even the mystic. He was convinced that his experience had brought him close to those primordial experiences that have been experienced by the mystics of all times and all places and that are actually the essence of every form of mysticism.

The highest goal toward which the Zen Buddhists strive is that illumination of the divine self that they call *satori* or enlightenment. They emphasize again and again that this "enlightenment" is to be understood as an indescribable personal experience to which the uninitiated have no access and that mocks every attempt at intellectual definition or analyzation. Admittedly, there have been repeated attempts at certain descriptions or definitions of its essence that stimulate comment. Kaiten Nukariya, for instance, an expert who is himself a professor at the So-To-Su Buddhist College in Tokyo, gives the following explanation:

> Having set ourselves free from the misconception of Self, next we must awaken our innermost wisdom, pure and divine, called the Mind of Buddha, or Bodhi [the knowledge through which one experiences Enlightenment], or Prajna [highest wisdom] by Zen Masters. It is the divine light, the inner heaven, the key to all moral treasures, [the center of thought and consciousness], the source of all influence and power, the seat of kindness, justice, sympathy, impartial love, humanity, and mercy, the measure of all things. When this innermost wisdom is fully awakened, we are able to realize

that each and every one of us is identical in spirit, in essence, in nature with the universal life or Buddha, that each ever lives face to face with Buddha, that each is beset by the abundant grace of the Blessed One [Buddha], that He arouses his moral nature, that He opens his spiritual eyes, that He unfolds his new capacity, that He appoints his mission, and that life is not an ocean of birth, disease, old age and death, nor the vale of tears, but the holy temple of Buddha, the Pure Land [sukhavati, the Land of Bliss], where he can enjoy the bliss of Nirvana.

Then our minds go through an entire revolution. We are no more troubled by anger and hatred, no more bitten by envy and ambition, no more stung by sorrow and chagrin, no more overwhelmed by melancholy and despair. . . .[3]

If we accept these words at their face value, they affirm that man attains the state of final perfection when he attains the enlightenment.

Even at the risk of incurring the reproach of reacting crudely to a poetic flight of fancy, we cannot, since we are accustomed to critical integrity, simply overlook the palpable inaccuracies of this poetically exaggerated description of *satori*. Even less can we suppress the question: who is this "He" who arouses our moral nature, opens our spiritual eyes, besets us by His abundant grace, and appoints our mission? To the answer "Buddha, the Blessed One" there is appended the caution that this is not the historical Buddha, but the universal Buddha nature. In other words, this whole talk of Buddha is merely a poetic personification and is not to be understood literally. There is no god "Buddha" who actually bestows grace. "Buddha" is merely a name for our own eternal self, which—when it enlightens us completely—allows our identity with everything else in the world to shine forth. The poetic language should not be allowed to deceive us about the fact that we are speaking here of a strict monism.

Any attempt at critical analysis is, however, rejected as unsuitable to the subject matter. The objection is raised that *satori,* or the experience of enlightenment, in which the "perfect ones" find in the "self" their access to nirvana, is a totally extraordinary experience to which no ordinary person has access, for which reason the Zen Buddhists contest the right of every uninitiated person to enter the discussion. At this point, there is danger of creating a gulf that will preclude all passage to and fro; the bridge that would have made possible a common meeting of minds seems to have collapsed. Having halted the dialogue, the Zen Buddhist withdraws into the crystal palace of the "self" that is not only his own personal self, but, at the same time, the divine self, the Atman, that is identical with Brahman, the cosmic ground of being. He is inclined to consider it an unforgivable transgression if the uninitiated ventures to question the absoluteness of "Atman" or to ask reasons therefor. Such a level of questioning is "profane" in the mind of the "Exalted One," who, by reason of his *satori,* has placed the self in an entirely different dimension where it is no longer subject to doubts or criticisms. To doubt or criticize would be to "desecrate" what once was holy. It is precisely in this consecration of self that Zen appears to be a form of "mysticism."

But the dialogue does not have to founder on this danger point. This can be avoided if the attempt at philosophical definition is shelved and Zen is regarded primarily as a "way"—a "method"—of self-confrontation. For obvious reasons, the too rapid philosophical evaluation and definition of the enlightenment experience is more likely to be undertaken by the Westerner who is himself seeking access to Buddhism or by the "Zen philosopher" proper who deals with it thematically than by the Zen monk who practices it, but who neither inquires into its philosophical implications nor wants to do so, and who, because he lacks both the necessary education and the necessary interest, is actually unable to do so. If we define *zazen*, which is the form of meditation taught by Zen, as an effort to effect a meeting with one's own eternal self, it undoubtedly has a great significance today in a time of spiritual distraction and the attendant difficulty of finding oneself.

To understand Zen properly from within, Lassalle, the German Jesuit missionary to Japan, had the courage to let himself be practically inducted into *zazen*. In his report on the subject, he says: "Since it is impossible to understand Zen through theoretical study alone, I applied myself to the practice of it and joined in Zen exercises of meditation. In the process, Zen became a great help to me in my own religious life. The more I concerned myself with it, the more firm my conviction became that Zen—rightly practiced—can be of great advantage to the spiritual life of every man, whatever his religious persuasion."[4] To open for others the road to this method, to show them a road by which to arrive at a deep inner quiet amid all the disquiet of modern life, he published his impressions and experiences. The influence of Zen on the Japanese mentality is so great that it can be regarded, with justification, as a mode of access to the Japanese soul. Lassalle not only strove successfully to increase understanding of this key, but he also had equal success in awakening in the Japanese an understanding of Christianity, especially in the form of the Catholic church.

If, by following Lassalle's example, a too precipitous philosophical definition can be avoided (because *zazen* refers not to the content of any particular religion, but to the use and evaluation of the natural powers of the soul, and because the way of enlightenment, as Zen teaches it, is open to all), it must be assumed that contemporary efforts to become familiar with the methods of yoga and Zen can also help to prevent the premature failure of an incipient dialogue. The contemptuous rejection of the Western mind, which Suzuki, for instance, declares incapable of understanding the mysticism of the Oriental mind, will eventually cease to exist. Once Western man has himself had experience in this area, he can no longer be denied the right to enter into a discussion of it. Such discussion, certainly, need not degen-

God or Atman

erate into a rationalistically prejudiced criticism that loses sight of the Zen experience itself, but should be rather an openness to and a thoughtful consideration of those questions that are directly related to the Zen experience and the description of it.

The appeal to the truly unfathomable depths of the Eastern mind is, however, no adequate reason for expecting an a priori capitulation of Western thought or for denying its right to critical examination. However difficult it is to determine the exact meaning of Jung's often ambiguous language, it will not be unjust to him to say that he inclines to such intellectual capitulation. In his foreword to Suzuki's text, he deals disparagingly with Christianity, regarding it as mere "magic." On the other hand, he lauds the superlative qualities of *satori* and affirms the claim of Zen Buddhism that every attempt to explain or analyze Zen and its enlightenment is in vain. Yet, in contradiction to this view, he likewise accepts the thesis that the enlightenment "embraces an *insight into the nature of self,* and that it is an emancipation of the conscious from the illusionary conceptions of self. The illusion regarding the nature of self is the common confusion of the ego with self. Nukariya understands by 'self' the All-Buddha, i.e. simply a consciousness of life" (Nukariya, in Suzuki, p. 13; italics in original). Thus he adopts as his own a thesis of eminently metaphysical content that ought not to be simply excluded from critical examination.

Jung, however, always carefully avoided being classified as a metaphysician. What must be emphasized here is the intellectual predisposition that he shares with Buddha and Buddhism: his fundamental agnosticism. There has been much disagreement as to Jung's attitude toward religion and there is no easy way of determining it. As he says himself, he has been regarded not only "as a gnostic and its opposite, but also as both a theist and an atheist, as a mystic and a materialist."[5] What is certain about him, however, is his conscious opposition to all "metaphysicians," whom he describes as persons "who for some unspecified reason believe that they have knowledge of unknowable things about the hereafter." He added, "I have never dared claim that such things do not exist; but I have also not dared suggest that one of my predications can affect these things in any way or can present them correctly. I doubt that our conception of them is identical with the nature of the things in themselves—and this for very obvious scientific reasons" (Ibid.).

But Jung was compelled, by his very attempt to exclude the metaphysical, to exclude the question of truth as well and to take his stand upon relativism. The question as to the reality of the enlightenment and of the state of redemption thus becomes irrelevant for him. As he writes:

> We can of course never decide definitely whether a person is *really* "enlightened" or "redeemed," or whether he merely imagines it. We have no

criteria for this. . . . The imagination itself is a psychic occurrence, and therefore whether an "enlightenment" is "real" or "imaginary" is quite immaterial. . . . Yes, even if all religious reports were nothing but conscious inventions and falsifications, a very interesting psychological treatise could still be written on the fact of such lies, with the same scientific treatment with which the psychopathology of delusions is presented. (p. 15; italics in original)

But this is a theory that genuinely religious persons cannot accept without protest, as witness the English Orientalist Zaehner. The question of truth cannot and may not be excluded when religious matters come under discussion; to do so is to blunt the point of any genuinely religious experience.

In his fundamental agnosticism, Jung excluded those basic questions of human existence that lead, by their very nature, to God: the questions about the "whence" and the "whither" of human life. They are and remain the basic questions of man's religious existence and may not be simply brushed aside as insignificant and unanswerable. Jung never admits that Christianity's faith is faith in a personal God or that it is, for that reason, both much more than and quite different from mere "magic." For this reason, his whole comparison of East and West rests from the beginning on a scale with false weights.

He claims to limit his attention to the "reality of the soul" and to observe its "archetypal images," in order thereby to understand and be able to heal the neuroses that, in his theory, are pathogenic conflicts residing in the antithetical relationship of the unconscious to the conscious. As a result, however, he excludes from the start the possibility of a psychic disturbance that consists in a lack of order in man's relationship to a God who really exists. The fact that Jung remains firm in his agnosticism and seeks to limit himself to the only reality that exists for him, namely, the reality of the soul, is very revealing. He capitulates, moreover, before Suzuki's explicit statement that the absoluteness of the self is monistic. But explicit monism excludes theism. The result is—whether it is intended or not—a de facto atheism, however much Jung may protest the label.

Although Jung determines again and again to limit himself to psychology, he repeatedly and significantly transgresses this self-imposed limitation. In consequence, he cannot refer to it to defend himself against criticism. The person who has excluded one absolute even for tactical or methodological reasons will not be able to avoid introducing another absolute elsewhere. The vain renunciation of metaphysics for "critical" reasons merely facilitates the substitution of an uncritical metaphysics that demands our critical scrutiny.

When Jung compares the intellectual worlds of East and West, he praises the East with enthusiasm only to compare it with a caricature of the West. For Jung, Zen is

God or Atman

one of the most wonderful blossoms of the Chinese spirit, which was readily impregnated by the immense thought-world of Buddhism. He, therefore, who has really tried to understand Buddhist doctrine, if only to a certain degree— i.e. by renouncing various Western prejudices—will come upon certain depths beneath the bizarre cloak of the individual *satori* experiences, or will sense disquieting difficulties which the philosophic and religious West has up to now thought fit to disregard. As a philosopher, one is exclusively concerned with that understanding which, for its own part, has nothing to do with life. And as a Christian, one has nothing to do with paganism ("I thank thee, Lord, that I am not as other men"). (Jung, in Suzuki, p. 12)

For purposes of comparison, Jung introduced here some conscious parodies of "philosophy" and "Christianity." The philosopher who wants to do nothing but think and who therefore shuts himself off from life is, at best, but a rationalistic caricature of a true philosopher, who uses the power of his intellectually penetrating thought to make the probings and elucidations that are necessary if he is not to fall prey to deception. For him, truth is and remains a value that no one who is conscious of his own thinking can renounce. In like manner, the equating of a Christian with a Pharisee who exalts himself above other men is a falsifying caricature of the Christian image. Despite this devaluation of the Christian way of life, Jung is obviously unwilling totally to reject the support that can be gained for his position from Christian theology. On the contrary, he relies on certain bold and questionably orthodox sayings of Christian mystics that, when they are regarded in isolation, are seen already to have abandoned the safe ground of genuine Christianity and, for that reason, have repeatedly incurred the just criticism of the church and its theology. When these sayings are considered in conjunction with the whole of Christian mystical theology, on the other hand, they present the exact opposite of that monism that Jung affirms in Suzuki's writings.

If Zen Buddhism, in many of its forms, stops short of religion, it is, nonetheless, more than a mere ascetic preoccupation with oneself not only in those situations in which it claims to be a proper religion or in which it offers a philosophical explanation of itself, but also in the manner in which it is understood by Westerners. Huxley, for instance, insists that his experience with mescalin secured for him the mystical enlightenment of a blissful flowing into the All-Oneness, which, he believed, was the fundamental experience of every form of mysticism in all times and in all places. Many of the utterances of Zen Buddhism express a similar interpretation. The most immediate goal of meditation is described as reaching the "eternal in man," to use Max Scheler's expression. But according to Suzuki, the one who meditates finds in himself the true foundation of existence and loses himself in the infinite (Suzuki, pp. 44–45). Such a statement is an explicit polemic against a dualistic concept of religion.

With his hypothesis of a monistic mysticism, Huxley challenges all those who are concerned with genuinely religious experience. His essay on *The Doors of Perception* had the effect of such a challenge and was roundly criticized by Robert Zaehner. Zaehner understood Huxley's text as a challenge

> that no one with any religious convictions at all could afford to neglect, for Huxley did not seem to be merely advocating yet another variety of religious "indifferentism"; he was, simply by equating his own drug-induced experiences with the experiences of those who approach their goal by more conventional means, striking at the roots of all religion that makes any claim to be taken seriously. Such a challenge, when thrown down by an author of Mr. Huxley's standing and popularity, could not, with decency, be allowed to remain unanswered.[6]

Zaehner protests correctly against the inappropriate mingling of all forms of mysticism in Jung's contention that, in the last analysis, the same experience serves as the foundation of all of them. Such a statement cannot survive a critical scrutiny. In his comprehensive study, Zaehner comes to the unambiguous conclusion that three very different and extraordinary forms of experience bear the name "mysticism" and, more especially, that there is a distinct difference between a monistic nature mysticism and a genuinely religious dualistic mysticism.

As we can see plainly in Suzuki, Zen Buddhism tends toward a monistic mysticism. According to Suzuki, Zen is "not a religion in the sense that the term is popularly understood; for Zen has no God to worship" (Suzuki, p. 39). Suzuki is inclined, in any event, to regard the "self" (Atman) as an absolute, whereas it is more generally identified in Eastern thought with "Brahman," that is, with the actual cosmic ground of being.[7] Suzuki explains that Zen does not signify a denial of the existence of God; but such an explanation would gain more credence if Atman were not regarded as an absolute. When there also follows a deification of self, the denial of any other god is automatically implied. We shall not attempt to answer here the factual question about whether and to what extent the self is explicitly raised to the status of an absolute and the acceptance of the existence of God remains open. It is sufficient to have pointed out the danger that has certainly been realized in many instances.

If this is so, we should not overlook the final judgment of so competent a judge as August Reischauer, who defines Zen Buddhism in Japan as a "mystical self-intoxication" (quoted in Suzuki, p. 42). Suzuki dismisses this reproach too lightly. *Intoxication* refers not merely to the lower forms of intoxication of the senses or to the unleashing of life drives even to the point of clouding the conscious mind; there is also among the many forms of intoxication a kind of psychic intoxication.[8] There can be, in other words, a purely psychic intoxication that seems, when it is viewed from without, to have little in common with the more ignoble forms of intoxication, but that shares with them, nonetheless, the fact that the finite is exaggerated, by an emotional and intentional befuddling of limited, finite reality, and is divinized into an infinite. In its fullest form, even philosophical "idealism" is an intoxication of man with his own spirit, which it regards as the center and source of being. It causes man to be so inflamed by the potentiality of his own nature that he magnifies all creative spontaneity of the human spirit into a creative spontaneity of the absolute spirit that is the primary cause of all reality. This occurs, moreover, not as a result of any thought process, but as a kind of "primordial presupposition" or "a priori judgment." If actual human thought bears essentially the character of an "after-thinking" of what has already been thought in reality, of a statement of ideas already incorporated into reality with the result that the actual form of being has already been ordained and determined, then idealism is the attempt to circumvent this subsequentness of human thought, to begin before anything has been predetermined, and to make oneself the source and center of being. Eastern mysticism behaves in much the same way once the human self is glorified to an absolute self and raised, by the identification of Atman with Brahman, to the cosmic principle of being. It should be pointed out, however, that this does not occur in the Orient, as it does in the Occident, by way of philosophical categories or the discipline of dialectical thinking.

In his intoxication with his own self, man imputes to himself a divine eminence. The fact that he does so is, however, already an indication of his fall from the godlikeness that actually is the foundation of his being. The fall is occasioned by "pride," which, in the Christian tradition, is properly identified with "original sin." In his *City of God,* St. Augustine comments thereon:

> And what is the origin of our evil will but pride? For "pride is the beginning of sin" [Ecclus. 10:15]. And what is pride but the craving for undue exaltation? And this is undue exaltation, when the soul abandons Him to whom it ought to cleave as its end, and becomes a kind of end to itself. This happens when it becomes its own satisfaction. And it does so when it falls away from that unchangeable good which ought to satisfy it more than itself. This falling away is spontaneous; for if the will had remained steadfast in the love of that higher and changeless good by which it was illumined to intelligence and kindled into love, it would not have turned away to find satisfaction in itself, and so become frigid and benighted. . . . But man did not so fall away as to become absolutely nothing; but being turned towards himself, his being became more contracted than it was when he clave to Him who supremely is. Accordingly, to exist in himself, that is, to be his own satisfaction after abandoning God, is not quite to become a nonentity, but to approximate that. And therefore the holy Scriptures designate the proud by another name, "self-pleasers." (2 Pet. 2:10)[9]

Mankind was first lured into sin by the suggestion: "Ye shall be as gods" (Gen. 3:5). On this fact, Augustine comments:

> . . . they would much more readily have accomplished [this] by obediently adhering to their supreme and true end than by proudly living to themselves. For created gods are gods not by virtue of what is in themselves, but by a participation of the true God. By craving to be more, man becomes less; and by aspiring to be self-sufficing, he fell away from Him who truly suffices him. Accordingly, this wicked desire which prompts man to please himself as if he were himself light, and which thus turns him away from that light by which, had he followed it, he would himself have become light—this wicked desire, I say, already secretly existed in him, and the open sin was but its consequence. For that is true which is written, "Pride goeth before destruction, and before honour is humility" [Prov. 16:18; 18:12]; that is to say, secret ruin precedes open ruin, while the former is not counted ruin. For who counts exaltation ruin, though no sooner is the Highest forsaken than a fall is begun? (p. 461)

Like the Christian mystics, we can, of course, speak with a certain justice of man's "eternal self," but this is not to be interpreted as an absolute foundation of self in self. The person who, in conscious agnosticism, takes his stand on the human self and relegates God to the status of a purely psychic function of some archetype may perhaps not deny the reality of God in theory, but he does so in practice by the total ignoring of God in his own life. This is particularly so if, at the same time, he claims it is totally irrelevant whether "enlightenment" is genuine or merely imagined.

For Jung, *satori* is synonymous with the breakthrough to the unconscious, to wholeness, it is the "break-through of a consciousness limited to the ego-form in the form of the non-ego-like self" (Jung, in Suzuki, p. 14). It is unquestionably correct to see in the depths of human nature that reality of potential factors that also contains the norm for all that actually exists. Thus every man knows there exists in the depths of his being a better self that makes itself known through warnings and demands. In every man, the self that he ought to be complains about the self that he really is. The breakthrough of the better self is capable of transforming a man's whole attitude toward life by means of a "conversion." But this self that exists in the depths of man's being, which is for the most part unknown, and of which he becomes aware only fragmentarily, must not be simply identified with the "unconscious," which "is the matrix of all metaphysical assertions, of all mythology, all philosophy (in so far as it is not merely critical) and all forms of life which are based upon psychological suppositions" (p. 23).

In this case, too, Jung sees correctly when he ascribes a certain completeness to the workings of the unconscious on conscious life. Because

God or Atman

consciousness is so limited, conscious psychic life concerns itself with details and with parts whose connection with the whole is, in consequence, easily overlooked or ignored. The impulses that arise from the unconscious serve to eliminate fragmentation. The unconscious is in itself the complete totality of that human nature that can be endangered by fragmentation. Nevertheless, this totality of the unconscious is by no means the foundation of all being as such.

Even if there is an impulse in the depths of man's being that addresses to him its warnings and demands, it is and remains a piece of his own reality, which is a de facto reality, into whose origin and end the man genuinely interested in religion must inquire. He cannot and may not omit these questions merely to bolster his own illusion of an infinite self. The person who fails to ask the basic questions about his own existence will always be plagued by the unwelcome suspicion that he is bogged down in a lie that must eventually end in a monstrous disillusionment.

The illusion of an infinite self reduces man's de facto existence to a mirage or a dream that does not have to be taken seriously. Despite all the talk about an eternal self, the fact remains that man's de facto existence had a beginning and that it moves toward an end. For the religious man who is intellectually fully alert and capable of objective thought, the questions about the origin and end of human life are and remain matters of fundamental significance. But for one who directs all his attention to what is immanent and who raises the self to the status of an eternal absolute, they are obscured by dream phantasies even when they are not immediately rejected. Such a person acts as if these questions did not exist. He acts as if there were neither birth nor death. Or he attempts, in pursuit of a philosophy of immanence, to make his own death the occasion of a last self-enjoyment. This occurs in every instance of a pseudoreligion of immanence, just as it did in the case of the Stoics and their divinization of the human self by an exaggerated autonomy that raised man to the level of the gods. Man does not want to admit that the beginning of individual existence reveals that he was drawn out of nothingness by a great and preexistent being-as-power, or that the end of his human existence will restore him to this being-as-power laden, as it were, with the burden of a life that has been lived, of a life that has been successful or unsuccessful. Indeed, as Schopenhauer knew, it is precisely this added burden that lies at the base of man's very real fear of death, which is by no means a fear of his merely physical end. Thus any attempt to find the ultimate meaning of one's existence in oneself must be regarded as artificial and forced. The person who has shut himself up in the cocoon of himself is always threatened by death, for death destroys his cocoon.

Once the temptation to find the meaning of one's existence in oneself has been avoided, however, the methods of Zen Buddhism acquire great significance, for they lead man to himself. The German philosopher Eugen

Herrigel, who spent years in Japan as a professor of philosophy and studied the art of Zen, describes the process in stimulating terms. What Zen hopes to achieve might be compared to the first preparatory stage of Christian asceticism, which consists in the *via purgativa,* in the purification of the human self. Augustine, too, taught the entrance into oneself as the first step leading to God.

Zen strives for a "homecoming" into oneself in the conviction that man has lost his original state through his own fault.

> In the possibility that is open to man of living to a large measure by his own resources, Zen Buddhism sees the onset of a fall and, therefore, of guilt. Man feels and experiences himself as an ego. This ego-ness leads him to seek and affirm himself in sharp contrast to every non-ego and results in hardness of heart. He feels and makes himself the center of all things, if not consciously, then at least in the secret places of his heart. This development tends to become intensified. But it is not necessary for it to be carried to extremes. Zen Buddhism regards even the first impulses of the child toward self as unavoidable and destructive. Therefore, it is no excuse to point out that, unlike European man, the East Asian has never left his natural state; that he still lives in traditional modes. For this does not change the fact that he struggles nonetheless with the demands of his ego and is, consequently, not at all inclined to live to such an extent by his own resources as he would have done had he not changed his ways.
>
> The greatest danger is, however, that man is too naive to realize this fact and, when it is pointed out to him, cannot understand it. Linked to his ego-ness is a distortion of the reality of existence. His gaze is troubled. He finds it impossible to compare and to discover the difference between what he is and what he ought to be. For what he is and what he ought to be cannot be described beforehand. It is not a different style, a different direction of his daily life; it is not an image that he can realize; it is not something that he can accomplish by awareness and determination, by earnestness and a sense of responsibility. It is something quite different; something that eludes him totally and that can be reached only by fundamental change: by conversion.[10]

Thus Herrigel describes the meaning of contemporary Zen Buddhism on the basis of his own experience and insight.

Regarded from this perspective, Zen Buddhism demands our acceptance. It offers a methodology for the entrance into oneself, for something, then, that the distracted Christian in today's world has lost, but that he must learn before he can come to a new and living encounter with God. Zen Buddhism has long since freed itself from ancient Buddhism and its "truth" that all is suffering. It has long since cut its bonds to the historical Buddha. It has come to regard "Buddha" as a designation for man's own nature. It has abandoned the pessimistic doctrine of suffering and has begun to preach an active apostolate of good example. There is not as yet any clear rejection of the pantheistic identification of "self" and "Atman." But there is a clearly discernible moderation in discussing philosophical questions and a basic openness toward positive religions. For this reason, the dialogue between Christian missionaries and Zen Buddhists promises to yield much fruit. Perhaps in this way Zen Buddhism can be led to a genuine encounter with the Christian belief in God, an encounter for which Jung's recommendations were entirely unsuitable. On the other hand, the Christian's life of prayer can be significantly quickened by contact with Zen Buddhism.

A Zen bonze once said to Fr. Lassalle: "When you perform *zazen* (the meditation exercises), you will understood properly for the first time what Catholicism is." At first, this seemed erroneous to the Christian theologian. He could not imagine what Zen could teach him about Catholicism after his study of philosophy and theology and his long years of priestly ministry. "And yet," Lassalle says, "today I must admit that the bonze was right in a certain sense. The *zazen* methodology can really help one to see in three dimensions the knowledge that he had heretofore seen in only two dimensions."[11]

10

IN SEARCH OF THE ABSOLUTE

Man bears, in his finite being, the mark of the absolute. He cannot help himself: by his very nature, he is compelled to strive for the absolute and to seek a union with it. In this regard, Eastern man does not differ from Western man. But the ways by which each of them seeks the absolute diverge very quickly from one another.

"Nirvana," which is the Buddhist's goal, is described as "absolute nothingness." Nevertheless, it was not just the later Buddhist movements that developed it into a positive absolute. Although the fact is not frequently recognized, the absolute is not totally absent even from the teachings of Buddha himself. It is only because the Buddhist Scriptures decidedly overemphasize the innovative quality of Buddha's teachings that there seems to be an unbridgeable gulf between the teachings of the "Exalted One" and those of his masters and contemporaries. A more exact historical examination has since rectified these exaggerations. Buddha himself proclaimed, in fact, that he had rediscovered and renewed the "ancient" way. The ancient way was the way of Yoga, the way of liberation, of nondeath. Buddhism, which spread from India over all of Asia, is, as Jacques Albert Cuttat says, "basically nothing but Yoga expanded into a world religion and including Zen Buddhism, which is especially popular today in America and Europe." It is not only the "quintessence of the Hindu ways of spirituality, but at the same time typical, perhaps even historically exemplary, for the whole spirituality of Asia."[1] Buddha did not, in any sense of the word, repudiate the already existing ascetic and contemplative traditions to teach a new way. However innovative he may have been, his thinking was formed by ancient Yoga.[2]

Undoubtedly, Buddha was as opposed to Brahminic ritualism with its sacrificial magic as he was to exaggerated asceticism and the losing of oneself in metaphysical speculations. In fact, the Upanishads had already, even before his time, contained a criticism of fossilized ritualism. In the classic Upanishads, however, the claim was made that salvation could be attained only by means of metaphysical speculation. Buddha repudiated this claim. It should also not be overlooked that the central problem of Buddhism, namely, suffering and the liberation from suffering, is a traditional problem of Hindu thought. The Buddhist complaint that "everything is full of suffering because everything is transitory" was also raised by Samkhya-Yoga and Vedanta.

If Buddha accepted traditional spiritual premises even while he rejected the ancient doctrines and disciplines, it was because he refused to be satisfied with philosophical formulas or magic practices and mystical regulations and chose, instead, to revive the great common goal of freeing man from his sufferings and from the bonds of a constricted life and of opening to him the way to the absolute. He appropriated to himself from Samkhya and preclassical Yoga the merciless destruction of the concepts of "person" and "soul" to do away with an idol that had been preempted by speculation. His radical negations are due not to nihilism, but to his determination not to be satisfied with any temporary answer. His intention was simply to deny the possibility of learning anything about the absolute or the true self so long as no "awakening" had occurred. Until an awakening occurs, everything is "empty prattle" and without value. If Buddha also rejected the conclusions of the Upanishads that Brahman, the pure, absolute, immortal spirit, is identical with Atman, he did so because the searching intellect might too easily be satisfied by such teachings and cease to strive for its own awakening.

Buddha's agnosticism with regard to the phantom of absolute nothingness remains an unsolvable problem that will defeat every attempt at a solution until the shadow of this phantom has been explained away. But if modern scholarship shows that Buddha rejected the philosophies and asceticisms of his time only "because he regarded them as *idola mentis* interposing a sort of screen between man and absolute reality, the one true Unconditioned" (p. 164), at least the broad outlines of a solution to the problem are becoming visible. A better knowledge of the ancient Buddhist Scriptures reveals, in contrast to earlier theories, that Buddha "had no intention of denying a final, unconditioned reality, beyond the eternal flux of cosmic and psychomental phenomena" (Ibid.), but that he merely refrained from speaking on this subject. *Nirvana* is, then, the absolute par excellence, the "nothingness" of everything generated, composed, reducible; it is that which lies beyond all human experience, namely, "transcendence." In daily life, the sense organs of the ordinary man can perceive only transitory objects. If man cannot see nirvana with his bodily eyes, he can see it with the eye of the holy one, with a certain transcendent organ that sees beyond the transitory world. "The problem for Buddhism, as for every other initiation, was to show the way and create the means by which this transcendent 'organ' for revealing the unconditioned could be obtained" (Ibid.).

The message of Buddha and of Buddhism aims not at the solution of problems of understanding, but at the attainment of salvation, at the overcoming of the state of suffering by a kind of rebirth and conversion. Such salvation is to be won not by an isolated effort of the understanding or by intensive ascetic exercises alone, but by a very personal striving toward an "experience" that affects the whole person. From this point of view, both the pure will to grasp with the understanding as well as the pure, ecstatic will to know by experience are false paths that never lead beyond what is temporal. The salvation proper to nirvana is achieved only by the person who passes beyond the plane of the profane world and gains access to the very different plane of the unconditioned. This demands a kind of personal dying in the profane life to be born again into a different kind of life. Pascal would have said that it is a question of rising to a qualitatively new plane of human existence that is never to be attained by a quantitative multiplication of a lower plane, but only by a leap to a qualitatively higher one.

Buddha and Buddhism claim to teach both the way and the means of dying to the old human condition of suffering and transitoriness to be reborn to the freedom, happiness, and "unconditionedness" of nirvana. Buddha did not speak of this latter quality because he did not want to do so inopportunely. He attacked the Brahmins, in fact, because they claimed to be able to express the ineffable, to know the nature of the soul, and to define the absolute as Brahman and Atman. He likewise consistently refused to answer the questions of his disciples about the absolute because he was unwilling either to deny or affirm it.

Of the person who arrives at nirvana and the emancipation it entails, it is said that he reaches and feels happiness in himself and enjoys the perfection in which his soul has become identified with Brahman. It can also be said that Buddha believed, at least as it is understood in the mystic and ascetic tradition of India, in an emancipation in the absolute even though he refused to define it more closely. The "nirvana-ized" man is no longer of this world; he has become as unfathomable as the ocean.

If, then, the absolute is sought in the religions of the East, their manner of doing so is, nevertheless, very different from that of Christian thought, which believes that the absolute is realized in the Creator-God. This does not mean, however, that we see here an impulse in the non-Christian religions that is related to a similar impulse in Christianity as potency is to act, as presentiment is to knowing, as longing is to fulfillment; for there is no genuine faith that can be separated from its content, nor is there any purely natural religion that needs only to be developed to become Christian faith. What confront one another here are two concretely developed religions that differ so widely in their image of God and in their way of salvation that, after looking at them closely, "one is inclined," as Klaus Klostermaier says in his thorough study of Hinduism, "to doubt whether there is much point in classifying both Hinduism and Christianity under the heading of religion."[3] What Eastern and Western thought have in common is their search for the absolute, even though their manner of seeking it and

In Search of the Absolute

the very different terminology in which they clothe their thoughts render difficult any mutual understanding. Nevertheless, the attempt must be made.

Since it is easier to make abstract concepts comprehensible in symbols, we shall base our discussion here on the painting by an ancient Japanese Zen master that Heinrich Dumoulin chose—as a kind of logogram—for the cover of his book *Östliche Meditation und christliche Mystik* (Eastern Meditation and Christian Mysticism). It is a watercolor by the Abbot Hakuin (1685–1768). With economic strokes, it depicts blind persons groping their way across a bridge in a symbolic representation of the human condition, especially that of the aged. These blind persons symbolize those who, because of the unalterable lot of dying to which they are subject, find themselves cast back upon their naked existence and long to be transported to the opposite shore of eternity. In their blindness, they grope their way across the swaying bridge of this temporal world. In this fundamental human condition, they are stripped of everything that might serve to distinguish one from another. Here, Western man is like Eastern man; the enlightened is like the unenlightened. To make his meaning clear, the artist has brushed in the words: "Let the groping of blind men crossing a bridge be a symbol for the life of the aged." The Zen abbot was fond of this symbol of the bridge. He described it to young persons as a structure boldly spanning an abyss and used it as a warning to them to be concerned for the purity of their hearts. It is offered here as the wisdom of old age: "human existence, precisely as it is, full of danger, fragile and ill, creeping toilsomely over the bridge, close to eternity."[4]

A "bridge" is a road—but it is no ordinary road over firm ground that can be trodden in untroubled certainty; rather, a bridge—especially if one thinks of the often unstable hanging bridges of Eastern Asia—is a crossing that challenges him who uses it. It passes over abysses and rushing water. Yet the driving impulse to reach the other side suppresses the fear that the challenge evokes.

All fully developed religious premises and doctrines claim to be "road directions," that is, to point out the roads that lead to the fulfillment of the innermost demands of man's being. In the painful experience to which he was subjected, Buddha discovered that the mark of eternity has been imprinted upon man's very nature. In its beginnings, Buddhism is resignation produced by "dis-illusionment" *(Ent-täuschung)*. Buddha's youthful "pre-view" *(Vor-erwartung)* of life led him to expect a life that was full, that was as it ought to be, that would last forever. It anticipated the life of a person in absolute and eternal possession of self. It longed for the fulfillment of all the strivings of human nature. Because his expectation exceeded all reality and because he was "disillusioned" by the wretchedness and infirmity of an actual life that is constantly threatened in its very existence, Buddha simply clothed himself in a protective resignation; and rejected as "nothing" what life actually has to offer. Humble temporal existence had no value for him. It was "nothing at all."

No animal can be disappointed in its life and its world in the specifically human way of which man is capable because no animal approaches its life and its world with the same a priori expectation that man does. Because of his intellectual gifts, man is capable, after reflecting upon his experience of expectations and disillusionments, of making a transcendental analysis of his striving for the absolute, that is, he can discover the real goal of his natural striving. His transcendental analysis cannot, of course, reveal to him what it is in particular in the realm of reality that corresponds to his striving, nor can it deliver a judgment based on reality about whether what is sought is or is not reality. But it can examine the nature of the inner emptiness that calls for fulfillment and so discover the a priori knowledge of the absolute that is actually present in man's craving for infinity although much effort and many disappointments are needed to bring it to the light of consciousness.

As a matter of fact, unmistakable difficulties attend any attempt at transcendental analysis. For the immediate and natural will to knowledge directs itself toward objects that stand outside the knowing ego, but not to the voices that make themselves heard from within. Only a "turning back" *(reflexio)* can lead to a consideration of these nonobjective entities. To understand what forces its way up from the unconscious to the conscious and constantly incites man, but without offering him the possibility of comprehending it as he might comprehend an object, one must listen to what is trying to make itself heard here. The way of knowledge in this instance is meditation, reflection, that concerns itself with voices arising from within; that seeks to reflect on them and to raise them to the light. Words and language become, then, the further means of clothing in linguistic garb that which wells up without words from within—the means of rendering it communicable so it can be explained in speaking with others. Finally, that which has been explained in words must once more become an instrument, in the hands of those who are experienced in these things, for addressing and rousing those who are inexperienced so they, too, will not fail to hear what speaks to them gently from within, but will accept it, reflect upon it, and experience it inwardly for themselves.

Admittedly, this cannot occur without great danger. For an earlier interpretation already couched in fixed formulas can lead the experience of those who come after by a too narrow route so most of them will never come to understand and reflect upon the full breadth of interpretation of which the experience is susceptible. In this way, the original experience can become cramped, simplified, or even falsified. Interpretations once accepted can obstruct the way to the totality of the original experience for many generations, even for centuries.

In Search of the Absolute

Because this danger exists, the "road directions" of the various ways to religious salvation are in need of critical comparison. Only thus can a genuine dialogue arise; only thus can "byways" be avoided that lead to dead ends.

Road is one of the original words of the human language. In the depths of his being, every man knows he is, for all his life, a *homo viator,* a "traverser of roads." In the intellectual world of the East, there is much discussion of the "road" as such; the Chinese word *tao* also had the original meaning of "road." In time, however, the word was enriched beyond its original meaning by the addition of a symbolic meaning. It means the road of life that man must travel during his earthly existence from the relative and transitory to the definitive and absolute. For that reason the word *tao* can also be translated as "principle" or "doctrine" and even by the Greek word *Logos* that was appropriated by the New Testament and filled with new meaning.

In the intellectual world of both the Old and New Testaments, there is constant reference to the "ways [roads] of God." It is God who leads nations and men to the goal of their fulfillment. In the New Testament, it is Jesus Christ who says of himself that he is the "way [road] itself," just as he also identifies himself with the end of the road, with light and life. For the Christians of the first centuries, their faith was the new "road to salvation."

A transcendental analysis of man's striving for the absolute would make possible a clarification of one fundamental major difference between East and West. But it would require of each partner to the dialogue a positive evaluation of his intellectual awareness and his ability to shed light on the obscurities that would be questioned. However, even here there are differences of approach on each side. For the East has already decided, by a kind of prejudgment, that intellectual awareness is a negative value that it seeks to avoid. At this very point, the two roads diverge, never to meet again. The goal of the Eastern road to salvation is to retreat from the presently experienced moment to former times in order to move backwards through all time and thus to arrive once more *ad originem,* at the original absolute that, as the first to exist, set time in motion and brought forth the world; in order to come again to that state where time did not yet exist and where that which began in the beginning had not yet revealed itself in separate manifestations. The meaning and goal of the yoga technique is to roll world-time backwards—or better perhaps—to roll it up again. In this way, whatever has been particularized will be resumed into the whole. The human spirit with its consciousness has been most daring in its excursion into the realm of relative time. Accordingly, it must be suppressed so that it can pass backwards through all levels of consciousness even to that union with the absolute of which it dreams. For this intellectual position, the truly supreme wisdom consists in man's remembrance of all earlier existences and his reexperiencing of them in reverse order until he reaches precreation. In this way, one's whole past life is relived "against the current," and, at the same time, the "sins" of these past existences—that is, the sum of the misdeeds that were committed in the bonds of ignorance and that had been passed on from one existence to another—are consumed.

By this retrogressive movement along the road to salvation, it is believed, man will come again to the beginning of time, will arrive once more at nontime, at the eternal present from which human existence is, as it were, fallen. It is believed that man will thus regain the unconditioned state that preceded his plunge into time and the wheel of existence. If a person succeeds in emptying time retrogressively from the presently experienced moment, he sees his countenance before every birth, overcomes his human condition, and arrives at nontime, at eternity. This constitutes *nirvana*.

Buddha is said to have differed from many of his disciples and followers in that he succeeded in remembering all of his previous existences whereas the others, although they were able to remember a considerable number of their past existences, were yet far from remembering all of them and so did not achieve the perfection that Buddha achieved, but remained fixed in their earthly existence.

But this is not the whole road of salvation that is known to Buddhism. It is also possible to leave time behind and put an end to one's profane condition by taking advantage of the favorable moment of enlightenment in which this earthly life is dissolved and thus emerging from the realm of time.

In contradistinction to the West, the Buddhist technique of meditation repeatedly demands the emptying of consciousness, the suppression of object oriented thinking and willing, and the renunciation of all emotions and desires. In the world of the East, there is strong mistrust of man's intellectual self-possession with its potentiality for intellectual and intentional mastery of the world. Eastern man is inclined to view the world in which he lives as an illusion rather than as a positive starting point from which, penetrating the world intellectually, he can rise to become its "primordial being" *(Ur-sache)*. In late Hinduism the view is expressed that the supreme God prevents man by his *maya,* his magic arts, from knowing reality and thus from becoming like God. "He who recognizes Maya as illusion is God."[5] Nothing can express better than this sentence the obvious and flagrant difference between Eastern and Western attitudes, between the roads that are followed in the East and in the West and the goals to which they lead. Every presumptive confidence that the *lumen naturale,* the natural light of human reason, is a suitable torch for lighting the way to an intellectual conversion to the absolute is here thwarted by an equally presumptive mistrust that rejects the toilsome and difficult road and strives for a direct union with the absolute, that is, with the "eternal in man."

Although human nature, in its deepest *inclinatio*, tends toward the absolute, it does not follow that it knows from the onset in what the absolute consists. If it seeks it first in the things of its immediate life, it will require a radical disappointment before it can be brought to search for it behind these things. This result is attained more quickly when the world of appearances is regarded as a mere *maya*, as an illusion that must be destroyed before one can come into direct possession of the kernel beneath the deceptive shell. Genuine transcendence, however, is an activity of the intellect. It must be removed from the precritical sphere of mere supposition and opinion. It requires intellectual discipline, although not the restriction of logical formulas. If it is omitted, the human is divinized, the sphere of the human is not distinguished from that of the divine. From such concepts of God it is possible to learn more about what man thinks, strives for, and desires than about what God is. In his book on *Hinduism,* Klostermaier has documented this with many proofs.

For this reason, too, the thesis of Raymond Panikkar, which is also evident in the title of his book, *The Unknown Christ of Hinduism,* is too unrealistic; it fails to take into consideration the forces that pull in different directions and interprets Eastern thought too optimistically from a Christian point of view. This is an instance of an attempt by a Christian philosopher to initiate a dialogue by making the first advance to the intellectual world of the East. It remains to be seen, however, whether the Eastern partner will, for his part, respond to this step toward an intellectual encounter.

Despite many obscurities and attenuations, Brahman is basically the source of all genesis, preservation, and change in this world. In brief, "Brahman is the total ultimate cause of the world." [6] In strange proximity to Brahman stands Atman, the "self," perhaps best translated as "the eternal in man." The man searching for salvation is not at first concerned with Brahman; his attention is riveted on Atman. "It is in worrying about the self that a good part of Indian Philosophy comes to discover the problem of Brahman. But of course once this issue is raised, there is no way of avoiding the problem or of ignoring its capital position" (p. 76).

As long as no genuine reality of its own is admitted for the world of men, it can be no more than a deceitful mirage of the absolute. Fundamentally, Eastern thought begins a priori with the absolute. If this is conceived as *omnitudo realitatis,* as total and complete reality, a created being endowed with its own reality becomes an impossibility. If Brahman is primarily designated as the source of the world—even as the omniscient and omnipotent source of the world, and even as one possessed of a certain transcendence with regard to the world—the idea of creation in the Christian sense is totally lacking. Brahman is not regarded as the cause that brought the world into existence, as its creator. According to Sankara, existence cannot be caused, for there is no transition from being to not-being or from not-being to being. In an exact sense, only Brahman has existence, but its effect is nothing more than a determination of the cause itself and does not extend beyond Brahman. It follows that the world can be nothing but an illusion. Insofar as it is real, everything that is can only be a part of Brahman.

Nevertheless, it cannot be denied that all the Vedanta-Sutras teach above all that Brahman is the absolute, the highest principle, the cause of all things, although his nature is not knowable. We discover in ourselves as a first and basic fact the desire to comprehend the origin of all things, which, it should be noted, is not the same as "knowing." Nonetheless, this wish presumes that we already have some knowledge of Brahman to begin with, for if we did not, we could not strive toward him. Every striving is accompanied by a knowing. If our yearning for Brahman is to have any real meaning and content, we must know in some manner what we desire. If we had no knowledge of it at all, we could neither strive for it nor inquire into its nature. The *desiderium naturale,* the natural longing, that finds expression in us in the question about Brahman represents, if rightly interpreted, the bridge to transcendence.

Panikkar comments on this point:

> Thus, by one means or another, we have the desire to know Brahman. This "desire" is not the actual "knowledge" of Brahman, but yet it implies a certain cognition of Brahman—a cognition that somehow must be the necessary bridge on which the full realisation of Brahman has come down to us. It is, as it were, a thin thread that unites us already with Brahman, an ignition point, a certain identity or at least communication, not to say communion, that will grow and develop from Brahma-jijnasa, to Brahmajnana, from the "desire" to the "knowledge." And yet there is a gap, there is no continuity between them. (p. 85)

Here, also, Panikkar's thesis must be modified. "To know" does not mean the same in the language of the East as it does to the Western mind. For that reason, the longing for knowledge of Brahman cannot be taken as a common point of departure. Only with certain reservations is it possible to speak here of a "bond of unity between Hindu and Western philosophy" (p. 86).

What can be hoped for is a common effort toward a transcendental analysis of man's striving toward eternity that might reveal further points held in common. Let us explain this by a vivid image! To cherish a desire for something means to detect in oneself a tormenting inner space that must be filled. Even if we cannot know, in itself and for what it actually is, that which might fill the void, we nevertheless have, by reason of the emptiness that is within us, a certain prescience of what can fill it. We can more or less describe how it must be constituted if it is to correspond to the conditions that are present within us and that are, to a certain extent, known to us. This is the function of transcendental analysis—in meditative reflection upon our self, to probe the inner space that torments us by its emptiness to be able to determine what might fill it.

Such reflection, however, must not stop short of the critical questions: can the inner union that is sought with the absolute be found solely in the inner space of the human self, or is it rather a union of love that is sought with an absolute that lies outside and above the self? To these must be added the further question: what false paths leading to dead ends must be avoided; what roads must be taken to achieve the sought for and desired union with the absolute that is known?

At this point it must be noted, however, that Eastern man in search of salvation refuses to adopt this mode of thought. He regards every effort to provide a philosophical answer to whatever problems may arise as an unnecessary deviation from or retardation of his own natural inclination to achieve direct union with the absolute without the intermediary action of thought. A reasoned analysis is looked upon as a profanation, as a degradation of that holy of holies that can be revealed only in the feelings or in the experience of a great enlightenment. In philosophical probings, Eastern man sees not only an unnecessary delay, but even the danger of becoming mired in the penultimate.

It cannot be denied that there is a certain admirable consistency in Eastern thought. It is a way of thinking that begins with the absolute and takes the thought of the absolute so seriously that it would sooner deny the reality of the world around it than tolerate any diminution of the absolute. That is, there is implicit in the Eastern concept of the absolute the belief that it must itself be all being; that there can be no being outside it. But when the absolute is thus accepted a priori as the source of all being, the reality of the world must be denied. That is the inclination of the East, just as it is the inclination of every "pantheism" that refuses to admit that it thereby wounds the absolute in its absoluteness. A world with a reality of its own, it is objected, would limit the full reality of the absolute so it would no longer be the absolute. Every acknowledgment of a reality as such in the world and in man seems to the pantheist, with his single-minded concept of the absolute, to be a degeneration to a figurative mode of thought that is purely anthropomorphic, a concession to fantasy that does not rest upon the strong foundation of logical discipline. The consequence of this stubborn adherence to a belief in the possibility of only one absolute reality is contempt for those apparently all too popular attitudes in which man, as one who has being in himself, is compared with one or more gods. Such notions seem of their very nature to weaken the concept of the absolute and to refuse to take it seriously.

Except in the sphere of revelation, however, man is almost totally unaware of the existence of any mediative solution. On the one hand, such a solution would give full credence to the reality proper to the world and to man. It would not admit that the temporality of this world is the sign of a deceptive and illusory existence. On the other hand, it would give just as much credence to the concept of the absoluteness of the divine being. If God is acknowledged in all his divine—and to us incomprehensible—greatness, and if our own puny thought is not permitted to place a priori restrictions on the extent of his absoluteness, it cannot be denied that the almighty and absolute God can bestow a reality of their own even on those beings that already have their foundations in him—and with it a certain degree of personal freedom. Man's mind cannot comprehend how this can be. But the courage to acknowledge the reality proper to creation and, at the same time, to give equal credence to the absoluteness of a God who transcends our comprehension leads, by a kind of inner logic, to the concept of creation. However, it must be admitted that the thought of creation is so foreign to the man who is left to his own inner resources that, wherever there has been no revelation, it exists only as a certain kind of rudimentary presentiment, but never in the kind of clarity that it possesses in the realm of Christian thought.

Whoever lacks the courage to affirm that human self-consciousness is a positive value residing in the self-possession of the one who exists will also be hesitant about accepting the otherwise very natural conclusion that the highest self-possession, the highest form of the absolute possession of self, is attributable to the absolute. In fact, the disillusionment that lies at the root of all Buddhist experience leads the Buddhist to deny that man is a person simply because he does not possess himself absolutely. If there is an absolute reality, however, such possession of itself cannot be denied it. For an absolute that is neutral is an inherently contradictory concept. An absolute that was possessed only by others, but was unable to possess itself, to determine itself, would not be an absolute.

The tragic consequence of every failure to appreciate psychic awareness and of a too summary a priori dismissal of the concept of absoluteness is the divinization, the deification, of the "eternal in man." What is closest to man is Atman, the self: it bears within it the mark of definitiveness. For that reason, it moves into the sphere of the absolute and is identified with Brahman. But if this eternal is present in man himself, the goal of his religious striving is to become conscious of this eternal by means of enlightenment. If man shares in the eternal, he can comprehend it in himself. The result is a more or less clearly expressed monism that seeks the absolute in oneself. To achieve this, it requires no long philosophical approaches, but only that absorption into the self that leads to enlightenment. Its goal is the blissful awareness of being one with the absolute, even if only for an instant.

In Search of the Absolute

From the perspective of this striving for union with the absolute, a keenly alert consciousness is regarded as an alienation of man from his nature. Man no longer finds himself in that unquestioning unity with nature that he enjoyed in his primordial state; having abandoned this unity, he must now practice meditation to regain it. Goethe's sensitivity to nature seems to be for the Asians, and especially for the Japanese, the great ideal of an emotional union with nature. His inner accord is obviously very close to their own ideal.

Against the background of this monistic view of the world, man's striving for infinity cannot develop as a loving desire. There is no room for that. The highest ideal of Buddhism is an impersonal wisdom. All movements and demands of a loving desire are regarded as belonging to a preliminary level of being and must be reduced to silence before man can enter upon the road of enlightenment. Loving desire is relegated to the sphere of inordinate desire, the vanity of which must be perceived before man can truly understand the concept of all-in-one. In their goal of reaching the "ecstasis" of enlightenment—or, more exactly, the "enstasis," all Japanese Masters of Zen are influenced by the monistic and pantheistic metaphysics of Mahayana Buddhism, even though their allegiance to this form of Buddhism is not clearly stated.

In the "school of the spirit," the disciple learns how to become one with the spirit of Buddha. There is no question here of the historical Buddha, but of the Buddha principle, of the universal human nature that is supposed to be revealed during the *satori* (enlightenment) experience. Heinrich Dumoulin describes enlightenment in these words:

> Enlightenment, which breaks through with overwhelming suddenness, is experienced as a liberation from earthly chains. "On the border between life and death," the Enlightened One "possesses great freedom. In the midst of this world of the six ways and the four births, he enjoys untroubled recollection." The law of *karma,* to which all corporeal things are subject, is no longer binding upon him. For his enlightenment has raised him above the lower levels of existence. He is not affected by limitations of space. "He lifts his foot and springs over the waters of the southern sea. . . . His body clings to nothing." This state of absolute freedom and spirituality has perhaps never been more clearly expressed than in the words that the Japanese Zen Master Dogen spoke about the experience of enlightenment: "Body and mind are cast off; cast off are body and mind." The words reflect with admirable precision the totality of the experience. The absolute sphere of Buddha-reality that is attained in this experience is spiritual.[7]

Because we of the West place more emphasis on concepts, we are too prone to give Eastern views a definitive meaning and interpretation that they do not have in the East. The concepts of Atman and Brahman, for example, have many meanings even in the Upanishads. If we translate *Atman* simply as "soul" or "self" and *Brahman* as "highest being," we have established a meaning based on our own point of view and have, in the process, come to a decision about what is, for the most part, undecided in the Atman-Brahman teachings of the Upanishads. Yet the Eastern intent is unmistakable: Whoever knows Atman and becomes aware of himself through the deep sleep acquires all worlds and objects. The last stage of the Turiya state is the real and valid absolute. We must be careful, too, about using the label *pantheism,* for there is no question here of an absolute equating of the existent world with God, but only of a striving to reach the absolute by a laborious "climb"—or, more accurately, "descent"—into a deeper region of consciousness. Nor is Atman simply to be identified with Brahman. Only the final stage of a long ascetic struggle bestows union with Atman and Brahman. The search proceeds from Atman, the individual absolute spirit, to Brahman, the absolute cosmic ground of being.

Moreover, the direction in which the absolute is sought in the East is in direct contrast to the spiritual doctrine of Christendom. In the retreat from the known world, asceticism has the task of overcoming the painful imprisonment in the illusion of body and world and of plumbing the depths of primordial life, there to shed light upon the absolute. Despite significant differences of detail, nearly all the spiritual movements of the East have an inner relationship. According to Dumoulin, Patanjali describes the essence and purpose of the yoga technique as follows: "Yoga is the suppression of states of consciousness" (p. 73).

Because the asceticism of yoga demands the destruction of what is specifically human in man, it can be said to bear an antihuman character. It regards everything human as profane, as something to be suppressed so what is holy can break through. It does violence to man's status as a human being, most specifically as it is reflected in the core of man's being, whereas the efforts of Christian asceticism are directed only to the sinful accretions that must be removed if man's true essence, the primordial purity of his nature, is to be revealed, developed, and perfected.

There is operative in man's fundamental striving to bring his own essence to fruition and positive perfection a craving for the absolute that is clearly perceived only in Western thought. There, the approach to the absolute occurs not in the destruction of what is specifically human, but in the construction and realization of man's true nature. In the process, the spirit—as both knowledge and striving—is highly active. This is not true of the Buddhist's struggle to reach nirvana. Although it must be granted that, in the last analysis, the struggle involves something very positive, the first meaning of nirvana is, nevertheless, an absolute emancipation from everything; one who has attained it must be free from all the wishes, passions, emotions, reflections, anxieties, and goals of this life; he must be preoc-

In Search of the Absolute

cupied with "nothingness." If this "nothingness" is not an objective nothingness, but a subjective one, namely, the highest degree of inner freedom, the contemporary Zen Buddhist seems to see in it no contradiction to life. There is a question here, however, neither of a striving for perfection nor of perfection itself, but of an emergence from the cycle of births and thus from the world of becoming with a consequent end to the painful thirst for existence. In this sense, it is possible to achieve "enlightenment" even in the midst of this life and so to arrive at nirvana. In the state of nirvana, there is no longer any distinction between subject and object, between life and death, between past and present, between this world and the next. Everything is contained in the highest moment of inner freedom.

The precondition for attaining the goal of enlightenment is the destruction of all representational images and concepts, the silencing of *ratio* by emptying consciousness totally of all that it contains. Only in this way can the new eye of the spirit, which is able to contemplate reality directly, be opened. As a kind of undifferentiated comprehension of the whole, the contemplation that is reached through meditation is regarded as the antithesis of the activity of the individual intellect, which, it is said, must of necessity become mired in error. The objective world, it is claimed, has its origin just as necessarily in the activity of the differentiating intellect as does error or the concept of a permanent ego. By virtue of the radical conversion of the spirit, *ratio* is overcome and the emptiness of all things is experienced. In the Mahayana Scriptures, this process is called the awakening of *prajna*. "The eye of *prajna*, of universal transcendental wisdom, is opened and contemplates objects in their full likeness. Since *prajna* and wisdom, according to the Mahayana doctrine of all-in-one, are identical with each other in indivisible unity, there can be no intermediary link between them. The directness of the intuitive unity is complete. *Prajna* shines in its own light and functions as a mirrorlike wisdom" (p. 87).

What is contemplated in enlightenment is said to be one's own eternal nature or one's original countenance before all births. At the same time, one acquires an insight into the unity of self and all. The contemplation of one's own nature is called *reincarnation*. Enlightenment is an intellectual experience, not, however, of the kind in which a counterpart, an object, is recognized, but rather of the kind in which comprehension moves in the other direction, toward one's own condition as subject, which is understood as a oneness with the cause of the world. One can speak quite properly here of a nonrepresentational knowledge.

Such an intuition is a very subjective experience. Because it is nonrepresentational and referred to a subject, it cannot be expressed in words and there can be no question of justifying it. The person who retreats into his own experience thereby destroys the bridges of intellectual communication with others. There are actually "wise men" in the East who regard themselves as perfected in this way, as having become one with Atman and Brahman; who monotonously repeat this proposition and reject in advance any dialogue in which a basis in fact might be sought. They have withdrawn from the community of intellectual life with others and have retreated totally into themselves.

But such an action reflects a divisive lack of logic. The subjective experience does not claim to be only something subjective; on the contrary, it contains in itself the affirmation of another experience—of the experience of becoming one with Atman and Brahman. In the claim that one has or has had this experience, there is contained, accordingly, the affirmation of a thesis whose justification can properly be questioned.

From the example of certain related "ways," it is possible to show where subjectivism on this level can lead. The *Bhagavadgita* affirms that all "ways" are equally justified and lead to the same goal. *Bhakti* (devotion to God) seeks, as it were, to place man in the right "frame of mind." The identification of one's own self with the absolute and the consequent ascent above all that might be opposed thereto takes place, in this view, on the level of feeling.

> By emotional self-identification with a corporeal Absolute, man avoids the problems that arise from the perception of the multiplicity of things and their real claims upon him. For *Arjuna* [hero of *Bhagavadgita*], emphasis is upon man's natural feeling for what is right or not right; man sees that it is not right to precipitate a civil war in which he will be obliged to murder his nearest relatives and revered teachers in order to see his ambitions fulfilled and to be able to enjoy the life of a king. The traditional *dharma* (teaching) also opposes this kind of warfare: hell is reserved for those who murder their next of kin. The *Gita* clearly conceals the moral question under metaphysical speculation. On the one hand, it says, man is a *kshatriya* (warrior), and the *dharma* of the *kshatriya* is war. On the other hand, it is the same self that quickens both him and his relatives—the fate of the bodies is extremely secondary. "Nature" must run its course: death follows upon birth and rebirth upon death. The ideal is the man who thinks only of "God" and carries out simply and regardless of consequences all the activities that an "anonymous duty" lays upon him. Even if the whole world were to be destroyed, *bhakti* would rescue man's self. "Freed" from all dependence, he can murder even his relatives without incurring sin and its sanctions. The first half of the statement proclaims that it is the sign of a disciplined spirit to disregard heat and cold, hunger and thirst, honor and dishonor; the other half cites true—and in the same breath complete—indifference toward good and evil as the realization of the same ideal of freedom. The challenge to murder one's next of kin without qualms so long as one is careful to preserve one's *bhakti*, one's commitment to the "Lord," builds on the second half. (Klostermaier, p. 202)

This quick glance at a related religious movement shows most forcibly the danger of a religious subjectivism that rejects the absoluteness of the self. The denial of the reality of the human world community has been pushed to extremes here while the fundamental appreciation of good and evil has been suspended. The recognition of the unquestioned character of moral values is and remains the only basis on which a true human community can be erected. Movements that reject these values must be regarded as fanaticism, as aberrations of the human spirit, which thereby forfeits its right to appeal to an entirely subjective experience.

Another characteristic of a spiritual community is the recognition of a common truth that, despite all human error, must always remain the goal toward which its members strive together. For that reason, a purely intuitive contemplation that allows no possibility of objective verification can never reflect man's ultimate concern and, in particular, can never be the basis for an intellectual meeting of minds. Besides, such a reversal of the intellectual process cannot be completely accomplished. Even a nonrepresentational enlightenment claims to be a truth and demands acceptance. It affirms something by what it includes. At the same time, it exposes itself, as does every affirmation, to the possibility of criticism; it cannot and may not withdraw itself from such criticism. If it does so regardless of the consequences, it withdraws itself from the community. It is only in a community of like-minded individuals who all, in the same way, affirm truth as their foundation that a true life of the spirit can be unfolded.

When Western observers meet with Eastern sages who believe they are in possession of enlightenment, the former are often struck by the human isolation of these wise men. Their mysticism lacks the warmth of a uniting love. All possibility of a cordial community life is paralyzed by the icy breath of an aristocratically exclusive intellectuality.

Withdrawal into one's own self and coming-to-rest in oneself may be a high state of natural mysticism; but it bears within itself the great danger of wanting to remain fixed in this state of rest. Several forms of Eastern mysticism are quite similar to certain forms of a pseudomysticism that drew many persons into its ranks during the Middle Ages, but that Christian mystics rejected as an aberration. In the Middle Ages, there were also "mystics" who claimed to have found their final rest in an absolute self and so to have attained perfection; in consequence, they believed that they had been raised above good and evil and were incapable of sinning. The mysticism of the absolute self is often very difficult to distinguish from genuine mysticism. In this very similarity, however, lies the temptation to stop at the penultimate and to omit the last decisive step.

The Flemish mystic Jan van Ruysbroeck attacks the "Quietists" of his time in a manner that might well lead one to believe he had intended to single out certain forms of Eastern mysticism. He speaks of men who delude themselves that they can no longer be led astray in the life of the senses by any images, that they possess a great "inner emptiness" and so have found final rest in themselves. Such mystics resemble to an astonishing degree the Eastern sages who, being free from sensual images and having achieved "inner emptiness" and that great at-one-ness in which there are no secondary concerns, believe they have thus become one with the highest Brahman. Thereupon they crowd in upon themselves and become incapable of further progress.

> For those who make this mistake have wandered so far from God and all virtues that it is hardly conceivable that they will be able to reverse their ways. These are all those who, without practicing virtue and in an intellect devoid of representational concepts, experience within themselves and possess their essential being by virtue of the mere freedom from encumbrance of their spirit and their nature. For they succumb to a vain, blind disencumberment of their being; they despise all interior as well as exterior good works. They scorn all inner activity, that is, all willing, knowing, desiring, loving, and every active approach to God. . . . For this reason, these miserable persons are badly deceived. They fall asleep and sink into natural repose. And as they find this repose in themselves without love or the practice of virtue, they want to possess it and remain in this state. The result is a great lack of faith and a perverted, false freedom of the spirit.[8]

If Ruysbroeck sharply condemns Quietism, he does so from the point of view of a positive belief in God. For Quietism is consciously opposed to any such belief and is, precisely for that reason, an anti-Christian mysticism. But this cannot be said of Eastern mysticism, which is still a pre-Christian mysticism. For it too, however, the great discovery of Atman-Brahman represents a danger zone, the "danger-zone of introversion."[9] The repose of the mystic who has come to rest in himself is ambivalent. If it is regarded as final, then this repose is, as Ruysbroeck so incisively explains, completely opposed to the repose that one can possess in God. Viewed from without, no difference is apparent. Both use the same mode of expression. As Evelyn Underhill has pointed out, this "false idleness" is only too easily attained by men of a certain character and disposition.

> They can by wilful self-suggestion deliberately produce this emptiness, this inward silence, and luxuriate in its peaceful effects. To do this from self-regarding motives, or to do it to excess—to let "peaceful enjoyment" swamp "active love"—is a mystical vice: and this perversion of the spiritual faculties, like perversion of the natural faculties, brings degeneration in its train. It leads to the absurdities of "holy indifference," and ends in the complete stultification of the mental and moral life. The true mystic never tries deliberately to enter the orison of quiet. . . .[10]

In Search of the Absolute

Klostermaier comments here:

> If yoga were to be regarded as an end, it would have to be categorized with Quietism—as a falling short of the essential goal. If it is regarded as a means, the *kaivalya* [isolation] is to be considered not as a final isolation, but as an openness to what is above. Hinduism offers no possibility of setting a goal for which *kaivalya* might be a means. The "one who seeks" will be dissatisfied with the emptiness of "loneliness"—the complacent man will plume himself on his achievement and will be satisfied. *Kaivalya* is a relatively high stage of the spiritual life—for that reason, however, the danger is even greater of misunderstanding it as an end and of remaining fixed in it. (Klostermaier, p. 267)

The inauguration of a fruitful dialogue between representatives of Eastern mysticism and Christian dogma depends basically on whether the Eastern seeker after absoluteness remains fixed in a penultimate union with the absolute or whether he takes to the "road" again to carry his search further. In this regard, it is of fundamental significance to know whether the reality of man in his own right and with his own propensities will be recognized despite its nothingness vis-à-vis the absolute; whether man's own propensities are questioned as to their goal; and whether man can thus be roused to transcend his own self. In the Eastern mode of expression, union with the absolute means becoming one in an ontological sense, an entering into and being absorbed by the absolute substance, that is, an identification or fusion with the highest reality. Indispensable to this view is, as we have seen, that one-sidedly absolutistic interpretation of the absolute according to which no other reality can exist beside the absolute, but must always be a deceptive illusion. Added thereto is the lack of courage to take seriously the reality—even though it be a created reality—that is proper to man and to bring the inclinations of one's own being not to silence, but to speech. If they are brought to speech, they direct man's attention beyond himself to a personal encounter with an absolute, personal being and, untimately, to union with the absolute in the sense of a personal communion of love with the personal Creator-God.

The Western approach is also well-acquainted with a mode of thought that views objects in their totality, not with just an analytical division of reality by the *ratio*. The former mode of thought is directed by man's "heart," which detects within itself a craving for infinity and seeks gropingly for its fulfillment in the true absolute.

St. Augustine's unique significance lies in the fact that, as a seeker after the absolute in all the experiences and disappointments of his life, whose meaning he illumined by meditation, he unequivocally found the goal toward which man's striving for the infinite is directed. In the key sentence of his *Confessions,* he says, "Creasti nos ad Te, et inquietum est cor nostrum, donec requiescat in Te, Domine" ("Thou has created us for Thyself, O God, and our heart is restless until it rests in Thee"). In this inner restlessness, whose meaning became clearer to him as he reflected upon it at every stage of his life, he found the "way" that led through many perplexities to God as the absolute in whom his heart attained its full "rest."

The inner obligation to seek for the absolute is the common starting point for an interpersonal clarification in which all can participate—the believers and unbelievers of the West as well as the wise men of the East. This is that common ground that Cuttat designates as "spirituality"; that the Christian conceives of as a "restlessness unto God"; that the declaration of Vatican Council II on non-Christian religions describes as the "inquietudo cordis hominum" (the restlessness of the human heart). A common intellectual effort to understand this fundamental characteristic could form the narrow base on which men of the most varied religious persuasions could meet, broaden their perspectives, and find access to a new search and a new discovery of God. In my *Psychology of Belief in God*,[11] I have described and analyzed in more detail this phenomenon that is common to all men. This restlessness manifests its effects also in those who describe themselves as unbelievers. Despite all the skepticism that, for modern man, often bars the road to God; despite all the confusion of the various concepts of God that shroud him in darkness for the man of today; despite the vehement denial of God that fights with clenched fist against the old God and announces his "death," modern man carries within him, even in his alienation from God, a gentle, sometimes even a turbulent, longing for God. With his renunciation of Christian belief in God, man did not lose every need for the absolute. Even in the soul of the unbeliever who, to judge by externals, seems to have found his equilibrium in unbelief, an inner restlessness makes itself felt and, now and then, bursts forth unexpectedly. This phenomenon can be described more exactly through the medium of literary self-documentations.

Implicit in man's restless striving is a dull a priori knowledge of the goal. But because the conscious ego does not know this fulfilling goal; because it is, in fact, natural for seeking man to labor under a long and profound illusion about the concrete nature of the absolute that he seeks, his search must follow a path that is long and rich in dis-illusionments *(Enttäuschungen)*, a path that can stretch out through the whole of man's life. None of this alters the fact, however, that man's striving is linked to an a priori knowledge of the absolute that can bring him fulfillment, and that only his persevering effort and patient expectation will lead him to the goal. Indeed, the very dis-illusionment that seeking man experiences by reason of his erroneous and premature determination of the goal serves no other purpose than to inform the conscious ego out of the depths of the soul about the discrepancy between the false absolute toward which it presently strives and the real absolute whose nature it does not yet comprehend. To man's natural craving, the ego presents what it believes to be the absolute only to receive from that craving the disappointing answer: Not this; it must be something else! Only when the soul replies: This and nothing else! is man's restlessness stilled, has his search been transformed into the blissful repose of fulfillment. Like the experience of disillusionment, the experience of fulfillment can be properly understood only when that which shines forth as the absolute has been judged and "recognized as genuine" by man's natural craving.

There is no other way for man to discover the direction of his striving for infinity than through self-recollection, through attentiveness to the demands that arise from the depths of his soul to pierce the quickened surface of his consciousness. Those who have followed this way to its end and have found fulfillment there affirm again and again that it is the indispensable means of eventually arriving at the absolute. The man who does not listen to this deep place of his soul lives, for the most part, in direct dependence upon his senses and is consequently easily inclined to regard the experience of sensual ecstasy as a satisfaction of his uncomprehended striving for infinity. In the thrill of the first moments of ecstasy, the secret of the universe seems to have been disclosed to him. But the ego that believes it can lose itself in ecstasy is forced to acknowledge, to its sad disappointment, that the river of sensual enjoyment does not flow deeply enough, that only the surface of the soul has been stirred, that the striving for infinity only seemed to have been satisfied in the brief whirlwind of turgid consciousness, of ecstatic ravishment.[12]

Even when the ego hurls itself in a frenzy into the whirlwind of ecstatic enjoyment, it cannot "lose" itself therein as it would like to do; again and again, it is cast back upon itself. If man strives for an absolute communion of love, he discovers that every sensual embrace remains somehow "on the outside." Just as salt water only seems to be able to still thirst, so it is with sensual ecstasy. Instead of relieving thirst, it makes it more pressing until it becomes a painful search that cannot be satisfied by any forced union with the deified objects of one's drives. Significantly enough, we find sexual ecstasy present in many of the various Eastern religions although there are many others that reject it as an aberration. Even Augustine was not spared this false passage. The resultant dis-illusionment made him realize that a true fulfillment of man's striving for infinity is possible only in the spiritual sphere. What is the true intent of man's striving for infinity? It is a striving toward a being that can be to the ego its "one and all." The soul does not want to depend on a multiplicity of objects in time and space; it does not want an undetermined generality of unspecified content. It wants *one* reality, one self-subsistent, unparceled reality. But this one is to be conceived not as one of many other possible or actual "ones," but as a one that is, at the same time, an "all," that encompasses the whole universe, that is the absolute value from which all other objects derive their merely relative significance. The soul strives toward an absolute that combines within itself both the highest simplicity and the richest multiplicity; an absolute that does not possess its value partially and, therefore, subject to loss, but that contains within itself an absolute value that is subject to neither loss nor change.

Man's noblest possession is his spiritual possession of self, which is the most characteristic inner quality of the human person. But Buddhism does not recognize its significance. For this reason, the Buddhist too often misunderstands the demands of this inner core of his personhood. In the last analysis, it is not enough for man to cling to and become one with an impersonal absolute. On the contrary, his deepest striving is a yearning of love that seeks a personal encounter and a communion of love with an absolute personal being.

If Augustine, after years of inner growth toward maturity, comes to the realization that man does not find his satisfaction within himself, but is oriented toward a final goal that is absolutely superior to him, yet penetrates him utterly, that the subjective state of perfect fulfillment [*Voll-Endung*] consists in a communion of love between the finite creature and the divine Creator, it should be noted that this transcendental analysis derived from his experience of life is illumed by the light of a concept already familiar to him from Christianity. God, he discovers, is not something alien to man's nature; man's orientation is toward God; he has been made for God. As he looks back over the course of his life, Augustine makes his acknowledgment: "Creasti nos ad Te" ("Thou hast made us for Thyself"). The possession of God in knowledge and love is, therefore, something that corresponds to man's nature; committing oneself to God does not mean the sacrifice of one's own personhood, but rather its fulfillment and exaltation.

When no previously accepted intellectual belief in God illumines man's religious striving, on the other hand, it seems almost impossible for the man who must depend upon his own resources to achieve his goal. He is constantly exposed to the danger of projecting his own desires, of worshipping his own desires in the gods whom he adores, of seeking to affirm himself in his concepts of God. By his own resources, man cannot escape from his confusion. It is only God himself, as Klostermaier has said, who can so touch man's inmost soul "that belief in God is the deepest possible answer that can be evoked. Christ says that only that person can come to him who has been called by the Father" (Klostermaier, p. 107). This is, actually, the new doctrine of Christianity, that God, in his revelation through Jesus Christ, speaks to man's deepest being and calls for an

In Search of the Absolute

answer, calls personally, but without thereby compelling man to answer "yes." Man can also answer "no," or he can, in his spiritual sloth, neglect to respond at all.

The mystic Jan Ruysbroeck explains to us what constitutes the final experience of the Christian:

> In our simple being, where we are one with God in His love, there begins a praeternatural contemplation and experience, the highest that man can express in words. It is this: to live while dying and, while yet living, to die out of our being and into our supernatural bliss. This occurs when we gain mastery over ourselves by the grace and help of God so that we rid ourselves of all images as often as we desire to do so in order to arrive at our simple being where we are one with God in the bottomless abyss of His love. There we have all that we need, for we have God within us; we are blissful in our being by the action of God with whom we are one in love, though not in being or nature. But we are blissful and bliss in God's being, in which He rejoices Himself and all of us in His exalted nature. That is the kernel of love that is concealed from us in darkness and in a bottomless ignorance. . . .
>
> When I stated that we are one with God, I meant this: in love, not in being or nature. For God's being is uncreated; our being is created. There is an endless difference between God and the creature. Although they can be united, they can nevertheless not become one. If our being were to become nothing, we would be unable to know, love, or be happy.[13]

In these words, Ruysbroeck is clearly at variance with the teaching of Master Eckhart, who not only calls man's striving for infinity—which he designates as a "small spark in the soul"—unequivocally godlike, but also stresses man's eternal existence in the mind of God so strongly that the reality of man as it exists in time threatens to be swallowed up. According to Eckhart, the difference between God and nature, between Creator and creature, seems to have been overcome by the man who is mystically united with God. Yet Eckhart's teaching, as a thorough study by a Buddhist has recently revealed, remains in the sphere of Christianity and is unambivalently distinguishable from the ontological concept of becoming one with the absolute that is the usual interpretation in the East.[14]

In Hinduism and Buddhism, belief in a personal God and the religious goal of union with God in love are certainly not unknown. But they are regarded—in Amida Buddhism, for instance—as a descent from the height of pure spirituality to an anthropomorphically popular concept of God. More than other forms of Buddhism, the Amida school has remained a strongly popular religion. In it, we have a form of Buddhism that is averse to the concept of self-redemption and that directs man in need of salvation to the redeemer figure of the Buddha Amida, the Buddha of mercy. There are certain unmistakable parallels here with the Christian belief in God. The man who has fallen prey to the world, to suffering, and to sin seeks consolation and grace from the Buddha Amida and hopes, through the grace of Amida, to be received into the "Pure Land" of the next world.

A very similar form of piety is that of the Hindu Bhakti Buddhism, which cultivates a personal *devotio* to a God who is conceived of as a person, although it reveals, in its overwhelming hypertrophy of purely subjective feeling, shameful distortions of the image of God and of man's relationship to God.[15]

However, belief in Amida, the Buddha of wisdom and of great mercy, who appears even today in many forms of Buddhism, might well form a bridge of understanding between the Western and Eastern concepts of the absolute. Besides the "Buddhism of meditation" with its basically monistic Mahayana philosophy there exists, in noteworthy and thought-provoking actuality, the "Buddhism of faith," which seeks a divine object of its devotion that it often represents as female.

Despite the fact that there still exists a considerable difference between this faith and the Christian belief in God, nevertheless a great obstacle to transcendence to a personal God is here essentially diminished, though not totally overcome. This obstacle is basically the arrogance of an autonomy that rejects every redemption from without and consequently seeks the absolute only within itself. Only when the will to self-glorification and self-redemption has been transformed into a humble readiness to receive God can the Eastern way be further developed into belief in a personal God.

The search for the absolute that Cuttat calls "spirituality" is the common basis of all genuine religion; we find the marks of this spirituality in Yoga and Tao as well as in Zen Buddhism and, under another form, in the Bhakti and Amida schools also. There is then, as we have already noted, a common foundation that links all forms of devotion and that might become the unitive element of a genuine dialogue. This common foundation, it must be admitted, is not something as clearly discernible as, for instance, what used to be called "natural religion." Such a phenomenon is a rational abstraction with no historical reality. A common ground that has been overrun by the luxuriant growth of historical religious forms must first be stripped bare before a fruitful dialogue can begin.

The intellectual way to God must begin with man's concept of himself. As long as Buddhism lacks a full understanding of man's personhood, it cannot be expected to understand the concept of a personal God. Not until man knows that he stands in God's presence as a created person before a personal Creator-God will he have any real awareness of the uniqueness of his person and its immortal soul. It is not enough to ascribe certain personal aspects to a Brahman that still remains impersonal. For in that case that which man learns through meditation, that with which he wants to be ontologically one, will still belong to the apersonal sphere. It is a part of me or I am a part of it. But only objects that are conceived apersonally can thus enter into one another; it is not possible for persons to do so. Persons, in the proper sense of the term, have a personal inner space, a psychic self, that can never merge itself to the extent of becoming ontologically part of another person. Just as a man remains a person to his fellowman and affirms his fellowman as a person in his own right without wanting to absorb him into the self, so a personal encounter with God cannot consist of the merging of the one into the other. An encounter at the primordial level demands that the persons allow each other to exist, that they mutually affirm each other.

It is only when the individual himself discloses his interior, reveals to the other his thinking and willing, "opens" himself to the other that that unique meeting of persons, that standing eye-to-eye, is possible that is imcomparably exalted over every merely ontological union, which is understood as an entering into another. I can concentrate, in the sense of meditation, only upon myself; in doing so, I can reach as yet unknown and deeper levels of my self. But I can never meet another as person in this way. That can occur only when the other also reveals himself to me; when we, as it were, meet each other eye-to-eye. Every attempt to possess the other ontologically violates the free personal core of his being; it cannot fail to wound him most deeply and cause him to close himself entirely to this invader of his privacy. Persons can meet only on the level of free self-revelation.

If it can occur on the purely human level that a man comes to a totally new consciousness of himself through a loving encounter with a fellowman, it can occur in an even more extraordinary manner in man's relationship to God. Only the man who knows that he has been touched by the eye and the love of God is fully awakened to his eternal meaning. There can take place in him that which Eckhart calls the birth of God in the soul. At this point, the level of intellectual and spiritual technique has been left behind. What are important are self-revelation, commitment, requesting and receiving, gazing upward, and adoring. As long as the Eastern seeker after wisdom conceives of his own ego or that of the other as only a kind of microcosm, as a conscious synthesis of all the apersonal values of the universe, an apersonal explanation will be sufficient to explain it to him. Whoever, on the other hand, has become aware of the personhood of himself and others, whoever actually recognizes and acknowledges himself as a person who has been called into existence, cannot fail to realize that both he and the universe must have had their source in a personal omnipotence. By his primordial command, a divine person must have called both man and the universe out of nothingness and into existence, must have placed them before his face. God as Creator belongs to a personal concept of the absolute. Thus man is rescued from the comfortless notion of an eternally recurring life cycle. He is not a faceless mask progressing from birth to birth after birth. He is a unique creature called into being by the person who created him, set upon his life's course, not destined to end somewhere in nothingness, but to find in an eternally loving union with God his complete perfection.

The Yogi stops at the threshold of the full awakening of his person and of holiness. He remains closed within himself, a spirit monad, really open neither to his fellowman nor to God. "The paradoxical combination of a comprehensive monism and an isolating dualism marks yoga as 'monadism,'" says Cuttat. He continues,

> Asiatic spirituality includes a genuine, intensely spiritual depth, but it is a lonely depth, lonely in respect to God and, therefore, also in respect to the neighbor. When I visited the revered ascetic Purushottomanada at the foot of the Himalayas as he meditated motionless for hours at a time in the circle of his disciples before the cave in which he had lived almost without nourishment for twenty years as a hermit, both of the above-named dimensions of Eastern spirituality were clearly evident: on the one hand, a profound interiority that spiritualized the aged countenance of the Master and gave it a luminous repose; on the other hand, the restless self-orientation [*kailvalya*] of both Master and disciples, their complete lack of inner relationship to each other. To my repeated question as to whether even the slightest mutual relationship existed between the inner self of one yogi and that of another, I received always the same reply: at this stage, every relationship has been excluded; the self of all who have been liberated is a unique, unduplicated self; thus Christ, Shankara, and Buddha are indistinguishably the same person [*derselbe*]—or, perhaps, the same substance [*dasselbe*]. In the East, this radical monadism of Asian spirituality seems to me to lend all genuine contact between men, such as friendship or love, the paradoxical character of latent loneliness. Innumerable Europeans living in India—even those who prefer Hinduism to Christianity—admitted to me that they had tried in vain, even with the closest and most friendly Hindus, to reach that degree of psychic intimacy that we regard as the essence of friendship and love: it was as if the Asiatic avoided almost involuntarily in the deeper level of his soul any glance into the soul of another. Was he afraid that in this intimacy he might become fully aware of his radical finiteness? (Cuttat, pp. 109–10)

The will to autarky, the withdrawal into himself, the modest concealment of his own feelings, the attempt to be sufficient unto himself, to achieve a self-contained and self-centered perfection—these are signs of the cramped character of the unredeemed soul. It cannot be redeemed until it experiences the appeal of an absolute Thou whose self-revelation reveals his being to be that absolute love in which he created man and called him to himself. But this absolute love of God becomes credible to the person who has retreated into himself only when he experiences the appeal of fully selfless love in a Christian witness to the faith.

BUDDHA AND CHRIST

Comparisons between Buddha and Christ seem to present themselves unbidden. Human beings in vast numbers have followed both of these great figures in the history of mankind, calling themselves "Buddhists" or "Christians" according to their founder. At first glance, a comparison in the context of religious history reveals certain similarities. At approximately the same age, both left their father's house; both exchanged home for homelessness having first spent some time in solitude; and then, as peripatetic teachers, both gathered around themselves disciples who, after their death, carried on their work and caused it to spread throughout the world.

But the parallels that suggest themselves to a first superficial comparison conceal too quickly the decisive differences that existed between the two figures and affected their nature. It becomes suddenly clear to what extent they differed from one another when we consider the end of both their lives. Buddha, having lived his course, died at a ripe old age, probably of a natural ailment caused by the fragility of old age, although the suspicion of a malicious poisoning cannot be totally excluded. His peaceful death was attended by a great throng of his disciples; they honored the distinguished Master with their reverence, anxiously surrounding as he lay dying him whom they had made their hero in his lifetime. While still in the flower of youth, Jesus Christ, on the other hand, suffered the death of a criminal. Condemned to the most dishonorable of deaths, banned from the religious community to which he belonged, reviled by his triumphant enemies, surrounded by a gaping and mocking crowd, he died a slave's death on the cross. According to the words of Jesus as they have been transmitted to us by the gospels, this death on the cross was not an unexpected catastrophe, but stood in essential relationship to his mission. The first witnesses to the faith also affirmed and emphasized this fact.

In these very different kinds of death, we are confronted with a basic difference and a contrast. By his gospel, Jesus Christ attacked the "old"; he proclaimed something "new" and revolutionarily different. He opposed a firmly established spiritual tradition and, in doing so, met resistance from those who had been, until then, the religious leaders of the people. Deeply upset and angered, his opponents did not rest until they had "brought him to nought" *(ver-nichtet)*. This "annihilation" belongs—and on this all the first witnesses to the faith are unanimous—to the work of Jesus Christ; on it rest his personal resurrection as well as the future life of the church he founded. Jesus Christ forced those to whom he had come to a decision. By their "yes" or "no" to his teaching, they came to the parting of the ways—a parting that began at that time, but that would become a final parting in another world. He appeared as the light of the world, and it became evident that many preferred darkness to the light. His apostles and disciples shared his lot of forcing men to a decision and a parting of the ways and of being brought to nought by his opponents. Whoever confesses him must expect the same fate that befell him. In fact, nearly all of his first disciples died for him as "witnesses in blood."

Jesus Christ entered a world that was laden with intellectual, religious, and political tensions. Although from the perspective of the dominating Roman Empire the Jewish nation was but a splinter of people on the edge of the great world, it had behind it a long history of religious leadership. The Jewish believers were consciously the "sons" of their "fathers." They were proud of the fact that they were the bearers of a great promise from God. Thus they lived in expectation of the leader who had been promised and who would establish "God's kingdom" upon earth. While they sighed under the political domination of strangers—a fact they found particularly degrading because "heathens" exercised power over them, the "chosen people of God"—their expectations rose to fever pitch. Without their conscious volition, there had been added to their religious longing for redemption a craving for political freedom. Therefore they were looking for a liberator from their masters, for one who would help them to shake off the foreign yoke and restore the throne of dominion to those to whom, in their opinion, it belonged—to those who had been called and chosen, to the children of the nation whom God had called to power. In fact, this politically oriented longing for redemption had repeatedly aroused men who considered themselves called to bring this very redemption to fulfillment. They were inspired by the national spirit of the people, which had so colored their imaginations that they had deluded themselves into believing they had been called and, in this belief, they blindly and fanatically attacked the existing political power. In the process, they were destroyed.

Like these narrow-minded fanatics, Jesus was also concerned about the coming redemption. Salvation lies in the future. All that is past is a preparation for what is to come or, more exactly, for what he will bring. But he did not belong to the ranks of those who receive their "call" from the spirit of the people. He firmly rejected the political vulgarization of the concept of redemption and located the kingdom of God within man. He remained in the sphere of the religious and did not allow himself to be lured to the lower level of the political. In the end, it was this fact that caused his rejection by the people. The fanaticism of the national religious leaders had moved too far toward the politicization of the Messiah concept to permit them to accept with open hearts the message of Jesus. Rejected by the religious leaders of the people to whom he had been sent, he was condemned to death and executed. An essential element in the teachings of Jesus and Christianity is the intellectual orientation toward the future. This, too, Jesus had in common with his opponents. But he differs from them about the source of the salvation that is expected.

In contrast, Buddhism has no comparable orientation toward the future. On the contrary, it is, as we have already shown, directed toward the past; it wants to destroy what is present to lose itself once more in the beginning.

It is characteristic of the intellectual climate in which Buddha and Buddhism throve that it was a time without great tensions. Men did not suffer under foreign domination; they needed no popular leader who would direct their urgent affairs toward a goal. In this predominantly peaceful and intellectually exhausted period, there were no great political or intellectual or religious goals around which men might have united. There prevailed instead, especially in noble circles, a boredom with that life of which man longed to free himself, but from which he could find no escape. The Hindu was inclined to flee the world. Surfeited with a stagnant culture, many waited for the announcement of a way in which they could cast off their burden. They longed for release, for a loosening of the bonds of life, which they called "fetters," but not for the liberation of energies that would press for realization in deed.

Buddha's greatness lies in the fact that he followed the path of liberation from the world in a way that many regarded as exemplary and therefore adopted for themselves. But Buddha did not urge, as Christ did, a discernment of spirits. He did not appear as the light of the world that compels men to decide whether they will follow the light or darkness. The discernment that Christ demanded of men had as its counterpart the separation from sins that they were no longer willing to bear; Buddha required this separation only of those of his disciples who became monks. Buddhism proper is a community of monks who have cut themselves off from the world and who regard the imparting of their doctrine to those still in the world as a regression. Buddha had no desire to offer something "new"; he wanted only to point out the "ancient way." Of course there were opponents who disapproved of him and found much in him to which they took exception; discontentment existed even among some of his disciples. But these oppositions did not become a matter of life and death. They were, in fact, settled rather peacefully.

Nietzsche, who often made an excellent point with one caustic remark only to weaken it with the next one, is right when he says of Buddha as a religious founder that he discovered the kind of men who were attuned to him, and discovered them, in fact, "scattered through all the classes and social strata of his people, who were good and good-natured (and above all inoffensive) out of sloth; who were abstinent, likewise out of sloth, and lived almost without needs: he understood how men of this kind must inevitably roll, with the whole *vis inertiae*, into a faith that promised to guard against the recurrence of earthly toil (that is, of work, of action in general)—to 'understand' this was his genius." [1]

It is possible to prove that Buddha, as he himself knew and emphasized, introduced no new teaching; from the most ancient traces of Hindu monasticism and of Brahminism, "the historical development proceeds in a direct line to Buddha, who abandoned his loved ones and all that he possessed in order to wander homeless in the yellow garb of a monk and contemplate redemption." [2] This explains to some extent the fact that what we discover behind all we hear about Buddha is not a concrete individual person, but only a type.

In the case of Jesus Christ, the opposite is true. He does not belong to that group of persons who, because they are the product of their age, can be understood only in terms of that age. Popular favor did recognize him briefly as the national leader and political liberator who would fulfill men's expectations. But Jesus disengaged himself unequivocably from those expectations. Because of his intellectual superiority, he neither let himself become entangled in the cunningly devised questions of his antagonists nor allowed the well-meaning advice of his disciples to distract him from the clearly defined path of his unique mission.

With his serenely authoritative declaration: "Amen, I say unto you . . . ," he penetrated the barriers that men had erected to preserve themselves from a direct encounter with the living God and addressed the conscience that established every man in a direct relationship to God.

A political leader addresses himself first to man as a member of the collective, to the man who meets with others en masse on a lower level. But for Jesus the political sphere is the sphere of the temporary, which must yield before that which alone is important, before man's decision in favor of God and the recovery of the sinner from his alienation from God. Those who have been disappointed in their short-sighted hope, who do not want to penetrate into the secret chamber of conscience where they will have to stand naked before God, become angry and cannot forgive Jesus because he does not remain on their level.

Yet in all that is essential—in their belief in a personal God of the universe who calls men to himself—Jesus is one with the people from whom he comes and to whom he has been sent. His relationship to his Father, on the other hand, is a "unique" one that is not to be simply equated with the relationship of others to their fathers. Because of the uniqueness of this relationship, his words possess a crystal clarity and relevance that illumine the hidden places of the motives by which men are led to shun the light. He rejects, for instance, as an aberration principally due to the blindness engendered by sin the particular interpretation that his own age had conferred on its longing for redemption and opposes it to address sinful man on a deeper level, to redeem the "sinner" from his forlorn entanglement in worldly things and return him to the house of that Father of whom he is, in a unique way, the emissary and son.

Jesus Christ is merciless in his destruction of self-made religious guarantees, relentless in his attack on the Pharisaism that seeks salvation in a self-imposed legalism while it ignores the definitive moral demands that the divine Creator has imposed upon men. Jesus Christ tears away the masks of moral and religious hypocrisy to restore man to a direct relationship to God, to tell him that he is nothing in himself, that his justification consists, above all, in the grace that emanates from the personal love of God. To Jesus, a religious self-justification that renders God's commands ineffectual by bending them to its own will is "nothing." He reorients man totally to God and promulgates his demands for an intensification of moral and religious concern as a new gospel, distinct from what had been said to men of old.

What poses the greatest obstacle to man's redemption is, in fact, the blindness of the sinner. It is only the recognition of his "nothingness" and sinfulness before God that predisposes man for the redemption that comes to him through grace. But because the religious leaders of the people had fallen into the error of believing that their racial membership in the nation whose fathers had received God's promise of a redeemer relieved them of all necessity of moral conversion or penance, they saw the position they had arrogated to themselves endangered through Jesus, who revealed their hypocrisy publicly before all the people. They became obdurate in their attitude, plotted his death in their official capacity, and sought for a means of putting him to death legally so they might afterwards continue undisturbed in their self-justification.

In the end, these blind men were condemned by their own deeds. For Jesus came into the world as judgment, as the light that was to show men the way out of the darkness they had created for themselves. But the majority preferred darkness; they were unwilling to take upon themselves the toil and self-conquest of a conversion; they were unwilling to make the painful admission of their nothingness and sinfulness. Therefore, they became angry in their hearts and planned to assault God's emissary. They plotted evil and carried it out. Without willing or intending it, they thereby cooperated in the work of redemption. For it belongs to the work of redemption that Jesus should deliver himself as a victim to his enemies and should die the sacrificial death required of him by the Father. Through this death, the blind are to be shaken out of their self-justification and are to come to conversion. By it, they are again faced with a decision. But if they reject even this last offer, they will have called down upon themselves the blood of the just one and will have subjected themselves to the lot of eternal and final damnation.

The deepest reason for sinful man's alienation from God is his disobedience; from it, as from their deepest root, proceed all sufferings. If Jesus Christ proposes to heal men even to the very roots of their being, his person and his work form the constitutive elements of redemption. To the man who denies God out of pride and disobedience and in an effort to be something by his own efforts, Jesus Christ, as God's son and emissary, opposes his "kenosis," his emptying of self, the voluntary suppression of the likeness to God that is his by nature, to repair by his obedience the disobedience of men.

In a pregnant formula, the apostle Paul summarized the basic meaning of the act of redemption in his letter to the Philippians: "Christ Jesus . . . though he was by nature God did not consider being equal to God a thing to be clung to, but emptied himself, taking the nature of a slave and being made like unto men. And appearing in the form of man, he humbled himself, becoming obedient to death, even to death on a cross. Therefore God also has exalted him and has bestowed upon him the name that is above every name, so that at the name of Jesus every knee should bend of those in heaven, on earth and under the earth, and every tongue should confess that the Lord Jesus Christ is in the glory of God the Father" (Phil. 2:6–11).

What Jesus Christ taught is more than just a neutral and objective way of wisdom that frees those who follow it from all toil and trouble. What he revealed is more than just the order of a universal law that might as easily have been discovered and taught by someone else. In his own person, he presented himself to his Father in heaven in place of man who had fallen into sin. Through his sacrificial and loving act, he effected man's redemption and won for him, not only in the universe but even in the history of man and his world, a central position that binds him also to the Kingdom of God. Jesus Christ is the "alpha" and the "omega" of all history, which is not merely a world process following its natural course, but a history of that decisive choice in which weak and sin-laden creatures in need of redemption encounter God's judgment and his will to save.

Jesus Christ is not just another of the countless gods of the Hindu heaven, who resemble man in many respects, especially the moral one, and who, like man, are transitory. He is the preexistent one through whom the world was created. He is the "brightness" of God's glory, "the image of his substance" (Heb. 1:3). "For even if there are what are called gods, whether in heaven or on earth (for indeed there are many gods, and many lords), yet for us there is only one God, the Father from whom are all things, and we unto him; and one Lord Jesus Christ, through whom are all things, and we through him" (1 Cor. 6:5–6). This unique Son took upon himself the nature of a powerless slave. Christ voluntarily emptied himself of his divine mode of existence, in the sense of sacrificing the manifestation of his power, and exchanged it for the mode of existence of man, whose historical existence is one of obedient service. "For you know the graciousness of our Lord Jesus

Christ—how, being rich, he became poor for your sakes, that by his poverty you might become rich" (2 Cor. 8:9). This self-despoliation is founded on Christ's loving will; through his loving deed, he becomes the Head of the redeemed church: ". . . He is the head of his body, the Church; he, who is the beginning, the firstborn from the dead, that in all things he may have the first place. For it has pleased God the Father that in him all his fullness should dwell, and that through him he should reconcile to himself all things, whether on the earth or in the heavens, making peace through the blood of his cross" (Col. 1:18–20).

The debate about the so-called demythologizing of the gospels that is carried on with every means of modern philological textual criticism has shown that if we cannot write a biography of Jesus Christ, we can, nonetheless, point with certainty to a historical Jesus. Today, we possess so many verified results of New Testament research that we can study the real historical Jesus without running the risk of ending with a modernized reconstruction of what Jesus was like.

As the Göttingen exegete Joachim Jeremias has shown, there are five achievements of contemporary research that save us from constructing a picture of Jesus too hastily. They are the findings of literary criticism; the conclusions resulting from research into the history of (literary) forms, which distinguishes the individual levels of tradition one from another; our enhanced knowledge of the milieu in which Jesus lived; the identification of his mother tongue; and the realization of the eschatological character of Jesus' gospel. It was ascertained only a few years ago that Jesus spoke a Galilean Aramaic. Careful philological attention to detail has had its reward. In many instances, it is possible for us to determine, from an extant translation, what the original Aramaic expression must have been. "By this method, the Pater Noster, for instance, which contains many variations in the Greek texts of Matthew and Luke can be reproduced in the language of Jesus with a high degree of probability."[3] "Of particular importance in this regard is the discovery that this kind of study is able to determine individual characteristics in Jesus' speech habits that do not correspond to contemporary usage. The word "abba,' for instance, by which Jesus addresses God, has no parallel in the entire literature of late Jewish prayer. Nor are there contemporary analogies for his introduction of his comments by the word 'amen.' Yet these two characteristics of the *ipsissima vox* of Jesus, we may well believe, contain *in nuce* both his gospel and his consciousness of mission" (p. 22).

Jesus' whole gospel rested on his knowledge of God's approaching entrance into human history, on his knowledge of God's coming in judgment. In speaking of it, he proclaimed the advent of the Kingdom of God in the present. Jesus was not merely a Jewish rabbi, a sage, or a prophet. His message from God, who even then bestowed upon the despised, the maltreated, the hopeless, their share in salvation, contradicts all the religious tendencies of the time and even reflects the end of Judaism.

Joachim Jeremias has summarized for us the conclusions of a critical research that has made careful and discreet use of the methods at our disposal today. We come upon

> a unique claim to sovereignty that transcends the limits of the Old Testament and of Judaism. Throughout the gospel of Jesus, we encounter this latter claim, that is, we encounter the same demand for faith [in his person and mission] that we find in the *kerygma*. It is necessary to speak explicitly here of what is simplest and most obvious because the meaning is no longer obvious. That is to say: Every sentence of the sources witnesses to it, every verse of our gospels emphasizes it: something has happened, something that is unique, something that has never happened before. One can heap up parallels and analogies gleaned from the history of religion. . . . Yet the more analogies we heap up, the clearer it becomes. Jesus' message has no analogy. There are no parallels to Jesus' revelation that God wants to commune with sinners, not with the just, and that even now he permits them to share in His kingdom. There are no parallels to Jesus' sitting at table with tax collectors and sinners. There is no parallel for the sovereignty by which He dares to address God as Abba. Anyone who accepts the fact—and I do not see how it can be rejected—that the word 'abba' is the *ipsissima vox* of Jesus, anyone who understands it correctly and does not detract from its meaning, is faced with Jesus' claim to sovereignty. Anyone who reads the parable of the Prodigal Son, which belongs to the bedrock of tradition, and observes in the process that Jesus uses this parable, in which he depicts the incomprehensible and forgiving goodness of God, to justify his sitting at table with tax collectors and sinners—such a person is also faced with Jesus' claim to be the representative and plenipotentiary of God. Examples could be multiplied, but the result is always the same: if we use with discipline and conscientiousness the critical means that are at our disposal, our efforts to discover the historical Jesus are repeatedly reduced to one truth: we stand before God himself. That is the unique truth to which the sources bear witness. A man appeared, and those who heard his message were convinced that they were hearing the word of God. It is not as though faith were taken from us or even made easier when exegesis reveals to us that behind every word of Jesus and every one of his deeds there stands his claim to sovereignty. . . . (pp. 23–24)

From the reports of the Evangelists, there emerges a completely individual person who cannot, however, be placed in any of the usual psychological categories. Every psychological explanation of the person of Jesus in terms of these or those analytical principles is repeatedly contradicted or supplanted by another, yet in such a way that no explanation ever totally suffices.

In his mission of salvation, Jesus Christ, as the Good Shepherd, searched for and found the man lost in sin just as the anxious shepherd searches for and finds the sheep that is lost, frees it from the thorn hedge, and brings it back to the flock. His mission, therefore, is a mission of person to person. For many, the encounter with him is the beginning of a long process of choosing and becoming, as it was for his apostles, whose individual characteristics and vocational histories are plainly illumined for us in the concise reports of the gospels. Jesus Christ had the courage to consort openly with known "sinners"; even prostitutes were not driven away from his protective presence. He came as a physician who treats not only those who are physically sick, but also those who are sick in the very core of their beings. He knew how to exert every variety of influence upon men, from gentle reminders to thunderous threats of judgment. In their personal relationship to him, men come to the full consciousness of their religious calling. Yet he left man his full freedom; he tyrannized over no one; he was never fanatical; he aroused no frenzy in the masses; he drove no one to fanatical excitement by overzealous ideas. His action was like a ray of light that brightens and warms without noise. Just as light makes visible what is bright or dark, so his action makes visible both the bright and the dark places of man's soul. For this reason, he is the judgment that has come among men.

The intellectual world in which Buddha appeared is entirely different from the world of Jesus Christ. The differences are readily apparent. The most formative influence on Buddha was his origin. He was not descended from the caste of Brahmins, who were the religious leaders; no special Vedic learning has ever been ascribed to him—a fact that perhaps explains why he derived no preconceived ideas or modes of thought from the Brahmins. Like his contemporaries, on the other hand, he was influenced by the general religious spirit of his age. The fact that he belonged to the caste of the nobles explains the initially esoteric circle of his disciples. It is characteristic of the religious attitude of the time that it had no living belief in a personal God although it believed that Prajapati had created the world. This belief recurs again and again. But Prajapati was no longer regarded as a religious figure. There was no active link to him, no hopeful confidence in him as God, not even an anxious fear of him. Like the other gods, he had become a figure of speech that man might indeed use again and again, but the reality of which he no longer took seriously. For that reason, Buddha, too, could not become a "redeemer sent by God," for man "did not expect his redemption from a God" (Oldenberg, p. 301).

It was a time, however, in which man queried the "whither" and the "whence" of man and the world. From Buddha's broadly conceived sermons, we learn that these questions were often raised even in the circle of his monks. But it was impossible for them to do more than measure theory against theory, personal opinion against personal opinion, for there existed a complete lack of ability to think through objective reasons and thus to reach a decision based on thought. In Buddha's eyes, unproductive discourse prevented those engaged in it from attaining the reality that was his heart's goal, namely, the "enlightenment." For that reason, he renounced all such questioning, which, in his opinion, brought only restlessness, strife, and confusion; which was a contradiction to that which alone he sought, namely, the unshakable peace of emotions that can no longer be stirred by anything at all. With unwavering agnosticism, therefore, he rejected all questions about the metaphysical grounds of being; if anyone questioned him explicitly on that score, he kept silent in order not to give the impression he had decided for one or other side of the question. To this area that he labeled *tabu,* there belongs every attempt to arrive at a decision about ultimate truths by one's own effort. "Criticism," in its real sense, "the scrutiny of basic positions and concepts, and the attempt to arrive, by way of different opinions and counteropinions, at universal principles or syntheses"[4] was unknown at that time, as it is, for the most part, today.

Once the Brahmins had dissolved every active relationship to a personal Creator-God, the burden of religious activity was transferred entirely to their own actions. They became magicians who believed, by reason of their mastery of the holy word and the sacrificial rites, that they possessed, through their magic practices, more power than the gods themselves. The pedantry and exactitude to the point of absurdity that marked their reading of the *mantras* (true words) "becomes understandable against the background of the view that the *mantra* as such, that is, the exact sequence of certain letters in a certain manner or way, not the meaning of the words or any deity, produces the effect" (p. 62). The "word" that the Brahmins possess has existed as such from all eternity; it owes its origin to no person; it is unfailing in its efficacy. This is true as well of sacrifice: "God" is necessary only "as the *terminus ad quem* of the sacrifice" (p. 125). The effect is produced mechanically as an impersonal result of the rites and the *mantras.* The person who offers sacrifice stands at a critical point in the affairs of the world and so is able to influence the course of the release from *karma.* In a certain sense, the magician-priest of the sacrifice has control even over the deity. Thus the Brahmins could believe that priests were mightier than gods and that their power lay in their mastery of (religious) customs. Again and again, their poets praise rites, ceremonies, sacrifices, and hymns as the real givers of what is good.

Under the influence of this kind of thinking, Buddha was compelled to seek redemption in man himself, in man's own activity. Because he was not a Brahmin, their magical practices were meaningless to him. He had to find a substitute for them. This substitute is knowledge or, more precisely, the self-knowledge that produces self-redemption. But we must not understand this "knowledge" as a critically self-observant knowledge in our sense of the word. So-called objective knowledge is a relatively late phenomenon in the history of mankind; it was preceded by a mode of thinking "in which feelings, ideas, wishes, facts, experiences, and their effects are inseparably linked" (p. 77). What Buddha sought as he strove for salvation was a knowledge that would descend upon man like a supernatural power and overwhelm him.

For Buddha, who opposed an irremediable agnosticism to all metaphysics, even though in his innermost being he believed in an absolute, the knowledge that is salvation is concentrated in a very narrow sphere: in the realization of the painfulness of life, of inordinate desire as the root of all suffering in life, and of the renunciation of all desire in order to achieve peace of mind and to reach the state of nirvana in which nothing will ever again arouse one's desires—"nothing"—literally, "absolutely nothing."

When Buddha declared that all life is nothing but suffering, such a thesis already presumed a whole metaphysics, although such a metaphysics had never been clearly enunciated. In fact, it presumed as well a (likewise not enunciated) metaphysical concept about the origin of suffering, for according to ancient Hindu belief Brahman himself was responsible for the fall of the world and had incurred the necessity of permanent reparation. At the time, however, man's intellect lacked the trained power of critical thinking necessary for examining even this notion and testing its validity; moreover, it was rejected by Buddha himself as unessential and misleading.

Instead, a rejection built on sensitivity to and resentment of man's toil-laden life led to the further conclusion: all life is suffering; all life is nothing but suffering. Instead of attacking a single concrete suffering in the world and working to eliminate it, instead of attempting to master world and life, there is only the single, peremptory admonition: flee the world, extinguish the thirst for life, and suffering will cease.

Basically, Buddha's teaching consists of this one point. In monotonous and almost endless repetition, his sermons expound this one concept with no evidence of reflective or progressive development of thought. Again and again, the one universal doctrine is: everything is transitory and, therefore, full of suffering; to overcome suffering, desire must be put to death. But the reference is never to a single, actually concrete suffering of one man who might be helped if someone would come to his assistance. This constant circling around one point creates, in fact, the impression that what one is hearing is the stereotyped complaint of persons who in reality have nothing to endure, are well nourished, and cannot quite conceal a certain satisfaction with themselves—an impression created also by most of the statues of Buddha. Buddha, then, is not a savior who really heals man's concrete suffering. He does not, like Jesus Christ, receive the sick, the leprous, the exiled, the tax collectors, the sinners, the anxious, the confused, the seeking, the children. Jesus Christ not only showed his concern for those who suffered pain, hunger, thirst, illness, imprisonment; he identified them with himself and promised that he would reward what was done to them as though it had been done to himself. On the other hand, he threatened to punish those who neglected such help as if they had neglected to help him. In this way, he released a latent force that has continued to affect sub-

Buddha and Christ

sequent human history with ever new impulses. This spiritual force, once accepted into the hearts of men, changed the lot of slaves—not by organized efforts, but by a fundamental conversion of the human heart. In the Middle Ages, it changed the lot of lepers, the social outcasts; for the saints of the Middle Ages, for a Martin of Tours or an Elizabeth of Thuringia, those who had heretofore been outcasts became the "good people." At the beginning of the modern era, the same force exerted an influence that completely changed the lot of the mentally ill.

From these examples, it is clear how the Christian gospel produces its effect. There is no one-sided concern about knowledge or about a change in one's manner of thinking; concern is for a change of attitude in the human person as a whole, whose most exalted characteristic is the ability of the heart to love. For this reason, the principal commandments of Christianity are not simply demands for obedience to an established order, but commandments to love: first, to love God with one's whole heart, with one's whole mind, and with all one's strength, and then, according to the second commandment that follows immediately from the first, to love one's neighbor as oneself.

In contrast to Jesus Christ, Buddha was not a well-defined individual person from whom there issued positive impulses for the genuine healing and conversion of mankind. In the reports about Buddha, it is impossible to discern any concretely individual person. Buddha is the personification of a certain system. As Hermann Oldenberg has shown in detail in the classical work about Buddha that has been frequently quoted in these pages, Buddha is not an independent intellectual person who taught new truths. On the contrary, what came to fruition in him was rather the seed that had long been present in ancient Hindu asceticism and that has merely forced its way to a fuller consciousness in him. What is true of Buddha is true also of his circle of disciples. They are types, generalizations, interchangeable with one another. They possess very few individual traits that hint at a life history peculiar to themselves. The disciples are but reflections in miniature of Buddha himself. "In the time between Buddha and the establishment of the tradition, India was perhaps more lacking in creative personalities who might have given this great movement a new direction and impressed upon it the stamp of their own individuality than it had ever been before; the ancient Buddhist church had no Paul" (Oldenberg, p. 135).

In Buddha's sermons, there is unmistakably present the fixed type, the bloodless generality.

> The rhythms of these sermons, with their rigid and inflexible uniformity on which there falls neither light nor shadow, are reflections of the world as it appeared to the eyes of those communities of monks, of the gray world of comings and goings that pursues its pain-filled course with an eternally even pace and behind which lie the motionless abysses of *nirvana*. No inner activity, no seeking, echoes through the words of this teaching. All seeking

lies at a distance, behind him who has overcome. . . . This preaching never penetrates to the hearer with the force that resides in the words of a dominant personality, or with the firmness that is inseparable from such a force. No fierce compulsion to believe; no bitterness against the disbelief that remains aloof. One word, one sentence, follows in monotonous quiet after another, regardless of the significance or lack of it in what is expressed. . . . Thus there are multiplied those endless repetitions that Buddha's disciples never tired of hearing again and again and that they honored at each repetition as the indispensable garment in which the holy thought was clothed." (pp. 172–73)

When we open the Christian gospels by way of comparison, "we find there the tenderest and deepest traits of Jesus' action as it penetrates—caring, comforting, healing, and restoring—from his person to the persons of those around him. How different is the picture that the Buddhist community has preserved of the action of their master; how poor in every detail that touches upon personal life and its mysteries. The living human traits disappear behind the outline, the formula; it is the suffering of the whole world that diverts his gaze again and again from every individual personal suffering so that the spirit may thus be fortified to follow the road that leads beyond all suffering" (p. 178).

There was no dramatic penchant in the monks who wrote these reports—a sign that they had no intention of writing a personal biography of the life of an individual. Buddha's disciples serve no purpose other than to say "yes" to the words of the Master, to hold their tongues in confusion if malevolent opponents are present, or to be converted if they are as yet unconverted. There is no indication whatsoever that a conversion had a history of personal decision and change.

In Buddhist sermons, the theme of "suffering" never refers to the genuine and actual sufferings of an individual. It does not refer to the sick man, sinking into despair after being lame for thirty-eight years; it does not refer to the widow who has lost her only son; it does not refer to the woman who has fallen into sin, but whose heart is burning with shame and repentance. It does not refer to the slow and pedagogically skillful guidance of a Simon Peter who is thereby weaned from his stormy temperament and his overpowering vision of the Kingdom of God to an intellectually deeper understanding and to an insight into the necessity of the sacrifice the Messiah must endure. It does not refer to the winning back of a Thomas from his own obstinate wrong-headedness to a joyously luminous belief in the Resurrected One.

Anyone who compares Jesus' farewell address with that of Buddha soon recognizes the essential difference between the two. Jesus knows what awaits him; but he also knows whither he is going. Jesus knows the dreadful fate that will be his; yet he can promise his followers that he will remain with them to the end of the world. The dying Buddha, on the contrary, when he knows he is approaching his end, can offer his disciples no consolation except the single thought that, since it is all transitory, it serves no purpose to excite oneself about it.

What makes Buddha Buddha is his knowledge of the four holy truths. Because he has received this knowledge in its full greatness, he is the "Enlightened One." In this knowledge, which was later disseminated in fixed formulas, lies redemption. All unredeemed suffering, moreover, comes from ignorance, whereas all redemption depends on the knowledge of the basic truths and their formulas. Buddha brings no redemption that is linked to his own person. Without his person, as Oldenberg has pointed out (p. 300), Buddhist doctrine could still be what it is in all its essentials; it is conceivable apart from the person of Buddha. If Buddha does, in fact, play a great and significant role in Buddhism, his person is, nonetheless, theoretically unimportant. His name is not mentioned in the four holy truths.

If redemption lies in recognizing the four holy truths, it follows that every disciple is basically able to attain this knowledge and so to become a Buddha. In the parable of the chickens that emerge from the hen's eggs, Buddha makes it clear that, in the opinion of the Master, every disciple can actually reach the same rank. The first to emerge is the oldest of identical offspring and is different from the others only in the fact that it was the first in time to escape from the egg. It was the first to break the eggshell of ignorance; but the others do so in precisely the same manner.

If Buddha in his departure from the world freed himself, as he said, from all arrogance of life, all arrogance of riches, and all arrogance of health, it should not be overlooked that he also exposed himself to a new arrogance—the arrogance of his knowledge of the enlightenment. If it cannot be clearly determined whether the elevation of the "Exalted One" was accomplished only at a later time by his disciples or took place in his own time, Buddha himself seems nevertheless, according to the reports, to have been filled with a consciousness of his own uniqueness as a result of his knowledge of salvation. He seems to have considered himself the only fully Awakened One—that is, the only Buddha—of his age. In the eternal revolution of world events, in which there is no beginning and no end, every age is supposed to have its Buddha. There is, then, not one, but, if we regard all times, an infinite number of Buddhas.

Buddha's disciples fostered Gautama's elevation to the dignity of a Buddha. Intellectually dependent as they were, they needed the firm ground of infallibility. By raising Buddha to the status of an idol, the community of his disciples transcended all the boundaries of earthly and human reality. The communal belief that was in the process of formation did not hestitate to set upon Buddha's head the radiance of a glory that illumined the universe.

Buddha is only the first to have experienced an enlightenment that his disciples could gain in the same manner. For that reason, the dying Buddha was able to answer the complaint of his disciples that they were losing their teacher with the words: "After my death, the doctrine and order that I have shown you, have explained to you, will be your teacher."[5] Through his deification by his disciples, however, Buddha was raised above the simple role of teacher, above the gods themselves, even above the most sublime of the gods, above Brahman himself. It was customary for Hindu thought to transform a natural, earth-bound event into the fantastic contexts of infinite space and time. The longer the disciples made the person of their master the subject of their respectful reflection, the more often their thought reverted to it, therefore, the more the human element tended to disappear to make place for the dream component, the typical, the fantastic, and the universal.

Therein lies one of the reasons why the figure of the historical Buddha was multiplied into a limitless number of past and future Buddhas. Because man wanted the satisfaction of having a redeemer for his own lifetime too, his thought, as it roamed in fantasy in the endless vistas of time and space, gradually transformed Buddha into a type that would reappear in every age of the world. Buddha himself did not promise that his teaching would endure forever. He promised his closest friend Ananda that it would endure for five hundred years, after which time belief in him would disappear and a new Buddha would arise to set in motion once more the wheel of doctrine.

In the minds of believers, the idealized Buddha became the seat of all perfections, the image of supreme power, supreme knowledge, supreme peace, supreme mercy. The real Buddha was an agnostic who had nothing to say about the foundations of being and purposely cut short any questions on that subject. But the idealized Buddha says: "I am the conqueror of all, the all-knowing, untouched by all that is. I have abandoned all things; I am without desires, one who has been redeemed. Of my own power I possess knowledge; whom should I call my master? I have no teacher; there is none who can be compared to me. In the world with its gods, there is no one who is my equal. I am the Holy One in the world; I am the supreme Master. I alone am the perfect Buddha; the flames have been extinguished in me; I have reached *nirvana*" (Mahavagga I6, 8; quoted in Oldenberg, pp. 304–5). Descriptive epithets are heaped upon him; he is called the "Exalted One," the "Bringer of Joy," the "Bringer of Peace," the "Eye of the World," the "Prince of Victory," the "Supreme Master of the World," the "Perfect One."

The fundamentally rather banal and ordinary experience that all existence is transitory and painful is glorified into a "supreme insight" and a source of wonder to men and gods. After Buddha's "enlightenment" under a tree, the "gods" pay homage to him. "Now in this community of gods, my disciples, thousands of gods came to me and after they had come they greeted me respectfully and placed themselves at my side. . . ." (quoted in Dahlke, p. 86).

Even Brahman, heretofore the greatest of the gods, becomes in this apotheosis of Buddha a mere figurehead whose only role is to serve this glorification. Because the "Enlightened One," after experiencing his great enlightenment, wants to keep and enjoy it for himself and is not prepared to proclaim his holy truths to men, even Brahman grieves that the world will be destroyed if it does not learn this truth. He bestirs himself in all haste, humbles himself before Buddha, folds his hands, and pleads insistently with the "Exalted One," the "Blessed One," the "Lord," to reveal the truth that he has discovered. But Buddha does not yield quickly; at first inclined to refuse, he then surveys the world with his "Buddha vision," allows himself to be stirred to pity for impure men, and, after Brahman has made his threefold petition, grants him his request.

Buddha addresses his disciples in this fashion:

> Conqueror of All, Omniscient am I,
> untouched by all things,
> having left all things, liberated and
>   freed from thirst!
> I have understood by my own power—whom
>   shall I follow?
> For me there is no teacher; there lives no one
>   who is my equal.
> In the world with its gods, I have no rival.
> I am worthy of veneration in the world,
>   I am the incomparable teacher.
> I alone am the fully Awakened One,
>   I have grown cool, I have gained *nirvana*.
> To turn the Wheel of Doctrine, I go to Kasi, the city.
> Beating the drums of the Deathless One in a blinded world. (p. 42)

Here, too, it is relevant to compare Buddha with Jesus Christ. As it is reported in the gospels, the attitude of Jesus Christ to his Father in heaven, to whom he is utterly obedient, is far different from the relationship of Buddha to Brahman, who, although he is actually the highest of the gods, has become a theatrical figure whose only function is to confirm Buddha in his self-elevation to the dignity of Buddhahood.

In the case of Jesus, however, obedience unto death on the cross is followed by glorification. For that reason, he can demand an unconditional confession of faith in his person. Only one who confesses him before men will he confess before his Father in heaven. One who denies him before men, on the other hand, he will also deny before his Father. He knows himself as the one to whom the coming judgment of the world has been entrusted. Precisely this knowledge makes him superior to those who cause his death. When he comes on the clouds of heaven to judge the world, all mankind will be compelled to appear before his judgment seat. Buddha can demand no such belief in himself. He dies because he is subject to the transitoriness of all things. He can do no more than refer those whom he leaves behind to the doctrine that will be their substitute for his teaching.

It remains to compare the reports of the miracles wrought by Jesus Christ in his lifetime with those reported in accounts about Buddha. Here, too, the difference is plainly visible. In the gospel reports, the miracles of Jesus form part of his work of salvation. The reports of miracles in the legends about Buddha's life, on the contrary, are obviously later additions and often stand in direct contrast to what we know about the historical Buddha. If Jesus Christ performs miracles, they are intended as proofs that he has really been sent by his Father. His miraculous deeds are often inseparably linked with utterances that have survived the sharpest critical scrutiny. From no point of view are they to be regarded as belonging on the periphery of his mission or as a secondary work added by popular belief or as a later tradition of the believing community. Jesus performed his miracles in full public view, without the magic struggles of a medicine man or a shaman, but rather in majestic sovereignty. He performed them, moreover, despite an icy atmosphere of mistrust and disbelief. Hate has the keenest vision, and there were no keener critics of Jesus' miracles than the contemporary religious leaders of the people. They were men who, by their education and training, were well-fitted to reveal false miracles for what they were and to expose publicly the occasional failure of a practicer of magic. Yet they never denied the actuality of Jesus' miracles, but only misinterpreted them. They accused Jesus of being in league with Satan. In the case of some of the miracles, the words by which Jesus commanded the sign were so deeply impregnated in the memories of those who heard them that even in the Greek text of the gospels the original Aramaic sounds have been preserved as an erratic sequence. Thus Jesus once bade an already dead girl to arise with the words "'Talitha cumi'. . . . And the girl rose up immediately. . . ." (Mk. 5:41–42). On another occasion, Jesus restored hearing to a deafmute with the command to ear and tongue: "'Ephpheta,' that is, 'Be thou opened'" (Mk. 6:34).

It is otherwise with the reports of miracles in the legends about Buddha's life. It is significant to remember that Buddha's activity was directed to something quite different from miracles or the healing of the sick and sinners. Such activity does not fit the historical Buddha, who saw his task as setting in motion the Wheel of Doctrine. The reports about Buddha's miracles are, as we have said, obviously later additions. According to the *Mahapadana Suttanta,* a "Great Sermon about Legends," Buddha was not regarded as one who had achieved perfection by way of inner struggle and enlightenment after years of searching; on the contrary, he was already, at the time of his birth, the perfected Buddha who had descended into this world from a world beyond. His descent was accompanied by the most fantastic miracles. Upon the descent of the future Buddha into his mother's womb, "there appeared in the world with its gods, with its Maras and Brahmans, its gods and its men, an immeasurably great splendor, surpassing the divine Majesty of the gods" (p. 68). The future Buddha was surrounded in his mother's womb by four sons of gods at each of the four points of the compass. It is said repeatedly that the mother-to-be was thus protected from every sickness so she might remain healthy and free from all physical complaints. By way of contradiction, there exists, however, the fact that Buddha's mother was by no means free from physical complaints and sickness; a few days after the birth of her son, she fell victim to them. This fact was later reinterpreted and construed as a necessity: It had to be thus!

In a fantastic vein and contrary to all probability, it is said of the newly born Buddha: "Immediately after his birth, the future Buddha strides forward in seven long steps, his feet pointing straight ahead, his face turned toward the north, while a white parasol is held over him; he looks in all directions of the compass and speaks the mighty word: 'I am the most excellent in this world! I am the first in this world! I am the highest in this world! This is my last birth! No further existence is required of me! . . . Then there appears an immeasurably great splendor, surpassing the divine majesty of the gods . . . and this system of ten thousand worlds trembles, shudders, and quakes" (pp. 70–71).

At the death of the venerable Buddha at the age of eighty, some sources mention a sickness, bloody discharges, and violent pains—an account that has aroused the suspicion that he had been poisoned. A doctor was summoned to the fatally ill patient. Other sources recount, however, that the gods assembled in great numbers around his deathbed; that they wept at his passing and mourned because the eye of the world had disappeared.

The later apotheosis is, then, clearly distinguishable from the actual facts, which reveal the objective reality with which Buddha regarded himself as a transitory being, no different from all other men. Nevertheless, this later apotheosis tended more and more to place Buddha on the throne of the personal Creator-God whom ancient India revered under the names of Prajapati and Brahman, but who were later driven from their places—or, more accurately, whose significance was later shrouded in forgetfulness. In many Buddhist sects, Buddha has become a substitute for the forgotten God of the World. Prayers are offered to him and mercy is expected from him.

The result of our comparison of Buddha and Christ is unambivalent: It is not permissible to place the two side by side on the same level as "religious geniuses." Jesus Christ claimed to be the only Son of his Father in heaven, sent by him as a mediator of salvation. As the mediator affirmed by the Father through his miraculous deeds, he brings men religious salvation in a positive sense. He is the only mediator, the alpha and omega of history. Buddha, raised above all gods by his apotheosis, does not even lay claim to such a mission. He claims to be the Buddha of only one age in the history of the world. Before and after him, there are countless others.

FROM EMPEROR WORSHIP
TO BELIEF IN GOD

Japan did not inherit its religious mien from Buddhism alone. Before Buddhism came to Japan, another religious force—Shintoism—was already there. Shintoism did not remain long in the shadow of its at first intellectually superior rival. Although in the beginning it often formed strange alliances with Buddhism, it later resumed the religious leadership of the Japanese people. Its essential tenet was the belief that the emperor was the son of God. If Western Christianity hopes to enter into fruitful dialogue with the religions of Eastern Asia, and especially of Japan, it will do well not to limit its intellectual encounter to Buddhism.

When, in the middle of the sixteenth century, the zealously proselytizing Francis Xavier and his first companions stepped onto Japanese soil after inexpressible hardships and heard of the indigenous emperor worship, the saint quickly formed a plan: to seek out the emperor in his palace in Kyoto and, through discourse, to convert him and the bonzes of the nearby imperial university to the Christian belief. Obviously he envisaged a Japanese emperor who was as powerful as the king of his native Spain and the Buddhist university as similar to the Spanish university at Salamanca. The journey on foot through Japan to Kyoto was fraught with unbelievable difficulties. But when he arrived barefoot and ragged in the vicinity of the imperial city, his Basque blood flowed faster. He danced for joy; he had reached his goal; the emperor would be converted and the people would not be slow to follow.

But he was doomed to disappointment. No one was willing to admit into the presence of the emperor this ragged stranger who arrived with no attractive gifts. He learned, moreover, that the "son of heaven" enjoyed no real power. The emperor's children were even compelled to beg and it was obvious that he had no means of exerting his influence over the people as Francis Xavier had hoped. Xavier was compelled to change his missionary techniques. He did so with quick decisiveness and was successful.

Until Japan's defeat in World War II, official Japanese emperor worship persisted in Japan. It was the victorious Americans who insisted that the ancient cult of the emperor, as the force that had driven the Japanese people to such wild fanaticism during the war, should be abolished. The Christian missionaries expected to be able to breathe freely thereafter. A strong bulwark seemed to have fallen and the way seemed free for successful missionary work. But they were deceived. Although in nearby Korea after the war a spiritual and religious revival brought many seekers to the Christian church, missionaries to Japan did not enjoy the same success. Even today, the number of Christians remains an infinitesimally small minority that seems to grow, percentage-wise, more slowly than the population as a whole.

In searching for the reason, we propose an answer that has yet to be proven in all its details: The soul of the Japanese people is not receptive of Christianity because it is still deformed by the aftereffects of the ancient emperor worship. To understand this, we must turn back the pages of history.

The official history of Japan begins with the year 660 B.C. Japanese historians explicitly emphasize, however, that this year indicates only the beginning of the earthly dominion of the most ancient imperial dynasty. Even before that time, the emperor's ancestors had held sway in heaven. In Japanese mythology, no God is recognized as the absolute lord of the world and its moral order. The gods are believed to have had their origin in chaos.[1] According to a primitive myth of creation, the primeval god Izanagi and the primeval goddess Izanami created the first island so they might settle on it. But Izanagi surrendered his ruling power to the sun goddess Amaterasu. It was she who sent her grandchild Ninigi-no-Mikoto to earth and established him as the first emperor of Japan. He brought three things with him from heaven: a jewel, a sword, and a mirror. Even today, these imperial insignia are preserved in Japan: the jewel in the imperial palace in Tokyo, the sword at Atstuta Jingu, the mirror in the great shrine of Ise. This shrine is regarded as the holiest in Japan. Under a chief priest, seventy-four priests serve in this holy place. Until the present day, the three treasures are passed on from emperor to emperor. At least once in his lifetime, every Japanese is expected to visit Ise and to pray at the holy shrine. According to an ancient tradition, every prime minister visited Ise at the beginning of his time of office.

Until very recently, Shinto sages have sought, with every evidence of scholarship, to prove that the Mikado is an "Arahito-Kami" ("a god incarnate") and that the cult of the emperor represents the soul of Shintoism.

When the first Christian missionaries were turned away from the entrance of the imperial palace in Kyoto, however, the Mikado was almost totally without political power and was living in abject poverty. He was obliged to live on the money sent him by some of the great ones of the realm. In his "palace," which was little more than a pile of masonry, he and his numerous retinue led a distinctly uncertain life. Nevertheless, the mysterious and unapproachable son of god lived in the hearts of his people.

Fr. Cosme de Torres, a companion of Francis Xavier, has given us the first account of the emperor:

The ruler who holds the post of honor is called Vo. The honor is hereditary. He is held in the same veneration as if he were one of their idols and they worship him as such. He is not permitted to set his feet on the ground. If he does so, he is removed from office and his place of honor. Therefore, if it is necessary for him to leave the seclusion of his home, he does so in a palanquin or in slippers or wooden sandals a span in height. He does not leave the seclusion of his home and it is difficult to meet him face to face. Usually, he sits with his sword on one side, his bow and arrows on the other. . . . Although this Vo is so venerated and holy, there are, nevertheless, three conditions on which he can be removed from office: 1) as we have noted above, if he sets his feet on the ground; 2) if he kills someone; 3) if he is not a very peaceful man. For each of these reasons, he can be removed from his office and the dignity that pertains to it, although he cannot be put to death for any of these reasons.[2]

For centuries, Japanese emperors lived in a mystic half darkness, scarcely recognized by the powerful princes, yet venerated by the people as a *kami,* that is, as a supernaturally divine being. "In many regions of Japan, the veneration of the Mikado as the divine successor of Amaterasu was deeply entrenched in the hearts of the people, who clung tenaciously to the old Shinto belief despite the progress of Buddhism and despite the Mikado's centuries-long powerlessness and helpless poverty. This fact was revealed at one time by the appearance of the bonze Nichijo Shonin, about whom we have Frois' report of 1569" (p. 133). On the pretext of wanting to help the emperor regain esteem, position, influence, and riches, he sold every particle of the false imperial relics for precious money and built with it a Buddhist monastery.

Whereas the emperor, shrouded in an unapproachable nimbus, was the highest divine authority on earth, whom no one ever saw or heard, it was the great lords who exercised the real power under which the people humbly bowed. Liege lords and vassals took advantage of the emperor's weakness. Whenever the opportunity presented itself to elevate themselves at the expense of another, they did so. To their subjects, the lords showed inhuman cruelty. The missionary Fr. Valignano of Chieti reported in 1583: "On the slightest pretext, they kill their subjects and regard it as no more serious to bisect a human being than a dog. This is true to such an extent that many, if they can do so without danger to their own persons, bisect any poor person whom they happen to meet in order to test the keenness of their *katanas* (swords)." In war they raze villages and murder the inhabitants. To escape misfortune and imprisonment, they readily lay hands on themselves. "But what is more horrible and against all natural order is the fact that mothers often murder their own children, either while they are still in the womb or by drowning the newborn infant after birth. And they do so merely to avoid the trouble of rearing them or, as they say, because they are poor and cannot feed so many children."[3]

In a world of ancient feudal traditions—until the Meiji reform, there were some three hundred royal courts in Japan[4]—the subject had no rights in respect to his lord, the child had no rights in respect to its parents; only that individual could survive who humbled himself and bowed in polite subjection. Hypocrisy is the weapon of the weak who are deprived of their rights. Valignano had already noted with reference to the Japanese character that the self-controlled friendliness and politeness of a Japanese is a mask that conceals his true feeling and causes his words to be ambiguous and deceitful. It is best—or so the Japanese seems to think—to have no opinion of one's own, but to bend as a single reed with the collective motion of the whole grain field. This typically Japanese worldly wisdom has its classical expression in the three famous monkeys over the temple entrance in Nikko; one covers its ears, another its mouth, the third its eyes. They symbolize the three "no's": "Hear nothing," "Say nothing," "See nothing." For the Japanese, Christ's demand that man's speech be a simple "yes" or "no" is something foreign; he finds it crude and lacking in refinement. His ambiguous thinking is reflected in the confusion and ambiguity of Japanese writings. The Japanese offers deep-seated resistance to the long-overdue reform that would bring unambivalent clarity to the literary language and writings.

The concept of an authority exercised from above is reflected in the whole hierarchical social order even to the smallest social group, the family. Here it is the father who "lords it over" wife and children as their absolute master; in consequence, the Japanese regards the father as a curse and counts him among the five great evils of the world, placing him immediately after earthquakes.

A century ago when Japan became a modern state and began to write its constitution, a German professor of constitutional law was invited to assist in the undertaking. The choice fell on Hermann Roesler who, in the *Kulturkampf* under Bismarck, had had the courage to become a Catholic and had thereby lost his professorship in Rostock. Even his patient efforts, however, were not sufficient to remove the mythological nimbus from the first article of the Meiji constitution. He had proposed the reading: "the Japanese Empire is a forever indivisible hereditary monarchy." But his suggestion was not accepted. The final version read: "The Great-Japanese Empire is ruled by a Tenno of the continuously unbroken line of descent (bansei ikkei)." It ran counter to Roesler's scholarly integrity to include the myth of the eternity of the imperial dynasty in the basic first article of the constitution, but he was unable to prevent it. The public regarded his views as completely untenable.[5]

Other occurrences that are totally incomprehensible to Western man reveal how reluctant even the enlightened modern Japanese is to allow the myth of the eternity of the imperial dynasty to be destroyed. The following is an experience of the Englishman A. Morgan Young, editor of the *Japan*

Chronicle, a newspaper highly regarded throughout Eastern Asia for its fearless criticism. In 1935 the director of a school perished in a fire in his school—a not unusual occurrence since most of the schools were built of wood—because he considered it his duty to rescue from the flames the portrait of the emperor. Young added to his report the comment that such self-sacrifice was sad and certainly contrary to the will of the emperor. On the following day, Young was summoned before the head of the police force who explained to him with great earnestness: "I understand very well that an Englishman or an American might think in this way; the Japanese view is incomprehensible to them. For us, it is God (and he struck the table with his fist). A Japanese would be severely punished if he had written what you have written, but since you did so out of a lack of understanding, I shall merely warn you." [6]

This was not a case of overreaction by some backward provincial official or insignificant civil servant. On the contrary, the head of the police force represented a view that was held even in the highest scholarly circles. This is further proven by the fact that, in the same year, a professor of political history at the Imperial University in Fukuoka taught that the mythological thesis of the "eternity of the imperial dynasty" was possible on historical and constitutional grounds alone and that it was indispensable to the existence of Japan. He taught without circumlocution: "According to our religious conviction, the emperor is not merely a man, but the personification of the goddess of the sun, who bestows life, light, warmth, and hope upon men and all other creatures. For this reason, our emperor is always inspired by the ardent desire to contribute in every way possible to the general good of mankind." The goddess of the sun, so the professor taught, had given Japan to her grandson and his successors in perpetuity to be ruled in the spirit of her own "limitless creative love." Since the goddess had constituted the emperor as ruler, the professor continued, his will was never dependent upon the people; the Meiji emperor who had given the new Japan its new constitution on February 11, 1889, had presented it out of the fullness of his power as a more exact explanation of the task entrusted to him by his ancestors and, clothed in the garb of the supreme Shinto priest, had sworn in the holy place never to allow the hereditary line of imperial descent to be destroyed.

Despite the extraordinary regard in which he was held, an "enlightened" professor of constitutional law like Minobe, a professor at the Imperial University in Tokyo who designated the emperor as the "organ" of the state—albeit the "highest"—saw his books relegated to the flames and the old belief reinforced by a government decree proclaiming that Japan's emperor, who is descended in an unbroken line from the goddess of the sun, is the bearer of the highest authority and that any constitutional theory that would make the emperor an instrument of the state was contrary to national policy. The decree was supported by the military leaders, who regarded the current ideology as indispensable for their purposes.

As Joseph Roggendorf, who is well acquainted with conditions in Japan, has remarked:

> The tendency toward a military dictatorship was an accurate reflection of the attitude of the people, who enthusiastically joined martial youth organizations, gymnastic clubs, and partiotic women's societies; who took part in the denunciation of leftist agitators and foreign spies; and who turned their backs in scorn on party politics. The leaders, moreover, were careful to cultivate throughout the nation the atmosphere of the ritualistic emperor cult that had gradually become customary in the barracks. Schools were required to make constant pilgrimages to the national Shinto shrines; instruction was preceded by a common prayer recited in respectful obeisance toward the imperial palace; the Imperial Edict on Education had to be read on festive occasions by the school director clad in formal dress and wearing white gloves; and the "sacred likeness of the emperor" could be possessed only by those schools that could give proof either of a fireproof place for displaying it or of a perpetual guard.[7]

The cult of the emperor was the ideology that flared into fanatical chauvinism and gave the impetus for Japan's last war, which the Japanese call the "Great East Asian War." It began with the destruction of the American fleet lying at anchor in Hawaii in a daring attack that was camouflaged with great cunning up to the very last moment by prolonged diplomatic negotiations.

"No one who knew Japan at that time," Klaus Mehnert reports,

> will ever forget the impression: the eruption of more than seventy million people, equipped with the machines of modern warfare and the mentality of a race that entered battle clustered around their leader, believing in his divinity and in their own likeness to God. At that time, I spent some years in regions occupied by the victorious Japanese. The least Japanese soldier regarded himself as the offspring of the goddess of the sun, as vastly superior to Chinese, Americans, French—and Germans. We learned, then, to know the Japanese from a side that we recall without enthusiasm. It was almost the opposite of the modesty, charm, high culture, and sensitivity that we had hitherto encountered in Japan.[8]

From a German university professor who spent the war years in Japan, we hear the following: "The tremendous initial victories served only to strengthen the military in their stubborn arrogance. Prisoners of war were treated with a terrible ruthlessness that resembled the barbarity of the feudal wars of the Japanese Middle Ages rather than the chivalry with which the Japanese had behaved toward the Russians even at the beginning of the century or toward the defenders of the German colonies in the First World War. Even the civilian population in conquered regions fell victim to a crude chicanery that must have created the psychological conditions necessary for guerilla warfare" (Roggendorf, p. 57).

What happened in Japan happened in a similar way in Germany during the years of the Third Reich. From what we experienced ourselves, therefore, we can acquire some understanding of those events in faraway places that at first seem so alien and inhuman to us. It is easy to speak with a too hasty facility about "Asian fanaticism and Asian cruelty" and, whether or not they express it, there are many among us who believe, in their pharisaical arrogance, that such a thing could not happen in Germany. Yet the atrocities of German "war criminals" and "criminals against mankind" are scarcely less monstrous than the deeds of the Japanese in their last war. It is too easy, moreover, to regard these deeds merely as the acts of sadists who were driven to their atrocities by their perverse natures. In the ambivalence of their natural impulses to good or evil, men are alike the world over. During the juridical actions against war criminals immediately after World War II and the later processes against the major National Socialist criminals, those who were present were repeatedly astonished that the accused so seldom gave the impression of being criminals, that nearly all of them regarded themselves as innocent and claimed only to have performed their duty of obedience to the "Führer." Doctors who had tortured prisoners to death by testing their endurance to cold, for instance, remained undisturbed before the court even when they saw films recording their experiments, explaining that doctors cannot afford to be moved too readily to pity. Others disappeared again after the war into private life as harmless and sometimes even kindly citizens, whose "peaceloving nature" was doubted by no one. Their often gruesome crimes against the individuals who were delivered to them are comprehensible only in terms of a complete bypassing of an ethically formed conscience in favor of a fanatical "belief" in one man who was raised by mass suggestion to be the idol of a nation. By their belief in the absolutely definitive word of the Führer, every cruelty was transformed into a "hard measure," an indispensable "sacrifice" that was essential for reaching the great goal set by the Führer. The shocking thing is how fully men can call upon an idol to justify their proceeding "with good conscience" against the most fundamental demands of conscience and can later defend their conduct as a duty demanded by obedience to their Führer.

We are confronted here with the typically and universally human phenomenon of creating "false gods." It is not only primitive "fetish worshipers" who serve false gods. The scholarly study of "nature" religions has shown that the "fetish cult" is by no means as primitive as it was once believed to be. It is not normally the self-carved "fetishes" themselves that are worshiped; they are merely the symbols of powers that exist beyond and above the world. In its proper meaning, a "false god" is a divinized creature that is deified and to which man binds himself in the fanatical belief that he will thereby, without any secondary considerations whatsoever, receive precisely the results for which he hopes. Only such a fanatical belief in false gods can lend men the diabolical strength to trample in the most brutal manner upon their fellowmen.

In every man there dwells a primitive need to bind himself in faith to an absolute with which he rises or falls. Even in the world of modern man, who is often alienated from the religion into which he was born, there exists the need for at least a substitute religion, however different it may be in type from any genuine religion. In his study of "disguised religions," Carl Christian Bry has investigated the aberrations to which the need for substitute forms of religion can lead.[9] A specific characteristic of a "disguised religion" is the fanaticism that is lacking in genuine religions. A genuine religion, in its consciousness of an essential dissatisfaction with this world, seeks the goal of human life in the next world and therefore accepts earthly things as they are in their insufficiency. The person who is fanatically devoted to an idol believes that paradise can readily be achieved in this *aevum* provided that which is already present and hidden in the world, but not yet recognized as a bringer of salvation, can be brought to victory in a fanatical religious struggle. This paradise that lies hidden behind the present moment seems to be his justification for demanding every sacrifice of himself and others. Precisely the infatuation that hopes to see and realize the absolute in the things of earth drives the person who serves false gods to the humorless fixation of a fanaticism in which he remains characteristically removed from every genuine religious attitude.

The comparison of Nazi fanaticism with the Japanese cult of the emperor, which provided the impetus for the last war, must be corrected in one aspect, namely, that it was not merely the two-thousand-year-old cult of the emperor that drove Japan into the senseless war, but a mass ideology that, although it rested upon the cult of the emperor, was nevertheless fostered by the military and geared for quick action. Since the opening of the country in 1868, the people had been indoctrinated with the belief that, in the last analysis, the nation could not survive without war, "and so there followed in the last fifty years a whole series of wars. . . . In fact, Japanese history is a history of warfare. From the time of Jimmu Tenno to the days of the atom bomb, only men of prowess were numbered among the really great of our country. Our people allowed themselves to be persuaded to this value judgment; they had been educated to it," wrote the Japanese X-ray scholar Nagai in his *Notes from My Deathbed*.[10] Actually, none of the ruling families who had exercised their power for seven centuries had disavowed the mythical authority that had come down to them from their heavenly origin, but the Shinto myths about heredity were no longer regarded by most Japanese as binding religious beliefs. It was the nationalistic strivings of the military leaders that revived and reconfirmed these beliefs and used them as a quick means of rousing the people to fanaticism.

Just as in Nazi Germany, there was a tyrannizing of consciences in chauvinistic Japan that forced Christians into severe conflict with their consciences. Throughout the country, training officers supervised the political formation of young people. Students at the Catholic Sophia University in Tokyo, for instance, were obliged to take part in the general veneration at a shrine for those who had died in battle. On one occasion, when the training officer ordered an obeisance, three Christian students remained erect because the obeisance seemed to them to be a service of false gods, a participation in a heathen cultic ritual. Immediately press and radio magnified the incident, presenting it as proof that the Catholic church was hostile to the fatherland. The existence of the whole university was thereby threatened. Only an official declaration that an obeisance at a Shinto shrine held no religious significance and a permission to church members to perform it created the possibility of survival. The Old Christians of Nagasaki were painfully affected by these latter events because, as they said, "It is now permitted to do something that was forbidden to our ancestors and for which they died by the thousands."

The pseudoreligious character of the chauvinistic ideology was most clearly revealed toward the end of the war by the senseless slaughter of thousands of civilians in occupied regions and the mass suicides that reached what can only be called hysterical proportions among the Japanese. Under the threatening shadow of defeat, the only acceptable conduct was the heroic death extolled as "gyokusai," the "Shattering of the Diamond."

On August 14, 1945, when the Japanese for the first time heard on the radio the voice of their Tenno as he announced to them the end of the war and the collapse and capitulation of Japan, there were many who felt the ground on which they stood was being removed from under their feet and they were falling into a bottomless abyss. Many, indeed, were so numbed by the catastrophe of losing the war that they were not aware of the full meaning of what they had lost. The political structure itself did not fall apart, although the Americans demonstrated before all eyes that the emperor possessed no divine attributes. The Japanese accepted without opposition the fact that the Shinto cult of the state had been stripped of its former character.

The answer to the riddle of why the capitulation was effected so smoothly, why all weapons were laid down at the emperor's command over the radio, and why the fiercely warlike nation became overnight the most peaceful and friendly of people lies "in the unique Silbe Chu—in the absolute and undisputed duty to obey the command of the emperor. The emperor had spoken and the war was over."[11]

Both the defiant heroism before the capitulation and the extreme servility after it are evidence that the Japanese had no individualistic awareness of self. They had preserved, even into the present era, the character of a large family "whose patriarchal and sovereignly ruling head was the emperor. Japanese collectivism, which consists of tradition, poverty, and insular inbreeding presumed the leadership of the emperor, who was honored as both God and father'' (Mehnert, p. 284). Awareness and the will to personal responsibility were little developed, whereas the will to obedience was all too strong. Shintoism was both the policy and the religion of the state; the people were neither inclined nor prepared to distinguish between them. There was lacking, besides, any kind of independent morality; what had hitherto existed was no more than the sum of those regulations that had been established by those who held the first places in the social order, by the elders, by parents, and, of course, by the emperor.

Hence it would have been possible to believe—and many Christian evaluators of the scene did so believe after the capitulation—that all the conditions were ripe for an encounter with the Christian belief in God. After the collapse of the former idol, the place that it had occupied in the Japanese soul seemed to be empty for a belief in God. But this expectation was not fulfilled. The feudalism that had persisted for thousands of years, spearheaded by the cult of the emperor, had produced such great deformations in the Japanese soul that they are still the greatest hindrance to a Japanese acceptance of a belief in God.

The real difference between the Christian God and the Japanese *kamis* (gods) lies in the fact that "kamis" are only numinous supraworldly beings who possess no moral authority whatsoever; on the contrary, what the myths report about them is often more offensive from a moral point of view than the normal behavior of the ordinary citizen. The Christian God, on the other hand, is the absolute moral authority. He is the absolutely Holy One, the guarantor of unconditionally valid moral duties that protect every single individual in his basic rights. In Japan, however, the individual had been too long trampled upon by feudal lords to have the courage to believe in inalienable and absolute basic rights whether for himself or for others. All education had been directed too exclusively to the mere drilling of rules whose meaning was never unambivalent. But the true road by which man finds his way to God is man's own conscience, that is, his awareness of absolute duties behind which the divine source of these duties gradually becomes clearer. Japanese history helps us to understand that the Japanese people have no such conscience, or—more accurately—that it has not been developed. The Japanese has no understanding for the concept of "sin" as a religious category, as an offense against absolute duties. But when all morality is contained in the sum of certain inculcated moral regulations, the conscience is deformed. The determination to make one's conduct right before men has impeded that other will to make one's conduct right before God.

The concepts of sin, guilt, and divine justice are almost meaningless to the Japanese. His "ethics" is limited to offenses against the social code, which prescribes penances of a particular kind for all such offenses. The notion that the individual must render an account of his actions to a divine judge has been totally suppressed by the duty imposed by society of justifying oneself before its representatives. For this reason, the need to win the acclaim of others is not, as it is in the West, a sign of weakness or vanity, but the essence of moral behavior. "To win approval and avoid disapproval is the quintessence of the Japanese ethic since they have no transcendent system of values" (Koestler, pp. 264–65).

The Japanese national epic, The Forty-Seven Ronin (*ronin:* retainers deprived of a master), proves that the worst offense for the Japanese is the offense against etiquette. It reveals before our eyes, in a way that is truly shocking, how completely the Japanese feeling for morality has come to be centered in the social code. According to Western standards, the content of the epic is "non-sense"; yet this epic is still a favorite with young and old, in the kabuki theater as well as on television. The epic is based on a true happening in 1703.

Having been summoned to court, a count who was unschooled in court etiquette failed to bring the expected gifts; in consequence, he was falsely instructed and appeared in court without the prescribed garb. For this failure, he incurred a twofold obligation. For the honor of his name, he had to kill his opponent; but his relationship with this lord obliged him to refrain from doing so. The customary social resolution of such a dilemma would have been for him first to kill his opponent and then to commit harakiri. But whereas his suicide was successful, his attempt to kill his opponent proved unsuccessful. As a result, his three-hundred-man retinue became ronin without a lord, obliged by the moral code to follow their dead lord in harakiri. Forty-seven of the most loyal among them decided, however, upon another course: to avenge their lord by killing his opponent although this, too, was a breach of their *chu,* of their duty to their highest lord. Since the opponent was difficult to reach in his fortified castle, there followed a whole series of criminal and cunning deeds by which the goal was finally achieved. They were at last able to storm the opponent's castle and kill him. In the end, all the survivors committed suicide. "Verily," says a Japanese proverb, "etiquette is weightier than a mountain, but death is lighter than a feather."

Even to the present day, the burial places of these ronin have been preserved and constitute a favorite goal for pilgrimages. It is customary to leave one's visiting card on the graves.

Among the people, the concept of honor once adopted by the samurai lives on. For that reason, the Japanese has no understanding for or definitive rejection of a moral misdeed. From his own experience, Arthur Koestler cites some examples that may be allowed to speak for themselves. He happened to be in Tokyo when the Russian writer Pasternak, whose book *Dr. Zhivago* had been forbidden by the Russian government, was called, in a resolution by millions of Russian citizens, a "swine that had sullied its own sty." The Japanese public refused to take a stand in the matter. Pasternak's novel was not translated into Japanese. When asked by Koestler, the Japanese PEN Club gave an explanation that contained the sentence: "I do not know if it is wise always to hold to principles" (p. 285). In a like manner, no Japanese ventured to judge Hitler's criminal actions as immoral; they contented themselves with the judgment "unwise." Unequivocal moral judgments are regarded as "unrefined." A clear "yes" or "no" is avoided in favor of a less definitive utterance.

The Biblical command, "Let your speech be 'yes, yes' or 'no, no,' " is, as we have noted, something shocking to the Japanese, who regards it as unutterably crude and "insincere." The Japanese has given the word *sincere* an entirely new connotation. It is quite possible to lie and still be "sincere" provided one observes the rules of politeness. To say directly and frankly what one thinks is "insincere." If someone wants to ask his neighbor to keep his chickens in his own yard so they will do no further damage, he pays a courtesy visit to the neighbor and speaks of every conceivable topic except chickens. Only after the farewells have been said does he say, as though by way of afterthought, "Your chickens are very amusing; they even visit us!"

The Japanese feel obliged to display absolute perfection before others, before society. For them, there is nothing worse than "to lose face." But this was easier to avoid under the old feudal order than in the complicated life of a modern industrial state. The result is endless complications in professional life and social interchange, for the Japanese are so sensitive that some persons have even spoken of a moral disease of the blood among them. They live in constant fear of being insulted, for even the smallest wound can be fatal.

The first command of the Japanese ethic is: "thou shalt not become an object of laughter." The Japanese know no humorous self-irony, but only a fatal ability to be insulted. The American anthropologist Ruth Benedict has proposed a distinction between a "guilt culture" and a "shame culture." The members of a society that possesses absolute standards on which the judgments of conscience are based have an inner understanding of "guilt" and "sin." Such ethical cultures are properly called *guilt cultures*. In quite the opposite direction, the ethical judgments of a *shame culture* are based simply on the values established by society. In judging another, the individual's inner sensitivity reacts not to the inner components of actual "being," whether or not it is known, but to the components of "appearance," of what is reflected. "Shame" is not experienced because of one's own transgressions, but as a reaction to the criticism of others. For the member of a "shame culture" there is nothing worse than to be laughed at publicly or to believe that this is the case. In both cultures, there reigns a very effective control factor that resides either inside oneself, as in a "guilt culture," or outside oneself, as in a "shame culture." The one who is ashamed is dependent, for his psychic integrity, on the judgment of those around him. For this reason, social regard is the Japanese counterpart of the pure conscience of the Western world. The deformation of conscience has led the Japanese "to see mortal sin in the poor fitting of a sash, but only a small gaucherie in mass murder."[12] For the Japanese, it is difficult to believe that a subsequent reincarnation is dependent on the merits of this present life or that in the next world heaven should be the reward or hell the punishment for things done in this world.

The absence in the Japanese people of an inner understanding of absolute values, of good and evil as such, has its foundation in thousands of years of deformation under the oppression of the feudal system at whose head stood the emperor as the son of heaven. Consequently, the Japanese ethic has concentrated on the pragmatic and the relative. The concept of one who stands behind man's absolute duty as its divine cause and source has been lost to the Japanese. He has no feeling for or understanding of God as the absolutely Holy One.

Now that the Japanese has lost, with the cult of the emperor, his intellectual center, his last point of ethical orientation, the great question arises whether the preconditions have thus been established for a new spiritual uplifting and an awareness that is referred to the individual conscience. If so, the Christian mission will have a new opportunity.

Japanese moral instruction in the old sense was forbidden after the war, but public discussion about it has not yet led to any clear results. New conditions in Japan seem, moreover, to urge the introduction of a genuinely moral instruction directed toward absolute ethical standards. For there are clear indications, among the youth of Japan, of an early acquisition of corporal and psychic maturity (acceleration) accompanied by a slower acquisition of intellectual and moral maturity (retardation). The consequent moral endangerment of Japanese youth finds expression in the growing numbers of juvenile delinquents. Ethical instruction is plainly a necessity—but how, if there is no clearly defined concept of man? There is no value-based morality or obligation to any particular basic insight into human life, human nature, or human goals. If these are not found, morality will sink once more to the level of training in the rules of etiquette. Japan is faced, then, with the great task of overcoming its former "shame" culture and replacing it with a "guilt" culture that has still to be won.

This also implies an understanding of the religious concept of God as it exists in Christendom. It is already evident that a new concept of God is slowly taking shape in Japan. The spiritual influence of Christendom is subliminally at work in the process—the Bible is read frequently. Equally significant is the fact that, in the minds of the Japanese populace, "the understanding of the transitional concept of God (Japanese: kami) is shifting from a polytheistic personal/impersonal to a monotheistic concept. Bishop Noguchi of Hiroshima sees in this phenomenon one of the deepest and most significant of the results that have been evoked by Japan's encounter with modern Christendom. From this perspective, it is also possible to understand the reasoning that led the Japanese Bishops' Conference, some years ago, to follow the long-standing example of the Protestants by at last permitting the word 'kami' to be used also in the Catholic Church as a designation for the Christian God."[13]

The Japanese X-ray scholar Takashi Nagai exerted, in this regard, an exemplary influence that had its effect in far-flung Japanese circles. His wife had lost her life when the atom bomb was dropped on Nagasaki; he himself had been so severely injured that he gradually wasted away. He not only pursued personally the road from the positivistic materialism of the age to a Christian belief in God, but also bore witness to his belief by his heroic attitude on his death bed. Hundreds of thousands of copies of his book *Notes from My Deathbed* were published in Japan. Nagai set the Japanese people an example by his own living of the Christian faith, thus showing his countrymen the way. He demands that those who were once the "sacrificial victims of a totalitarian Moloch" become critical students of their own national history, thereby to achieve a new self-awareness. The "cadet school philosophy" that had been forced upon them had demanded "depersonalization" to such an extent that they had "lost" their ego. "To sacrifice, destroy, or lose the adult, mature ego is the basic concept of this depersonalization." The reason why the demand for "depersonalization" had such drastic consequences for the Japanese people is primarily because, even before that time, "the value of the individual had been basically ignored." Intoxicated by the philosophy of depersonalization, the Japanese had come to believe that "life weighed no more than a down feather." After the collapse of his former intellectual world, Nagai had to rediscover his ego, learn to appreciate the freedom on which the ego depends, form his self, and let it come to maturity. "In order to rid ourselves of the remnants of totalitarianism and to exchange it for genuine democracy, it is above all necessary to reject in principle and in practice the notion that the individual is but a possession with no worth of his own. Only when the individual member has matured into a selfsubsistent organ does any undertaking develop into what may be called an organically controlled operation. Discover, then, your own ego!"[14]

For Nagai, the rediscovery of the ego was linked to a determination to envisage the final goal of human life and to "put oneself on the right course" that leads to the goal. That was his interpretation of Christian belief in God.

The last entries in the dying man's notebook reveal how little his faith was shaken by the explosion of the atom bomb and its fearful consequences:

> We who have survived, the eye witnesses of all that has occurred, are firm in this conviction: The catastrophe wrought by the atom bomb was no

punitive judgment of heaven upon us; on the contrary, it opened for us a glimpse of that sublime Providence that had some as yet deeply concealed but lofty goal in store for us. And I myself—I became on that day a totally impoverished cripple, left standing in the burning ruins with two small children in my arms. Yet faith told me beyond the shadow of a doubt that these occurrences contained a revelation of Providence although I could not yet discern the how or why. Now the months and weeks and days of three long years lie behind me. From the perspective of today, it becomes daily clearer how rightly my faith saw at that time. The atom bomb had to come to remove from my side those obstacles that blocked my way. Now at last I have reached the point at which I can begin to taste true happiness. It will not be long now before death visits me. But he, too, is but a gift, a messenger of God's love for me, its latest and greatest proof; a gift of God Who is love itself. (p. 222)

NOTES

Chapter 1

1. Ingeborg Y. Wendt, *Geht Japan nach links?* [Is Japan Turning to the Left?] (Reinbek bei Hamburg: Rowohlt, 1964), p. 146.
2. Heinrich Dumoulin, *Östliche Meditation und christliche Mystik* [Eastern Meditation and Christian Mysticism] (Freiburg: Alber, 1966), p. 35.
3. Cf. "Japanische Bonzen beim Papst" [Japanese Bonzes Visit Pope] (News Briefs from Church and World) in *Die Kirche nach dem Konzil* 12 (1966): 1.
4. Quoted here from *The Documents of Vatican II*, ed. Walter M. Abbott, S.J. (New York: Guild Press, 1966), p. 660. Further page references to this document are given in the text.
5. Heinrich Dumoulin, "Exkurs zum Konziltext über den Buddhismus" [Excursus on the Second Vatican Council's Text on Buddhism], in *Das zweite vatikanische Konzil* [The Second Vatican Council], pp. 482–83.
6. Kurt Schmidt, *Buddhas Lehre, eine Einführung* [Introduction to Buddha's Teaching] (Kreuzlingen: P. Christiani, 1946), p. 9.
7. Klaus Klostermaier, *Hinduismus* [Hinduism] (Köln: Bachem, 1965), p. 17.
8. Gerhard Rosenkranz, *Der christliche Glaube angesichts der Weltreligionen* [Christian and Other World Religions—A Comparison] (Bern: Francke, 1967), p. 19. Further page references to this document are given in the text.
9. Wilhelm Guntert, *Japanische Religionsgeschichte. Die Religionen der Japaner und Koreaner in geschichtlichem Abriss* [History of Religion in Japan. Historical Outline of Religions of Japanese and Koreans] (Tokyo, 1935), p. 165.
10. Klaus Mehnert, *Asien, Moskau und wir. Bilanz nach vier Weltreisen* [Asia, Moscow, and Europe. Assessment after Four World Trips] (Stuttgart: Deutsche Verlags-Anstalt, 1961), p. 43.
11. Arthur Koestler, *Von Heiligen und Automaten*. With an Epilogue by Carl Gustav Jung, trans. Hans Flesch-Brunningen (Bern: Scherz, 1961), p. 206. For the English text, see Arthur Koestler, *The Lotus and the Robot* (London: Hutchinson, 1960).
12. Hugo Makibi Enomiya-Lassalle, *Zen, Weg zur Erleuchtung* [Zen, The Road to Enlightenment] (Wien: Herder, 1960). Hugo Makibi Lassalle (Hugo M. Enomiya), *Zen-Buddhismus* [Zen Buddhism] (Köln: Bachem, 1966).

Chapter 2

1. Maurus Heinrichs, *Katholische Theologie und asiatisches Denken* [Catholic Theology and Asian Thought] (Mainz: Matthias Grünewald, 1963), p. 33.
2. Cf. André Bareau, "Der indische Buddhismus" [Buddhism in India], in André Bareau et al., *Die Religionen Indiens* [The Religions of India] (Stuttgart: Kohlhammer, 1964), p. 11. Further page references to this work are given in the text.
3. Günther Schulemann, *Die Botschaft des Buddha vom Lotos des guten*

Gesetzes [Buddha's Teaching about the Lotus of the Good Law] (Freiburg: Herder, 1937), p. 17.

4. Hermann Oldenberg, *Buddha, sein Leben, seine Lehre, seine Gemeinde* [Buddha, His Life, His Doctrine, His Community], 13th ed., ed. Helmuth v. Glasenapp (Stuttgart: Cotta, 1961), p. 10. Further page references to this work are given in the text.

5. Jean Paul Sartre, *The Words,* trans. Bernard Frechtman (New York: Braziller, 1964), p. 149. Siegmund quotes from the German translation: *Die Wörter. Aus dem Französischen mit einer Nachbemerkung von Hans Mayer* [The Words. From the French with an Epilogue by Hans Mayer]. Further page references to the English translation are given in the text.

6. *Das Leben des Buddha von Asvaghosa* [Asvaghosa's Life of Buddha], ed. in Tibetan and German by Friedrich Weller (1926), p. 14. Further page references to this work are given in the text under the rubric *Asvaghosa.*

7. Cf. Georg Siegmund, *Sein oder Nichtsein. Die Frage des Selbstmordes* [To Be or Not to Be. The Problem of Suicide] (Trier: Paulinus, 1961), pp. 88f.

8. Cf. ibid., pp. 192–93.

9. Anguttara-Nikaya III, 38 as quoted in Kurt Schmidt, *Buddhas Lehre, eine Einführung* [Introduction to Buddha's Teaching] (Kreuzlingen: P. Christiani, 1947), pp. 21–22.

Chapter 3

1. In the text, Siegmund quotes from the German translation of Pascal's *Pensées*. I have quoted from the English translation: Blaise Pascal, *Pensées,* trans. W. F. Trotter (New York: Random House, 1941), p. 23. [Translator's note.]

2. Jean Paul Sartre, *L'être et le néant* [Being and Nothingness] in *Bibliothèque des Idées* [Library of Ideas], 5th ed. (Paris: Librairie Gallimard, 1937). Page references to this work are given in the text.

3. Hans Jürgen Baden, *Literatur und Selbstmord* [Literature and Suicide]. *Cesare Pavese. Klaus Mann. Ernest Hemingway* (Stuttgart: Klett, 1965).

4. Søren Kierkegaard, *Fear and Trembling and Sickness unto Death,* trans. with an Introduction and Notes by Walter Lowrie (Garden City, N.Y.: Doubleday, 1954), p. 200. Further page references to this work are given in the text.

5. Maurus Heinrichs, *Katholische Theologie und asiatisches Denken* [Catholic Theology and Asian Thought] (Mainz: Matthias Grünewald, 1963), p. 50.

6. Hermann Oldenberg, *Buddha, sein Leben, seine Lehre, seine Gemeinde* [Buddha, His Life, His Doctrine, His Community], 13th ed., ed. Helmuth v. Glasenapp (Stuttgart: Cotta, 1961), p. 153. Further page references to this work are given in the text.

7. Cf. Daisetz Teitaro Suzuki, *Die grosse Befreiung. Einführung in den Zen-Buddhismus* [The Great Liberation. Introduction to Zen Buddhism], 3rd ed., trans. into German by Felix Schottlaender (Zürich: Rascher, 1947), p. 58.

Chapter 4

1. Cf. Wolfgang Pfeiffer-Belli, *Europa und das grosse Asien. Studien zur Geistesgeschichte* [Europe and Great Asia. Studies in Intellectual History] (Speyer: Pilger, 1949), p. 58.

2. Cf. Fritz Mauthner, *Der Atheismus und seine Geschichte im Abendlande* [Atheism and Its History in the West], 4 vols. (Hildesheim: G. Olms, 1963), vol. IV, pp. 290–95.

3. Arthur Schopenhauer, *Sämtliche Werke* [Complete Works], 8 vols., ed. M. Frischeisen-Köhler (Berlin: Weichert, 1921), vol. III, p. 97.

4. Friedrich Nietzsche, *Complete Works,* vol. X, trans. and ed. Oscar Levy (New York: Russell & Russell, 1964), p. 307.

5. Schopenhauer, *Sämtliche Werke,* vol. III, pp. 175–76.

6. Ibid., vol. IV, p. 624. Further page references to this edition of Schopenhauer's works are given in the text.

7. Norbert Lohfink, *Das Siegeslied am Schilfmeer. Christliche Auseinandersetzungen mit dem Alten Testament* [The Song of Triumph at the Red Sea. Christian Encounters with the Old Testament], 2nd ed. (Frankfurt: Knecht, 1966), p. 86.

8. Hermann Beckh, *Buddhismus (Buddha und seine Lehre)* [Buddhism (Buddha and His Doctrine)], vol. I (Berlin: Göschen, 1916), p. 123.

9. Günther Schulemann, *Die Botschaft des Buddha vom Lotos des guten Gesetzes* [Buddha's Teaching about the Lotus of the Good Law] (Freiburg: Herder, 1937), pp. 35f. Schulemann's reconstruction and translation of the other three "holy truths," quoted on pp. 52–56, is also taken from this source.

10. Hermann Oldenberg, *Buddha, sein Leben, seine Lehre, seine Gemeinde* [Buddha, His Life, His Doctrine, His Community], 13th ed., ed. Helmuth v. Glasenapp (Stuttgart: Cotta, 1961), p. 344.

Chapter 5

1. Seneca, "De Vita Beata," *Moral Essays,* vol. II, trans. John W. Basore, *The Loeb Classical Library* (Cambridge: Harvard University Press, 1932), bk. V, sec. 1. Further references to this work are given in the text.

2. Seneca, "De Providentia," in ibid., vol. I (1928), bk. III, sec. 9 and bk. II, sec. 4.

3. The reference is to Mephistopheles, who thus identifies himself in Goethe's *Faust,* Part One. [Translator's note.].

4. Epictetus, "The Enchiridion, or Manual," in *The Discourses of Epictetus,* no. XVI, trans. George Long (New York: Crowell, n.d.), pp. 393–94.

5. Max Pohlenz, *Die Stoa—Geschichte einer geistigen Bewegung* [The Stoa. History of an Intellectual Movement] (Göttingen: Vandenhoeck & Ruprecht, 1948–49), p. 156. Further page references to this work are given in the text.

Chapter 6

1. The reference is to the song "Freudvoll und Leidvoll," which is sung by Klärchen as she awaits her lover in the scene "Klärchens Wohnung" [Clara's Home] in Act III of Goethe's *Egmont.* [Translator's note.].

2. Cf. Georg Siegmund, *Schlaf und Schlafstörung* [Sleep and the Disturbance of Sleep] Dülmen: Laumann, 1948). See also Georg Siegmund, *Der Mensch in seinem Dasein. Philosophische Anthropologie* [Man and His Existence. Philosophical Anthropology], pt. I (Freiburg: Herder, 1953), sec. 4, "Geist und Natur in ihrem gegenseitigen Verhältnis beim Menschen" [Mutual Relationship of Spirit and Nature in Man].

3. Cf. Georg Siegmund, "Wolfkinder" [Wolf Children], in *Erdkreis*, vol. 1 (1967).

4. Cf. Georg Siegmund, *Der kranke Mensch. Medizinische Anthropologie* [Ailing Mankind. Medical Anthropology] (Fulda: Fuldaer Verlag, 1951), pp. 227f.

5. Adolf Portmann, *Vom Bild der Natur. Ein Beitrag der Lebensforschung zu aktuellen Fragen* [A Portrait of Nature. Contribution of Biological Research to Topical Questions] (Basel: Reinhardt, 1947), chap. V: "Die Werkstatt des Leidens" [Suffering's Workshop], pp. 43–52, passim.

6. Clive Staples Lewis, *The Problem of Pain* (New York: Macmillan, 1944), pp. 2–3. (Siegmund quotes from the German translation of this work.)

7. Cf. Georg Siegmund, "Die Herzerkrankungen und die Lebensgestaltung" [Heart Diseases and the Ordering of Life], in *Universitas* 19 (1954): 173–81.

8. Lewis, *The Problem of Pain*, p. 63.

9. Heinz Brasch, *Kyoto, Die Seele Japans* [Kyoto, The Soul of Japan] (Olten: Urs Graf-Verlag, 1965), p. 4.

10. *The Works of Oscar Wilde* (London: Spring Books, 1963), pp. 782, 793. (Siegmund quotes from the German translation of Wilde's works.)

11. Cf. Georg Siegmund, *Sein oder Nichtsein. Die Frage des Selbstmordes* [To Be or Not to Be. The Problem of Suicide] (Trier: Paulinus, 1961).

Chapter 7

1. Cf. Georg Siegmund, "Pawlows Kampf gegen die Seele" [Pavlov's Struggle against the Soul], in *Jahrbuch für Psychologie* [Psychology Yearbook] 15 (1967): 24–40.

2. Kokumen Nenju Gyoji, *Das Jahr im Erleben des Volkes* [A Year in the Life of the People]. Official Translation from the Japanese by Adolf Barghoorn, Ernst Keyssner, Heinz van d. Laan, Gustav Rudolf, and Erich Simonis, in *Mitteilungen der Deutschen Gesellschaft für Natur- und Völkerkunde Ostasiens* [Publications of the German Society for the Natural and Ethnic History of East Asia], vol. XX (Tokyo and Leipzig: Verlag d. Asia Major, 1926), p. 165. In quoting this text, Siegmund replaced the misleading expression "Mass of the dead" [Totenmesse] by "memorial service for the dead" [Totenandacht].

3. Davaduta Sutta as recorded in Hermann Oldenberg, *Buddha, sein Leben, seine Lehre, seine Gemeinde* [Buddha, His Life, His Doctrine, His Community], 13th ed., ed. Helmuth v. Glasenapp (Stuttgart: Cotta, 1961), p. 217. Further page references to this work are given in the text.

Notes

Chapter 8

1. Hermann Oldenberg, *Buddha, sein Leben, seine Lehre, seine Gemeinde* [Buddha, His Life, His Doctrine, His Community], 13th ed., ed. Helmuth v. Glasenapp (Stuttgart: Cotta, 1961), p. 257. Further page references to this work are given in the text.

2. As Georg Siegmund points out here, there is no agreement among scholars about the real connotation of the term *parinirvana*. Siegmund seems to use it to mean the "complete *nirvana*" reached at death. For another interpretation and a brief discussion of the problem, see Edward J. Thomas, *The History of Buddhist Thought*, 2nd ed. (New York: Barnes & Noble, 1951), pp. 121–22, n. 4. [Translator's note.]

3. Siegmund's discussion of the "just one" on this and the following pages, including his references to Plato's *Republic*, is closely patterned on the longer discussion by Ernst Benz in *Der gekreuzigte Gerechte bei Plato, im Neuen Testament und in der alten Kirche* [The Concept of the Crucified Just One in Plato, the New Testament, and the Early Church], Monograph No. 12, in *Akademie der Wissenschaft und der Literatur. Abhandlungen der Geistes- und Sozialwissenschaftlichen Klasse* [Academy of Science and Literature. Proceedings of the Division of Arts and Social Science] (Mainz-Wiesbaden: F. Steiner, 1950). Page references to this work are given in the text.

4. The discussion of justice and injustice on this and the following pages is based on Plato's *Republic*, bk. II, sec. 358E–359C and sec. 360. Cf. Plato, *The Republic*, vol. I, trans. Paul Shorey, *The Loeb Classical Library* (Cambridge: Harvard University Press, 1953). Further references to this work are given in the text.

5. Joachim Jeremias, "Der gegenwärtige Stand der Debatte um das Problem des historischen Jesus" [The Present State of the Debate about the Problem of the Historical Jesus], in *Der historische Jesus und der kerygmatische Christus* [The Historical Jesus and the Kerygmatic Christ], 2nd ed., ed. Helmut Ristow and Karl Matthiae (Berlin: Evangelische Verlagsanstalt, 1961), p. 18.

Chapter 9

1. Carl Gustav Jung, Foreword, in Daisetz Teitaro Suzuki, *An Introduction to Zen Buddhism* (New York: Grove Press, n.d.), p. 25. Jung's foreword is also to be found, under the title "Zur Psychologie westlicher und östlicher Religion" [On the Psychology of Western and Eastern Religions] (1963), in the eleventh volume of his collected works: *Gesammelte Werke* [Collected Works] (Zürich: Rascher, 1958–1978). Further page references to this work are given in the text.

2. Aldous Huxley, *The Doors of Perception and Heaven and Hell* (New York: Harper & Row, 1963), p. 69. Further page references to this work are given in the text.

3. Kaiten Nukariya, "The Religion of the Samurai," quoted by Jung in his foreword to Suzuki, pp. 10–11. The words in brackets have been inserted by Georg Siegmund. They are not in Jung's foreword. Further page references to this work are given in the text.

4. Hugo M. Enomiya-Lassalle, S.J., *Zen—Weg zur Erleuchtung* [Zen—The Way to Enlightenment] (Wien: Herder, 1960), p. 9. Lassalle followed his first study of 1960 with a very intensive presentation: Hugo M. Enomiya, *Zen-Buddhismus* [Zen Buddhism] (Köln: Bachem, 1966), p. 450.

5. Jung, *Gesammelte Werke* [Collected Works], vol. XI, p. 658. Further page references to this work are given in the text.

6. Robert Charles Zaehner, *Mysticism, Sacred and Profane*, A Galaxy Book (New York: Oxford University Press, 1961), Introduction, p. xii. Siegmund here quotes from the German translation of this text.

7. Cf. Georg Siegmund, "Heil aus dem Hinduismus?" [Salvation from Hinduism?] in *Erdkreis,* vol. 12 (1962): 63–117, and Klaus Klostermaier, *Hinduismus* [Hinduism] (Köln: Bachem, 1965).

8. Cf. Georg Siegmund, *Rausch und Religion* [Intoxication and Religion] (Hamm/Westfalen: Hoheneck, 1966).

9. St. Augustine, *The City of God,* trans. Marcus Dods, D.D. (New York: Random House, 1950), p. 460.

10. Eugen Herrigel, *Der Zen-Weg. Aufzeichnungen aus dem Nachlass* [The Zen Way. Unpublished Notes], with Gustie Luise Herrigel, 2nd ed., ed. Hermann Tausend (München: Barth, 1964), pp. 16–17.

11. Lassalle, *Zen—Weg zur Erleuchtung* [Zen—The Way to Enlightenment], p. 97.

Chapter 10

1. Jacques Albert Cuttat, "Die Spiritualität Asiens" [The Spirituality of Asia], in *Hochland* 59 (1966): 97. Further page references to this work are given in the text.

2. The following passages follow the thoroughly documented study of Mircea Eliade, "Yoga Techniques in Buddhism," in *Yoga: Immortality and Freedom,* Bollingen Series LVI, trans. Willard R. Trask (Princeton: Princeton University Press, 1969), pp. 162–99. Further page references to this work are given in the text.

3. Klaus Klostermaier, *Hinduismus* [Hinduism] (Köln: Bachem, 1965), p. 16.

4. Heinrich Dumoulin, *Östliche Meditation und christliche Mystik* [Eastern Meditation and Christian Mysticism] (Freiburg: Alber, 1966), pp. 278–79.

5. Klostermaier, *Hinduismus,* p. 134. Further page references to this work are given in the text.

6. Raymond Panikkar, *The Unknown Christ of Hinduism* (London: Darton, Longman & Todd, 1964), p. 75. Further page references to this work are given in the text.

7. Dumoulin, *Östliche Meditation und christliche Mystik,* pp. 60–61. Further page references to this work are given in the text.

8. Joseph Kuckhoff, *Johannes von Ruysbroeck der Wunderbare. Einführung in sein Leben, Auswahl aus seinen Werken* [Johannes von Ruysbroeck the Wonderful. An Introduction to His Life and a Selection of His Works] (München: Kösel-Pustet, 1938), pp. 226f.

9. Evelyn Underhill, quoted in Klostermaier, *Hinduismus,* p. 266.

10. Evelyn Underhill, *Mysticism. A Study in the Nature and Development of Man's Spiritual Consciousness* (New York: Noonday Press, 1955), pp. 322–23.

11. Georg Siegmund, *Psychologie des Gottesglauben auf Grund literarischer Selbstzeugnisse* [The Psychology of Belief in God on the Basis of Literary Testimonies], 2nd ed. (Münsterschwarzach: Vier Türme-Verlag, 1965), pp. 48–49.

12. Cf. Georg Siegmund, *Rausch und Religion* [Intoxication and Religion] (Hamm/Westfalen: Hoheneck, 1966).

13. Kuckhoff, *Johannes von Ruysbroeck*, pp. 125f.

14. Shizuteru Ueda, *Die Gottesgeburt in der Seele und der Durchbruch zur Gottheit. Die mystische Anthropologie Meister Eckharts und ihre Konfrontation mit der Mystik des Zen-Buddhismus* [The Birth of God in the Soul and the Breakthrough to Divinity. The Mystical Anthropology of Meister Eckhart in Relation to the Mysticism of Zen Buddhism] (Gütersloh: G. Mohn, 1965).

15. Cf. Klostermaier, *Hinduismus*, pp. 195–220.

Chapter 11

1. Friedrich Nietzsche, *Die fröhliche Wissenschaft* [The Joyful Wisdom] (Stuttgart: Kröner, 1956), bk. V, sec. 353.

2. Hermann Oldenberg, *Buddha, sein Leben, seine Lehre, seine Gemeinde* [Buddha, His Life, His Doctrine, His Community], 13th ed., ed. Helmuth v. Glasenapp (Stuttgart: Cotta, 1961), p. 38. Further page references to this work are given in the text.

3. Joachim Jeremias, "Der gegenwärtige Stand der Debatte um das Problem des historischen Jesus" [The Present State of the Debate about the Problem of the Historical Jesus], in *Der historische Jesus and und der kerygmatische Christus* [The Historical Jesus and the Kerygmatic Christ], 2nd ed. (Berlin: Evangelische Verlagsanstalt, 1961), p. 21. Further page references to this work are given in the text.

4. Klaus Klostermaier, *Hinduismus* [Hinduism] (Köln: Bachem, 1965), p. 53. Further page references to this work are given in the text.

5. *Buddha, die Lehre des Erhabenen* [Buddha, the Doctrine of the Exalted One]. Selected from the Pali Canon [Tripitaka] and translated by Paul Dahlke (München: Goldmann, 1960), p. 130. Further page references to this work are given in the text.

Chapter 12

1. Cf. Paul Aoyama, "Die Mentalität der Japaner vor der Einführung der hochentwickelten chinesischen Kultur" [The Mentality of the Japanese before the Introduction of the Highly Developed Chinese Culture], in *Annali del Pont. Museo Miss. Etn.*, XXX (1966): 339–54.

2. Quoted from Georg Schurhammer, *Shin-to. Der Weg der Götter in Japan* [Shinto. The Way of the Gods in Japan] (Bonn and Leipzig: K. Schroeder, 1923), p. 130. Further page references to this work are given in the text.

3. Quoted from Fr. Jos. Schütte, "Der japanische Volkscharakter in der Sicht Valignanos" [Valignano's View of the Japanese National Character], in *Stimmen der Zeit* 138 (1941): 84.

4. Reported in Olaf Graf's Introduction to (Paul) Takashi Nagai, *Notizen auf einem Sterbebett* [Notes from My Deathbed], translated from the Japanese by Olaf Graf (St. Ottilien: Eos-Verlag, 1954), p. 2.

5. Reported in Johannes Siemes, "Die Staatsgründung des modernen Japans: Die Einflüsse Hermann Roesler" [The Founding of the Modern Japanese State: The Influence of Hermann Roeslers], in *Das moderne Japan—Einführende Aufsätze* [Modern Japan—Introductory Essays], ed. Joseph Roggendorf (Tokyo: Sophia University, 1963), p. 10.

6. Reported in Jakob Overmans, "Der japanische Staatsgedanke" [The Japanese Concept of the State], in *Stimmen der Zeit* 130 (1936): 203.

7. Joseph Roggendorf, "Niedergang und Wiederaufstieg: Die Geschichte der letzten fünfzig Jahre" [Fall and Rise: The History of the Last Fifty Years], in *Das moderne Japan,* ed. Joseph Roggendorf, pp. 42–43. Further page references to this work are given in the text.

8. Klaus Mehnert, *Asien, Moskau und wir. Bilanz nach vier Weltreisen* [Asia, Moscow, and Europe. Assessment after Four World Trips] (Stuttgart: Deutsche Verlagsanstalt, 1961), p. 282. Further page references to this work are given in the text.

9. Carl Christian Bry [pseud. of Carl Decke], *Verkappte Religionen* [Disguised Religions] (Lochham: E. Gans, 1925), 3rd ed., 1964.

10. Nagai, *Notizen auf einem Sterbebett,* p. 286.

11. Arthur Koestler, *Von Heiligen und Automaten.* With an Epilogue by Carl Gustav Jung, trans. Hans Flesch-Brunningen (Bern: Scherz, 1961), p. 226. The English title of this work is *The Lotus and the Robot.* Further page references are given in the text.

12. Henricus van Straelen, *Asiatisches Tagebuch* [Asian Diary] (Würzburg: Echter Verlag, 1963), p. 150.

13. Hans Waldenfels, S.J., "Japans Gespräch mit dem Christentum Europas" [Japan's Dialogue with European Christendom], in *Stimmen der Zeit* 177 (1966): 84–85.

14. Nagai, *Notizen auf einem Sterbebett,* pp. 67–70. Further page references to this work are given in the text.

INDEX

Absolute (The), 126–51; Brahman as, 127, 128, 133–34; Buddha's concept of, 126, 127–28, 162; Christian identification of, with God, 128, 131, 136, 143–44, 146–47, 148; Eastern attitude toward, 128, 131, 132, 135, 136–37, 138–41, 143, 148; man's a priori knowledge of, 29, 130, 134, 144; man's striving for union with, 126, 128, 130, 131, 133–34, 136–37, 144, 148; and nirvana, 126, 127, 136; reality of creation, 133–34, 135, 136; self-possession of, 136. *See also* Atman; God; Jesus Christ; Man; Mysticism; Nirvana; Self

Aristotle, 65

Arrogance, 14, 23, 44, 165

Aryans, 12–13

Asvaghosa, 21–23

Atman (self), 14, 29, 62, 113–25, 127, 128, 136, 137–38, 140, 142. *See also* Brahman; Man; Self

Augustine, St., 49, 94, 121–22, 124, 143–44, 145, 146

Baghavadgita, 140

Bodhi, 27, 44, 114

Brahman, 15, 45, 62, 77, 83, 115, 120, 121, 127, 128, 133, 134, 136, 137–38, 140, 142, 166–67, 169. *See also* Absolute (The); Atman; God

Brahminism, 15, 25, 26, 39, 47, 48, 49, 87, 88, 155

Buddha, 6, 11–29, 30, 37, 43, 44, 45, 51, 52, 56, 57, 58, 84, 96, 100, 103, 106, 113, 114, 115, 117, 128, 129, 152–69; apotheosis of, 45, 115, 165–69; Aryan roots of. *See* Gautama, Siddharta; and Buddhism. *See* Buddhism; and Christ. *See* Christianity; Jesus Christ; disciples of, 11, 13, 43–44, 45, 96, 132, 154, 163, 165–66, 167; enlightenment of, 4, 11, 16, 25–29, 41, 44–46, 54, 114, 167. *See also* Buddhist experience; Enlightenment; Nirvana; Nothingness; Suffering; four holy truths of, 51, 52–56, 165; historical. *See* Gautama, Siddharta; legendary, 12, 26, 165–69. *See also* apotheosis of; manifold existences of, 132, 166, 169. *See also* Reincarnation; as man's eternal self, 115, 124; miracles of, 168–69; and Sartre, 11–29; teaching of, 11, 13, 41, 44, 57, 58–59, 89–91, 100–01, 106, 126, 127–28, 160–69. *See also* enlightenment of; four holy truths of; Nirvana; Nothingness; Suffering; as type, 11, 45, 155, 163, 166. *See also* Buddhist experience; Enlightenment; Gautama, Siddharta; God; Man; Nothingness; Suffering; Yoga

Buddhahood, 45, 46, 165–69

Buddhism, 3, 4, 13, 14, 15, 16, 95, 96, 117, 129, 170, 172; Aryan roots of. *See* roots of, in bourgeois satiety; Gautama, Siddharta; and Buddha. *See* Buddha; and Christianity, 5–6, 7–8, 11, 35, 37, 46, 47, 48, 57–58, 60, 68, 92, 101, 112, 128, 147–48, 152–69. *See also* Absolute (The); Original sin; Man; Nothingness; Soul; Suffering; and concept of God. *See* Absolute (The); God; and concept of sin. *See* and Christianity; Man, personhood of; Man, and sin; Original sin; fundamental truths of. *See* Buddha, teachings of; Enlightenment; Nirvana; Nothingness; Reincarnation; Suffering; impersonal character of, 11, 57–58, 85, 105–06, 115, 136, 137, 141, 146, 148, 150, 155, 161, 163–65; manifold forms of, 5, 147–48. *See also* Mahayana Buddhism; Zen Buddhism; monism of, 114, 115, 118, 120, 136, 137, 148; nothingness as concept of. *See* Nothingness; origin of. *See* Buddha; Gautama, Siddharta; redemption as concept of, 11, 12, 25–26, 29, 61, 98–101, 103, 127–28, 132, 160, 161–62; rejection of metaphysical speculation by, 2, 7–8, 94, 98, 99, 103, 114, 115, 126, 132, 135, 162; relativization of good and evil in, 7–8, 57, 140; roots of, in bourgeois satiety, 13, 14–15, 154–55. *See also* Gautama, Siddharta; Sakyas; Schopenhauer on, 8–9, 47–50; as search for absolute. *See* Absolute (The); Man, and search for absolute; Man, universal questions of; and Stoic philosophy, 60–66; and suffering. *See* Suffering, Buddhist concept of; ten commandments of, 56, 57–58; world view of, 27–28, 34–35, 48, 56–57, 61, 86–88, 101, 132, 133–34. *See also* Absolute

(The); Atman; Brahman; Buddha; Buddhist experience; Dialogue: East-West; Eastern religions; Enlightenment; Gautama, Siddharta; God; Nirvana; Nothingness; Original sin; Self; Soul; Suffering

Buddhist experience, 11–29, 30, 43–46, 89, 105, 115, 162; as disillusionment, 6, 18, 21–22, 23, 25, 27–28, 44, 56–57, 60, 129–30, 136; and Eastern mode of life, 11–29; as renunciation, 25–26, 27, 44, 45–46, 105, 129–30, 162; repetition of, as way of salvation, 11, 12, 44–46, 105, 114–15, 165; satiety as root of. *See* Gautama, Siddharta; Sakyas. *See also* Absolute (The); Bodhi; Buddha; Buddhism; Enlightenment; Man; Nirvana; Nothingness; Self; Suffering

Christianity: basic concepts of, 1, 6, 7, 30–36, 41, 43, 46, 79, 92, 128–29, 131, 152–69. *See also* God; Jesus Christ; and Buddhism, 5–6, 7–8, 11, 35, 37, 46, 47, 48, 57–58, 60, 68, 92, 101, 112, 128, 147–48, 152–69; and Eastern religions. *See* Dialogue: East-West; Eastern religions; free decision as fundamental to, 8, 40–41, 79, 80, 82, 90–91, 121–25, 146–47, 150–51, 153, 156; Huxley on, 113–14; in Japan, 1–7, 170–84; and Jesus Christ. *See* Jesus Christ; Jung on, 113; personal orientation of, 112, 149, 148, 151, 155, 160; Schopenhauer on, 8–9, 47–50; and sin. *See* Man, hubris of; Man, and sin; Original sin; and Stoic philosophy, 60–66; and suffering. *See* Suffering, Christian doctrine of. *See also* Absolute (The); Dialogue: East-West; God; Jesus Christ; Man; Nothingness; Self; Soul; Suffering

City of God, The (St. Augustine), 121–22
Confessions (St. Augustine), 143–44
Cuttat, Jacques, 126, 144, 148, 150

Declaration on the Relationship of the Church to Non-Catholic Religions, 4–5, 144. *See also* Vatican Council II
De Vita Beata (Seneca), 60
Dhammapada (The Way of Truth), 104
Dialogue: East-West, 1–10, 51, 68, 102, 112, 115, 116, 117, 128–29; basis for, 4–5, 125, 134; efforts toward, 2–5, 6, 9, 10, 133; obstacles to, 1–2, 5, 6–8, 96–97,

115, 116, 148; prerequisites for, 7, 8, 68, 116, 131, 143, 170; and Zen Buddhism, 116–17, 123–25. *See also* Buddhism; Christianity; Eastern religions; Lassalle, Hugo Enomiya
Doors of Perfection, The (Huxley), 120
Dumoulin, Heinrich, 3, 5, 129, 137, 138

Eastern Religions: absence of metaphysical concepts in, 2, 7–8, 94, 98, 114, 115, 126, 132, 135, 162. *See also* Mysticism; Soul; and Christianity. *See* Christianity; Dialogue: East-West; nirvana as basic goal of. *See* Nirvana; relativization of good and evil in, 7–8, 57, 140; Schopenhauer on, 8–9; soteriological orientation of, 7–11, 94, 95. *See also* Buddhism, redemption as concept of
Eightfold path, 55–56
Emperor worship. *See* Japan
Enlightenment: Buddha's, 4, 5, 9, 11, 12, 21–22, 27–28, 30, 46, 54, 114, 115, 116, 117, 119, 122, 132, 160–61, 165–66; absence of critical analysis regarding, 114, 115; Christian vs. Buddhist concept of, 30, 45–46. *See also* Jung on; and Christian mysticism. *See* Mysticism; Self; description of, 114–15, 116, 117, 137; and final perfection. *See* as redemption; Man, primal decision of; Self-perfection; Huxley on, 113–14; Jung on, 113, 117–19, 120, 122–23, 125; nature of, 26 28, 30, 114, 165–66. *See also* Buddhist experience; and nirvana. *See* Nirvana; non-representational character of, 139–40, 141; as redemption, 11, 29, 115, 117–18, 132, 138–40; and salvation. *See* as redemption; as self-confrontation. *See* Mysticism; Self; subjectivism of, 139–41; transcendence and, 126–51; Zen way of. *See* Zen Buddhism. *See also* Absolute (The); Man; Mysticism; Nirvana; Nothingness; Self-Perfection
Enûma Elisch, 50–51
Evil, origin of. *See* Original sin

Festival of the Dead, 2, 96–98. *See also* Soul
Fetish cults, 176–77
Four holy truths, 51, 52–56, 165
Francis Xavier, St., 6, 96, 170

Gautama, Siddharta: absence of struggle in early life of, 13–23; arrogance of, 14, 23,

Index

44, 165; Aryan roots of, 12–17; as Buddha, 11, 45, 51, 165; disillusionment of, 27–29, 101, 129–30; enlightenment of. *See* Enlightenment; life of, 11, 13, 15–18, 21–28, 152, 169; and Sartre, 14, 17, 18–19, 23, 25, 28. *See also* Buddha; Buddhist experience; Enlightenment; Nothingness; Sakyas

God, 11, 47, 49, 62, 63, 94, 106, 132, 138, 140, 143, 147; Eastern vs. Western concept of. *See* Absolute (The); Buddhism, and Christianity; man's freedom to affirm or deny, 8, 40–41, 50, 79, 80, 82, 90–91, 121–25, 146–47, 153, 156; man's search for, 30–46, 126–51; as personal Creator-God, 4, 50, 128, 148–51, 155–56, 161; in Zen Buddhism, 1–2, 11–12. *See also* Absolute (The); Christianity; Jesus Christ; Man, primal decision of; Man, universal questions of

Goethe, Johann Wolfgang von, 113, 137

Hartmann, Eduard von, 47
Hinduism, 4, 6, 7, 8, 132, 133, 147
Huxley, Aldous, 113–14, 119, 120

Islamism, 4, 49

Japan, 25, 42–43, 116, 120, 124, 137, 170–84; Christianity in, 1–10, 170–71, 182–83; concept of God in, 1–2, 176–77, 179–80, 182–83; emperor worship in, 170–84; Festival of Dead in, 21, 96–98; shame vs. guilt culture of, 170, 177

Jesus Christ, 8, 11, 92, 95, 107, 110–12, 131, 146, 152–69

Jiva (vital principle), 14

John XXIII, Pope, 2–3. *See also Pacem in Terris;* Vatican Council II

Judaism, 48, 49, 159

Jung, Carl Gustav, 113, 117–19, 122–23, 125

Karma, 18, 56, 87, 103, 137, 161
Kierkegaard, Søren, 35, 42
Klostermaier, Klaus, 6, 128, 133, 143
Koestler, Arthur, 9, 180–81

Lassalle, Hugo Enomiya, 10, 46, 116, 125
Lives: of Buddha. *See Asvaghosa*

Mahapadana Suttanta (Great Sermon about Legends), 168–69

Mahapajapati (Buddha's foster mother), 15
Mahayana Buddhism, 56, 137, 139, 148
Man: Biblical and Christian concept of. *See* Christianity, basic concepts of; Christianity, free decision as fundamental to; Original sin; Buddhist concept of, 28–29, 85–88, 91, 121, 127, 136. *See also* Soul, Buddhist concept of; debilitating effect of satiety on, 13–15, 16, 17, 20–21, 22–23; formative influences on, 13–16, 18, 19–22, 23, 25, 28, 67–74, 79, 84, 85, 86, 89–91, 122–25, 130–32. *See also* self-awareness of; Enlightenment; hubris of, 30–42; human acts of. *See* Soul; and ills of human condition, 16, 23, 30–46, 83–91, 124. *See also* and sin; Original sin; Suffering, man as cause of human; Suffering, and pain; personhood of, 14, 28–29, 48–49, 81, 85–87, 93, 95–96, 98–100, 101, 114, 124, 136, 143, 149. *See also* Sartre on; self-awareness of; Self; Soul; primal decision of, for or against God, 8, 40–41, 50, 79, 80, 82, 90–91, 121–25, 146–47, 153, 156, 163; Sartre on, 36–40, 102–03; and search for absolute, 126–51. *See also* universal questions of; self-awareness of, 14, 32, 41, 64, 68–72, 77–78, 79–83, 85–87, 121–25, 136. *See also* personhood of; primal decision of; Enlightenment; Mysticism; Original sin; Self; Self-perfection; self-possession of. *See* self-awareness of; and sin, 48–51, 77, 79–83, 86–87, 121–22, 155, 156–57. *See also* hubris of; Original sin; Soul; Stoic concept of, 60–66; and suffering, 76, 77–79, 83–91. *See also* and ills of human condition; formative influences on; Suffering; universal questions of, 4–5, 28, 30–46, 67–74, 81, 90–91, 92, 102, 103–04, 113, 121–25, 130–34, 143–51, 159–61. *See also* primal decision of; self-awareness of; Enlightenment; Meditation; Nirvana; Nothingness; Self; Self-perfection; Soul

Mantras (True Words), 161
Maya (Buddha's mother), 15
Maya (illusion), 132, 133
Meditation, 57; Buddhist technique of, 132; as transcendent analysis, 130–32, 133, 134; Zazen (Zen), 116–17, 125. *See also* Mysticism
Mescalin, 113–14. *See also* Huxley, Aldous; Mysticism

Mysticism, 9, 37; and Buddhist enlightenment, 114–15; dangers of false, 130–31, 141–43; Eastern vs. Western, 113–25; Huxley on, 113–14, 119, 120; Jung on, 113, 117–19, 120, 122–23, 125; mescalin and, 113–14, 119; of Middle Ages, 141–43; Nukariya on Zen, 114–15, 116, 117. *See also* Atman; Brahman; Enlightenment; Man; Meditation; Zen Buddhism

Nagai, Takashi, 177, 183
Nietzsche, Friedrich, 41, 47–48, 95, 113, 154–55
Nirvana, 4, 5, 6–7, 30, 45, 49, 54, 56, 57, 60, 61, 91, 99, 103, 104, 105, 115, 126–51, 162, 166; and parinirvana, 105, 189 (n. 2, ch. 7); and reincarnation. *See* Reincarnation. *See also* Absolute (The); Enlightenment; Meditation; Mysticism; Self; Nothingness; Suffering
Notes from My Deathbed (Nagai), 177, 183–84
Nothingness, 6–7, 23, 26–29, 30–46, 101, 103, 123, 126, 129–30, 156, 162. *See also* Christianity, basic concepts of; Enlightenment; Nirvana; Man; Sartre, Jean Paul; Suffering

Oldenberg, Hermann, 163, 165
Original sin: Babylonian concept of, 50–51. *See also Enûma Elish;* biblical and Christian concept of, 48–50, 51, 79, 80, 86, 87. *See also* God, man's freedom to affirm or deny; of Brahman, 49, 83, 88; pride as, 121–25. *See also* Man, hubris of; Man, primal decision of; and origin of evil, 48–51, 63; Sartre on, 50; Schopenhauer on, 48–49, 83; and suffering, 51, 77, 79–83, 86. *See also* Four holy truths; Suffering

Pacem in Terris, 2. *See also* John XXIII, Pope; Vatican Council II
Pain, 72–77, 85–86. *See also* Suffering
Panikkar, Raymond, 133, 134
Pascal, Blaise, 31, 32, 128
Paul VI, Pope, 3–4
Plato, 21, 63, 65, 95, 107, 109, 110, 111
Prajapati, 18, 160, 169
Prajna (highest wisdom), 114, 139

Questions of Melinda, 98–100
Quietism, 141–43. *See also* Mysticism

Rahula (Buddha's son), 26
Reincarnation, 56, 58, 91, 94, 104, 127–28, 131–32, 138–40
Republic, The (Plato), 107–10
Ruysbroeck, Jan van, 141–42, 143

Sakyas (Buddha's tribe), 13, 14, 15, 23, 26, 44
Samsara (cycle of rebirth), 86, 104. *See also* Reincarnation
Sartre, Jean Paul, 14, 17–18, 23–25, 28–29, 36–40, 41, 50, 102–03; absence of struggle in early life of, 17–18, 18–19, 23, 24, 25; being and nothingness in thought of, 36–40, 41; comparison of, with Buddha, 14, 17, 18–19, 23, 25, 28; disillusionment of, 17–18, 19, 23–25, 28–29; faith of, 24, 25, 28, 102–03; fear of death of, 17, 24. Works of, *Being and Nothingness*, 37; *The Words*, 17, 39
Satori (enlightenment). *See* Enlightenment
Schopenhauer, Arthur, 8–9, 43, 47–49, 50, 83, 123
Schulemann, Günther, 52, 56
Scriptures: Buddhist, 13, 15, 18, 21–23, 43–44, 47, 52, 56, 96–97, 98–100, 103, 104, 126, 127, 134, 138, 140, 160, 161, 168–69
Self, 12, 29, 36–40, 41, 42, 70, 87–88, 114–17, 120–25, 133, 137. *See also* Atman; Brahman; Enlightenment; Man; Mysticism; Nothingness; Original sin; Sartre, Jean Paul; Self-perfection; Zen Buddhism
Self-perfection: Buddhist concept of, 102–04, 105–06. *See also* Man, personhood of; Nirvana; Christian concept of, as mission, 102, 105, 106; as happiness, 60–66; Jesus Christ as Christian ideal of, 106–07, 110–12; of just man, 102, 106–12; man's craving for. *See* Absolute (The); Plato's concept of, 106, 107–10; and redemption, 60–66, 103–06; Sartre's concept of, 102–03; Stoic concept of, 60–66, 123. *See also* Man, hubris of; Man, personhood of; Mysticism; Original sin
Self-transcendence. *See* Mysticism
Seneca, 60, 62. *See also* Stoics
Shintoism, 2, 7, 170. *See also* Japan
Sin. *See* Man, and sin; Original sin; Soul, and human acts
Socrates, 8, 21, 95, 109–10

Index

Songs of the Elders, 43–44

Soul: Buddhist concept of, 92, 94, 95–96, 98–101; Christian concept of, 92, 94, 95; historical concepts of, 92–95; and human acts, 98–101. *See also* Man, personhood of; Man, and sin; and life after death, 96–98; striving of, toward an absolute, 146–51. *See also* Festival of the Dead; Man, personhood of; Man, and sin; Original sin; Self-perfection

Spontaneous Decomposition of Christianity, The (Eduard von Hartmann), 47

Stoics, 60–66, 123

Suddhodana (Buddha's father), 15

Suffering, 47–91; Buddhist attitude toward, 25–28; 51–59, 64–65, 68, 84–85, 86–89, 89–91, 124, 129–30, 162–63, 164; Christian attitude toward, 34, 56, 68, 79, 162–63, 164. *See also* Man, personhood of; formative influence of, 13–15, 16, 62–91. *See also* Man, formative influences on; Man, and ills of human condition; four holy truths about, 51, 52–56, 165; four kinds of, in Buddhist thought, 89–91; man as cause of human, 77–79, 80, 82–83, 84; meaning of, 68–91. *See also* Man, formative influences on; Man, and ills of human condition; nature of, 68–72; and pain, 72–77, 85–86; and sin, 48–51, 79–83, 86, 155–57; Stoic doctrine of, 60–66. *See also* Buddha; Enlightenment; Man; Nothingness; Original sin

Suicide, 19, 25, 33, 40, 66

Suzuki, Daisetz Teitaro, 9, 113, 114, 117, 119, 120

Tibetan Life: of Buddha. *See Asvaghosa*

Transcendental analysis. *See* Meditation; Yoga

Unknown Christ of Hinduism, The (Panikkar), 133

Upanishads, 47, 126, 127, 138

Vatican Council II, 2, 3, 4–5, 144. *See also Declaration on the Relationship of the Church to Non-Catholic Religions;* John XXIII, Pope; Paul VI, Pope

Veda, 15, 160

Vedanta Sutras, 134

Wheel of existence, 132. *See also* Reincarnation

Yoga, 27, 116, 126, 127, 131, 138, 148, 150

Zen Buddhism, 1, 3, 9, 10, 11–12, 46, 113–25. *See also* Buddhism; Dialogue: East-West; Lassalle, Hugo Enomiya; Meditation; Suzuki, Daisetz Teitaro